Unfettered Hope

Unfettered Hope

*A Call to Faithful Living
in an Affluent Society*

Marva J. Dawn

Westminster John Knox Press
LOUISVILLE • LONDON

Scripture quotations, unless otherwise indicated, are from the New Revised Standard Version of the Bible, copyright © 1989 by the Division of Christian Education of the National Council of the Churches of Christ in the U.S.A., and used by permission.

Excerpt from *Close to the Machine* by Ellen Ullman, copyright © 1997 by Ellen Ullman. Reprinted by permission of City Lights Books.

Excerpt from *The Singing Tree* by Kate Seredy, copyright 1939 by Kate Seredy, renewed © 1966 by Kate Seredy. Used by permission of Viking Penguin, an imprint of Penguin Putnam Books for Young Readers, a division of Penguin Putnam Inc. All rights reserved.

Excerpt from *The Technological Bluff* by Jacques Ellul, © 1990 by Jacques Ellul. Used by permission of William B. Eerdmans Publishing Co. All rights reserved.

Excerpt from *Technology and the Character of Contemporary Life* by Albert Borgmann, © 1984 by Albert Borgmann. Used by permission of The University of Chicago Press. All rights reserved.

Book design by Sharon Adams
Cover design by Pam Poll Graphic Design

First edition
Published by Westminster John Knox Press
Louisville, Kentucky

This book is printed on acid-free paper that meets the American National Standards Institute Z39.48 standard. ∞

PRINTED IN THE UNITED STATES OF AMERICA

03 04 05 06 07 08 09 10 11 12 — 10 9 8 7 6 5 4 3 2 1

Library of Congress Cataloging-in-Publication Data

Dawn, Marva J.
    Unfettered hope : a call to faithful living in an affluent society / Marva J. Dawn.—
    1st ed.
       p. cm.
    Includes bibliograpical references (p.) and index.
    ISBN 0-664-22595-0 (alk. paper)
       1. Christianity and culture. 2. Christianity—21st century. 3. Technology—
    Religious aspects—Christianity. 4. Wealth—Religious aspects—Christianity. I. Title.

BR115.C8 D26 2003
261—dc21   2002028898

This book is dedicated to

those enmeshed in the technological milieu who reject its paradigm;
the wealthy who search for meaning in a culture of commodities;
those who resist society's benumbing speed and emptiness;
those seeking to be engaged in relationships of caring;
the thinkers who keep asking new and better questions;
prophets who persist in exposing our idolatries;
disciples who disclose the presence of God;
churches who live by their focal concerns;
believers who radiate the hope of grace;

and especially Myron,
who sustains my hope;

and in prayerful memory of

the victims of the tragedies on September 11, 2001, and thereafter;
the victims of the continuing tragedies of world hunger and injustice.

Contents

Introduction

I t was a case of the biblical Tower of Babel in reverse—sort of. The original story narrated in Genesis 11 is of human beings speaking the same
language, building a tower to reach into heaven in order to make a name
for themselves lest they be scattered abroad over the face of the whole
earth (11:1 and 4). But the LORD[1] confused their language and scattered
them just as they had dreaded (11:7 and 9).

That story was somewhat reversed on September 11, 2001, after hijackers flew commercial airliners into the two towers of the World Trade Center in New York City—built, indeed, to make a name for an architect, a
city, a nation, and a people. Then the towers burned and crumpled, collapsed and plunged to the ground, and people of all ethnicities and lan-
guages were united in grief, stunned silence, overwhelming pain and loss.
As that day exploded into tangles of steel, conflicting emotions, and deeply
gashed lives, neighbors and even the masses (of strangers, nations, conti-
nents) were knit together. It was a sudden confrontation with evil, and we
all—even those of us living thousands of miles removed—were forced to
look directly into its horrid face and turn away into each other's arms.

The tragic events additionally linked Democrats and Republicans,
natives and immigrants, citizens and foreigners, wealthy stockbrokers and

---

1. This book follows the customary practice in Bibles of capitalizing all the letters in
the translations LORD or GOD when the Hebrew word to be rendered is the name
YHWH, often vocalized as *Yahweh*. At some places I will instead use *YHWH* to remind us
of the custom of the Hebrew people not to pronounce the word because of its infinite
holiness, which they did not want to profane. May the name constantly remind us of the
faithfulness of the "I Am," the covenant promise-keeper.

poor waitresses and janitors. Death is no respecter of persons, and people from all sorts of social locations faced it, passed through it, or mourned it together.

It was Babel in reverse, and we all were united, at least initially, in a common sickness of heart.

Usually our despairs are more divided.

Many have written about their loss of innocence on that September 11. I wonder instead why people in the United States hadn't lost their innocence much earlier—for certainly the daily news in all its forms regularly reports unjust wars, economic disparities, and other oppressions and terrorisms. Evil is all around us, and many "innocents" die weekly in U.S. cities from violence and poverty. The disproportions of our world cry out for us to notice them. Can we "innocently" not pay attention?

I am also concerned for how quickly much of the immediate unity caused by the crisis of September 11 passed away, for how swiftly we were told to "get on with our lives"—a process that, for many, involved a return to insulation from personal suffering and apathy toward the suffering of the rest of the world. For example, hearts and wallets were opened by the initial crisis, and donations poured in for the families of those who died in the plane crashes in New York, Pennsylvania, and Washington, D.C. But by the end of 2001 other charities not associated with the September 11 events were experiencing drastic shortfalls in their customary receipts, and the hungry and homeless in the United States were having trouble finding food and shelter.

Meanwhile, the U.S. military response to the 9–11 attacks, the so-called war on terrorism, returned to the habitual patterns of a "superpower"— utilizing the latest weapons technology to pummel the enemy into submission. When the enemy (in this case, Osama bin Laden) escaped instead, these old ideas of power left us without a clear-cut plan or justified goals for the "war." Consequently, the initial terrorist attacks raised, and many events and responses in the aftermath escalate, new fears about our previously unobserved insecurity.

In the midst of these and other forms of societal turmoil after the terrorist attacks, the catastrophe made apparent to many that they weren't really satisfied with their existence. Suddenly people wondered why they had chased after profits or possessions, power or position. Their optimism was dashed by the catastrophic events, and the revelation that their economic securities and social hopes were bogus robbed them of their determination to succeed in their chasing. I wonder, however, whether the questioning and dis-ease will persist long enough and if answers will be pursued to the point of change.

In the first several weeks after September 11, 2001, many planes from Portland, Oregon (from which I travel for speaking engagements), were crowded with tourists going to New York City to show solidarity and to "build the economy" there. Conversations with such tourists on their way home convinced me that for many (not all, of course!) the trip was more about taking advantage of vastly reduced prices for theater tickets and hotel rooms than about genuinely sharing in the suffering of New Yorkers.

Meanwhile, attendance at the events for which I spoke was lower than normal because people expressed a fear of traveling or the desire to stay home with their families. It seemed that the gifts of communal spiritual study were not seen as an important source of solace.

I'm not forgetting the spirituality of many houses of worship opening their doors for multiple prayer services and memorial events. It is true that huge numbers of people turned to vigils and special ceremonies in response to the disasters. But attendance at regular worship and Bible studies did not noticeably increase after the first week or two, and the numbers of engaged participants in faith communities were not perceptibly enlarged.

Is there no continuing, regular need for greater spiritual strength and continuous maturation? What sets of diversions attract us so that we don't face the deeper questions of life? Behind what sorts of facades do we hide our griefs, our fears, and our selves? What kinds of despairs engulf our lives? What kinds of questions should we be asking?

By the time you read this, there have certainly been other crises in your own life or the world—medical emergencies, other kinds of terrorist attacks, new sources of war or fear. Perhaps deeper searching is persisting and fresh thinking about the nature of the world is being done. If not, perhaps the questions and issues I raise in this book are all the more important.

For What Do We Hope?

If we asked that question of a random group of people, no doubt many of them would say, "I hope for peace in the world." That is a large concern right now as hostilities continue to flare in the Middle East, and battles and suicide bombs continue to claim lives. Throughout history there have been "wars and rumors of wars," so peace will always be on the list in conversations about hopes.

Other people might express more personal hopes—for happiness, for financial security, for an end to their immediate troubles, or for life simply to become a bit easier to handle. Some might say that they have given up hoping.

We use the English noun and verb *hope* in many ways—to signify what we anticipate or expect, what we would recommend if we could control things, what we most earnestly desire or wish for if we could have our own way, or what we truly believe in or in what or whom we have confidence. One of my purposes in this book is to raise questions about the nature of our hopes, about what hinders or fulfills them, and about correlating our daily bearing and behaviors with them.

When we look more closely at our hopes, we discover that they are often blocked. In this book I am using the image of *fettering* to summarize the many ways that our feelings of hope might be stifled or squashed, that our hopes in the form of a possible event might be prevented or spoiled, that our hope for a condition in the world might be thwarted or restricted, or that our hopes in things or people might be disappointed or dis-illusioned.

Through this book's exploration of various kinds of fetterings and of one method for thinking beyond them, I want to demonstrate the unique and unfettered hope of the Christian faith. Moreover, I believe that hope in the Triune God gives us the means for dealing with the diverse fetterings in our lives and frees us to be engaged in counteracting the fetterings of violence and injustices in our world.

Without such a hope, we are overwhelmed by the fetterings and injustices.

How Do We Cope with Being Overwhelmed?

The world overwhelms us in many ways—by the sheer quantity of information, by employment uncertainties, by multiple responsibilities or insecurities, by its pain and suffering and despair. David Ford, Regius Professor of Divinity at Cambridge University, suggests in his masterful book *The Shape of Living* that there are three imperatives for responding to being overwhelmed.[2] First we must name it, to acknowledge the truth that we are deluged. Naming the fact that we are overwhelmed brings it into language and enables us to think about the situation ourselves and with others (15).

Ford tells us that next we need to describe what overwhelms us. When we do this, we discover how common our situation is. Otherwise, we frequently "struggle against drowning in the bad overwhelmings and often feel guiltily responsible for not being on top of our situation." To

---

2. David F. Ford, *The Shape of Living: Spiritual Directions for Everyday Life* (Grand Rapids: Baker Book House, 1997), 13. Page references to this book in the following paragraphs will be given parenthetically in the text.

describe our situation and learn that it is much larger than our own personal problem "frees us from the wrong sort of guilt and from paralyzing isolation" (15).

The third step, Ford suggests, is to attend to "the whole shape of living" (16). This is the primary issue, he insists, for we don't "need to drown in what overwhelms us, nor is the solution to fiddle with some of the details, important though they are." Instead: "While doing justice to both the overwhelmings and the details, the main task is to stretch our minds, hearts, and imaginations in trying to find and invent shapes of living" (17).

Following Ford's Process

In this book—and for the sake of the world's future—I will name as a primary problem in our times *the fettering of human hope*. Later, this introduction will distinguish the two opposing categories of fetterings that overwhelm the wealthy and the poor of our world, but both kinds of hope's captivity were exposed by the events and aftermath of September 11, 2001.

All too soon, however, the blatant disquietude of those of us who are the world's wealthy was stilled, muffled, submerged, repressed. Too quickly things returned to "normal"—and genuine hope was again imprisoned by forces to be described in chapter 1.

To make Ford's second, descriptive step more helpful for all sorts of readers, I have designed chapter 1 as a multi-media collage. Some readers might resonate with descriptions from news sources; others might find the personal testimony of a software engineer more compelling. Some might discover commonality by means of an allegorical story, an excerpt from a young adult book, a specific conversation, or a magazine ad.

I do not try, in chapter 1, to describe exhaustively all the components of our fettering or to provide a thorough sociological analysis; that can be found in books listed in the bibliography. Nor do I insist that the elements suggested are most significant for understanding the accumulating dimensions of our hope's bondage. Instead, in the collage I offer examples of aspects of the technological, consumerist world that fetter us, to deepen our awareness of how unremittingly we are chained and how desperately we need a Rescuer from outside ourselves. Only when we know the grip of our bondage in our present milieu can we know the sweeping fullness of our deliverance and thereby be empowered to respond by setting others free to hope.

You don't have to agree with all the problems I've pasted on this collage from various sources—perhaps many of them don't cause you insecurity or despair. But they may be small pieces for you of larger frustrations, so their description will help you indirectly to attend to the larger shape of your own situation.

My descriptions in chapter 1 will not totally answer the questions posed at the head of each section. Rather, the questions themselves and my responses are intended to stir up your own perceptions and experiences of the fetterings mentioned. May these pages cast some useful illumination on the shackles that bind us even as our technological milieu promises through its stockpile of commodities to free us from burdensome work and "meaningless" pain.

My goal is to whet our appetites for a better way to think about such "stuff." If we know more clearly what overwhelms us, we will not feel the false guilt (mentioned by Ford) that we are not in control of our lives, and we will be set free to act more positively to counteract what fetters us.

To do so, we first must follow Ford's third step and attend to "the whole shape of living" (16). Therefore, in chapter 2 we will learn from philosopher Albert Borgmann an approach to our human situation that enables us to gain a vantage point from which to ponder the various elements of our lives that overwhelm us and to keep them from swamping us.

Borgmann's work will help us gain a larger view, first, of the main paradigm or pattern of operation in our technological society. Then we will see that we can become liberated from this paradigm by examining everything in light of our "focal concerns"—the most important aspects which give our lives meaning and purpose and toward which we direct our attention. Chapter 2 concludes with Borgmann's instructions for integrating more of our lives around our focal concerns.

Chapter 3 will elucidate the notion of focal concerns by means of literature for middle school children. To my great surprise, while perusing books that my husband might read to his fifth-grade students, I discovered that focal concerns can be easily found. Perhaps what really matters in life is more readily apparent in stories that are less complex. It is my primary thesis that Christianity provides focal concerns worthy of our lives, suitable for integrating them, and strong enough to counteract what overwhelms us.

David Ford noted, however, that we must both know clearly what overwhelms us and also take right responsibility for the situation. Consequently, in chapter 4 we will consider how Christians and their churches are themselves often caught up in the technological milieu's paradigm and therefore fail to help people break free of its fetters. The chapter will challenge all of us who claim to be Christian to rethink our focal concerns and how these could free us from society's patterns and commodifications.

The final three chapters of this book will elaborate positively Christianity's genuine hope and how it can be released—for ourselves and for others in the world—in the unfettered and communal life of faith. By means of brief sketches of the biblical narratives, chapter 5 will explore the fullness of Christian hope and its empowerment for appropriate Christian mission in light of the character of the Triune God.

Chapter 6 will outline numerous Christian practices by which congregations can equip their members to question our society's paradigm and counteract its commodifications and injustices. Both chapters 6 and 7 will discuss the shape for living we need at this time in history to find a truly unfettered hope and to spread that hope to others throughout the world.

David Ford deals with many kinds of overwhelmings. In this book, in sum, I am concerned primarily for three: first, the despair of the world (in all its forms), in relation to (second) the technological milieu and its paradigm, which furthers (third) the idolatry of the god Mammon and all its relatives. Then I am delighted to look to a different sort of three, the Persons of the Triune God, who, by their overwhelming grace, unfetter our hope and who, through their embodiment in the Church[3] community, continue to reach out to unfetter the hope of the world.

Naming the Problem: Two Kinds of Despair

To name accurately how deeply we are enslaved by our society's paradigm, we must begin with Roman Catholic thinker Raimon Panikkar's observation of the "crisis of humanity" that "three quarters of the world's population lives under inhuman conditions."[4] We should keep that figure in mind as we note theologian Douglas John Hall's discussion of despair as the primary sign of our times and mission, for he is not primarily referring to that three-quarters of the world.[5]

Rather, Hall distinguishes between the overt despair of members of affluent societies, whose hopeless situations lead them to resort to crime,

---

3. Throughout this book I will use capitalized *Church* to signify the ideal as Christ would have His Body be and uncapitalized *church* or *churches* to name concrete fallen (and seeking-to-be-faithful) realities.

4. Raimon Panikkar, *Christian Century* 117, 23, August 16–23, 2000, 836.

5. Douglas John Hall, "Despair as Pervasive Ailment," in *Hope for the World*, ed. Walter Brueggemann (Louisville, Ky.: Westminster John Knox Press, 2001), 83. Page references to Hall's chapter in the following paragraphs will be given parenthetically in the text.

violence, substance abuse, or suicide, and the covert despair of those who repress their hopelessness. The latter is more insidious, he claims, for it

> is well able to masquerade under a guise of well-being so persuasive as to deceive the wearers of the masks themselves. It can readily sub-limate itself through the pursuit of activities that seem to emanate from highly positive attitudes toward life and the future. Human beings cannot live with a conscious, unrelieved sense of the "vanity" (Koheleth) of their lives and endeavors. If their gods die, if their opti-mism is dashed by events, if the habit of hope languishes in them, they will likely construct bogus hopes out of thin air and sheer deter-mination. "If the world's a wilderness, go, build houses in it!" (86)

This is the despair that was unclothed by the tragic events of September 11. Suddenly people saw that relationships were more important than the profits or possessions, power or position that they had sought so intensely. News journals at first reported their laments of despair, as well as their efforts to turn back to prayer and/or to their families. Some revealed that they could do nothing but cocoon in their homes.

However, with a few exceptions the media did not allow the despair to remain nakedly exposed for long. Within two months, news magazines were reporting that sales were up for products related to the home—for toys and puzzles; for cookbooks and baking staples; for knitting/sewing materials and arts/crafts supplies; for DVD players and video rentals; for contraceptives and lingerie.[6]

Of course, it's great that people are slowing down and spending more time with loved ones. But it's important to note that many are pursuing these new goals by following habitual patterns of purchasing more commodities (even though they are of a different sort). Politicians, including the U.S. president, as well as "Money and Business" sections of news journals, name *more spending* as the remedy not only for recession, but also for the obvious despair people feel. Will we continue to run away from asking what under-lies this constant turn to financial solutions to hide or assuage our problems?

Moreover, a radio news report almost exactly three months after the hijackings noted that drug and alcohol abuse in the United States had increased markedly since September 11, 2001. Will we as a people con-tinue to drown our fears and hopelessness in self-medicated oblivions?

---

6. Betsy Streisand, "The Comfort Zone," *U.S. News and World Report*, 131, 21, November 19, 2001, 31.

Is there no source of genuine hope by which to surmount our despairs? Could such a genuine hope give us the courage to let the despair remain visible long enough to probe its deeper roots?

To probe the roots and discover true hope (as we will in this book) is crucial, for, as Douglas John Hall notes, covert despair "relieves itself at the expense of those in its environs" (87). When those who possess the world's goods suffer "the absence of operative systems of meaning" (88–90) and consequently attempt to find meaning in more materiality, the dispossessed are wounded more deeply.

My goal in this book is to make as vividly clear as possible the kinds of fetters we (who are the world's possessors) experience and to show as radiantly as possible the gloriously magnificent hope of the Christian faith, so that we are liberated from the former by the power of the latter and thereby enabled to work more urgently against the injustices that fetter the hope of the dispossessed.

Wake-Up Calls

My own personal wake-up call shook me to the core in the summer after my junior year in college, when I sang in a college choir traveling around the world to strengthen churches. During ten days in India I was overwhelmed by the thousands of beggars. I saw countless numbers of dead bodies in the streets, and I watched the workers who scooped them into large wheelbarrows and hauled them to the city dump to be burned. My naive life was turned upside down there; I knew as a Christian that I could not ever ignore the poverty and injustice I had seen. I felt called by God always to work to counteract world hunger and deprivation.

Since then I have become increasingly troubled by the state of wealthy U.S. churches. Why do we not pay more attention to God's commands to feed the hungry and clothe the naked? We seem to ignore the real situation of the unfairly divided globe. What kind of wake-up call would be effective?

While our relatively small part of the world eases its pain by means of the production of more commodities and the consumption of them, the rest of the world suffers an opposite kind of hopelessness—when persons are not able to secure what is necessary to live. Let us look at a few statistics to see the picture of world financial discrepancies more clearly:

- Almost 1 billion people in the world don't get enough to eat each day; several billion's poor diets provide enough calories but not enough basic nutrients. Meanwhile, an estimated 600 million people—mostly in North America and Europe—are overnourished and overweight. In the United States, 55% of adults—nearly 100 million people—are overweight. (Brian Halweil, "Malnutrition Still Prevalent," *Vital Signs 1999*, 146)

- Of the 100 largest economies in the world, 51 are corporations; only 49 are countries. The top 200 corporations' combined sales are bigger than the combined economies of all countries in the world minus the biggest 10. Their combined sales are 18 times the size of the combined annual income of the 1.2 billion people living in "severe" poverty (24% of the world population). ("Top 200: The Rise of Corporate Global Power," a report from the Institute for Policy Studies)

- In the last 50 years, almost 400 million people worldwide have died from hunger and poor sanitation—three times the number of people killed in all wars fought in the entire 20th century. (Bread for the World)[7]

- In developing countries, 6 million children die each year, mostly from hunger-related causes. (Bread for the World)

No one should die from hunger or suffer from malnutrition when you and I and many others have so much! Many lives could be saved for pennies a day. Look at another statistic:

- Ending hunger would not be expensive relatively. Basic health and nutrition needs of the world's poorest people could be met for an estimated $13 billion more a year. U.S.ers[8] and Europeans spend more than that on pet food yearly. (United Nations Development Program)

But we cannot really solve the problem of our world's injustices by merely giving a little more of our surplus to fight hunger. More deeply, we need to be freed from our reliance on material consumption to find

---

7. Bread for the World is one of the best places to find up-to-date information concerning hunger in the world; their Web site is http://www.bread.org/hungerbasics/international.html.

8. In this book I use the term *U.S.ers* to name residents of the United States in order to avoid the title *Americans*. The latter designation seems oppressive not only of Native Americans but also of the peoples of Canada, Mexico, Central America, and South America, who are all residents of the Americas.

happiness, especially because wealthy countries consume at a rate unsustainable by the earth.

That is made clear by population ecologist Bill Rees, from the University of British Columbia, who asserts, by means of the most objective data, that "in order to bring everyone on the planet to the same general level of consumption and well-being as the average Canadian, we would need four or five more Earths—right now!"[9] Those of us who live south of the 54th parallel might wonder how many Earths it would take to bring the entire world to our level of consumption.

Why do some people in the world need to expend the earth's resources to such a degree that the rest of the globe is deprived of its share and the earth is endangered? How did hope become so fettered that such behavior seems to be the only way to keep despair at bay?

I believe that hope in the Triune God is so strong (see chapter 5) that it breaks the shackles that fetter us. Consequently, we can face squarely the nature of our fettering, as I sketch several of its dimensions in chapter 1. My goal is to lay down the main colors of the problems, so that we can understand more clearly the breadth of the powers that fetter us and be warned to untangle their connections with each other and resist their potential to strangle us.

What Are the "Powers" That Threaten?

Before we look at specific aspects of our cultural milieu that bind hope, it is essential that we take note of the biblical notion of "the principalities and powers." As the Bible describes them, these powers are not little spirits flying around and spitting sulfur, as many millennial-turn novels (such as those by Frank Peretti) might have us believe.[10]

Rather, powers include human institutions created for good (Colossians 1), but they share in the fallenness of the world and thus overstep

---

9. Hall, "Despair as Pervasive Ailment," 91, quoting David Suzuki and Holly Dressel, *From Naked Ape to Superspecies* (Toronto: Stoddart, 1999), 42.

10. For a more thorough description of principalities, see Marva J. Dawn, *Powers, Weakness, and the Tabernacling of God* (Grand Rapids: Wm. B. Eerdmans Publishing Co., 2001) and "The Concept of 'the Principalities and Powers' in the Works of Jacques Ellul" (Ph.D. diss., University of Notre Dame, 1992: Ann Arbor, Mich.: University Microfilms, #9220614). Other descriptions are offered in Marva J. Dawn, *Is It a Lost Cause? Having the Heart of God for the Church's Children* (Grand Rapids: Wm. B. Eerdmans Publishing Co., 1997), and in chapter 5 of Marva J. Dawn and Eugene H. Peterson, *The Unnecessary Pastor: Rediscovering the Call* (Grand Rapids: Wm. B. Eerdmans Publishing Co., 1999).

their proper vocation. In chapter 1 we will be considering the fettering of hope primarily by technology and money. Of course, there is nothing inherently wrong with technology—it has been created for good—but its paradigm (see chapter 2) causes it to overstep its function of releasing us from burdens, and it becomes instead part of the commodification and consumerism of our culture.[11] Similarly, money is a good thing, but why does it exert such a force on people? It becomes a god, which Jesus called Mammon.

What power does Mammon have over us? Sometimes we idolize money because we don't have enough and therefore covet it. Sometimes it enslaves us because we have too much and hoard it. Sometimes we falsely sacralize it because we are such good stewards of it that we are not generous.[12] In some way, all of us have probably made Mammon our god.

This is the nature of principalities and powers: they tend to overstep their proper role. Money, technology, and various other elements of our wired world do this in many ways—even as they offer excellent gifts for the sake of human life and well-being.

Another important feature of the powers is that they continually interact with one another and amplify each other's ill effects. For example, hope is fettered by consumerism, and consumerism is increasingly fostered by the seductive influences of technology. Technology, in turn, is given added weight by misunderstandings cultivated by deceptive communications, media hype, and information glut; by political and economic confusions and violence; and by ignorance about God and "church." All of these together contribute to our general lack of satisfaction, which nurtures the need to keep grabbing for more, thus spiraling into more consumerism.[13] Each of these factors, furthermore, can be subdivided into various aspects (such as the dimension of political-economic confusions related to the military-industrial complex or related to elections and affecting U.S. budget allotments for world aid), and these all fortify one

---

11. Though Christopher Clausen argues convincingly in *Faded Mosaic: The Emergence of Post-Cultural America* (Chicago: Ivan R. Dee, 2000) that the term *culture* no longer has any real embodiment in the United States, I am forced to use the word in this book for lack of enough other suitable synonyms for the word *society*.

12. These three sacralizations are suggested in Jacques Ellul, *Money and Power*, trans. LaVonne Neff (Downers Grove, Ill.: InterVarsity Press, 1984).

13. One new text that combines political and economic analysis (but disregards religion and its institutions) is Robert Gilpin, with Jean M. Gilpin, *Global Political Economy: Understanding the International Economic Order* (Princeton, N.J.: Princeton University Press, 2001).

another's potency. Consequently, we are overwhelmed and suffer from our own lack of discrimination; we don't know what to value, how to choose what's important to us, how to weed out the rest—in short, how to prevent our enslavement and paralysis. We drown in too many options, too much stuff, too difficult choices, too new of a sense of our real insecurity, too little genuine meaning, too strangled hopes.

As I will elaborate in chapter 5, however, Christ has decisively conquered the powers and thereby sets Christians free in life and mission to value the powers and their gifts, to be grateful for the genius God gave to human beings to develop them, and yet also to restrict the powers to their true place and resist their overwhelmings. It is the same with all principalities and possessions; they are merely gifts. Similarly, we hold our own talents, skills, character, ministries as gifts toward which we manifest a proper humility that restricts them to their rightful limitations. This Christian understanding of ourselves and the powers gives us immensely profound—and practical!—guidance in our search for ways to end the fetterings (as we shall see in the last three chapters). And that will deepen our hope, even as the genuine hope of Christianity enables us to face the fetters in the first place and to work for true justice with all of our gifts.

Acknowledgments

Many persons have helped to make this book possible. To thank them here does not include them in my mistakes, but acknowledges debts too huge to pay. My father first taught me the importance of our focal concerns by turning down better-paying baseball-pitching contracts to teach children in Lutheran schools about Jesus. My mother imparted the significance of hospitality through her tremendous gifts for welcoming others and serving their needs. Both of them grounded me in the love of God.

My husband, Myron Sandberg, supports my passions, shares my intense concern to combat poverty with our resources, and keeps me alive with his tender care in the face of my escalating handicaps. Most of all, his character convinces me of God's love for me.

My brother, Glen Gersmehl, keeps me mindful of the world's injustices and violence through his superb work as Executive Director of the Lutheran Peace Fellowship and by our conversations, sharing of books, and his specific assistance with the catalog of inequities in chapter 1.

I owe Dr. Albert Borgmann an enormous debt of gratitude for his thorough inquiry into the paradigm that controls our culture. I could never do justice to his brilliant work, but I cite many of his insights in chapter 2 to help us understand why the fetters sketched in chapter 1 pile up on us so extensively and to enable us to begin to find an exit from this captivity. I hope readers of this book will follow up with more study of Borgmann's works, because he is an important prophet for our times.

Drs. Walter Brueggemann, Terence Fretheim, and David Gushee contributed information and inspiration through their outstanding presentations at the American Academy of Religion/Society of Biblical Literature annual meeting in 2001. Many other friends and participants in speaking engagements prodded me with ideas and comments they never thought would wind up on these pages.

Especially I must thank the research assistants at the Fort Vancouver Regional Library system—particularly Kerry Martin, who has frequently located and sent me materials. Because I am visually impaired and can't drive, the library's extensive help with mailing books and articles to me is indeed a God-send. Also, thanks are due to Cathy Heide, librarian at Crestline Elementary School, Vancouver, who has given my husband and me numerous suggestions for excellent children's literature.

Thanks are chiefly due to Stephanie Egnotovich, who first welcomed me into the collegiality of Westminster John Knox Press and then goaded me into what I pray is better writing. To all the excellent people at WJK I extend my hearty thanks for this first book together.

Above all, *Soli Deo Gloria!*

Chapter 1

Why Are Our Hopes So Fettered?

$\mathbf{A}$s the Introduction noted, the wealthy and the poor of our world experience two opposing categories of fetterings. This chapter's multi-media collage will ask various questions to help us all ponder in what kinds of bondages our society and we ourselves are entrapped. (As I will explain in chapter 3, I have intentionally reserved discussion about our churches until later chapters.) Here I have purposely used a wide variety of sources and made the sketches relatively brief so that each section can be a starting point for your own deeper thinking. I pray that recognizing the depth of our enslavement will propel us all to renewed efforts to make appropriate choices for our own good and the good of others in the world.

Why Does the Technological Milieu Make Us Feel Overloaded and Overwhelmed?

Fifty years ago French sociologist/theologian Jacques Ellul warned that technology, in spite of its many lauded gifts, also presented great dangers.[1] Its most important threat was its development into the totality of an unremittingly encompassing milieu. He realized that human beings would become immersed in, and completely subjected to, an omnipotence made possible by the intertwining of technology, money, politics, and

---

1. Ideas in this section and others in the book are developed in my two essays "Technological Devices or Engagement in Practices?" and "The 'Humiliation' of the Word or Its Restoration?" in *Proclaiming the Gospel in a Wired World: The 2001 Princeton Lectures on Youth, Church, and Culture*, ed. Amy Scott Vaughn (Princeton, N.J.: The Institute for Youth Ministry of Princeton Theological Seminary, 2001), 37–80.

other forces.[2] He protested that it would be vanity to pretend that this monolithic technical world could be checked or guided, for people would discover that they were too enclosed within their artificial creation to find an exit (428). (We will see later that we do have possibilities for exits, but that we must attend to them with extreme care.)

This situation of an overbearing environment would be new in the history of humankind. Ellul called it a "profound mutation" (431) because technology and its paradigm would become the defining force of civilization. Prior to the 18th century, technology was applied only in certain narrow, limited areas (64), such as the production of clothing or goods for homes.

There was also a limitation of technical means, which was compensated for by the skill of the worker. Efforts had historically been made to improve the *use* of a tool, not the tool itself, so that results varied according to the skill of the workers, but Ellul realized that in the modern technological world the goal would be to eliminate this variability (67). We can immediately recognize this danger that lies in improving gadgets rather than persons' skills: if our work does not require skill from us, it is not as satisfying. That, in turn, contributes to the increasing move to "entertainments" and consumption for our moments of enjoyment.

Two other dangers highlighted by Ellul were (1) that the primary criterion in a technological milieu is efficiency and (2) that the proliferation of means would bring about the disappearance of ends (80). Perhaps all of us in wealthier nations in the 21st century struggle with the pace of our societies and with this loss of ends because of too many means. We have so many things to do, we forget why we are doing them; we have so many things, we forget why they matter.

William Kuhns, an early commentator on technology, lauded Ellul's comprehensive analysis of modern technology and his pioneering perception that it would become a distinct and unique centralizing force, with repercussions on every aspect of life. He especially commended Ellul for being the first to discern that technology would control values rather than be controlled by them.[3] This is critical for our purposes in this book because, as chapter 2 will disclose, the problem is not technology and con-

---

2. Jacques Ellul, *The Technological Society*, trans. John Wilkinson (New York: Random House, 1964; French version in 1954), 411. Page references to this book in the following discussion are given parenthetically in the text.

3. William Kuhns, *The Post-Industrial Prophets: Interpretations of Technology* (New York: Weybright and Talley, 1971), 84 and 110.

sumerism themselves, but the way their connection reverberates in our thinking about other aspects of life.

Ellul later identified three disturbing aspects of the connection between technology and consumerism that have become my primary concerns:

a. The technical world is one of material things . . . [but] spiritual values cannot evolve as a function of material improvement.

b. Technical growth leads to a growth of power . . . [but] when power becomes absolute, values disappear. . . . Power eliminates, in proportion to its growth, the boundary between good and evil, between the just and the unjust.

c. . . . Technique [by which term Ellul signifies the conglomerate correlation of technology with capitalism, media, politics, the military-industrial complex, Mammon, and so forth] can never engender freedom. . . . The problem is deeper—the operation of Technique is the contrary of freedom, an operation of determinism and necessity.[4]

Ellul also thoroughly warned against the technological milieu's attributes of totalitarianism, rationality, artificiality, automatism of choice, self-augmentation, monism, universalism, autonomy, efficiency, and necessity.

Because of these cautions and Ellul's expansion and intensification of them in *The Technological System* and *The Technological Bluff*,[5] he is often thought to be overly pessimistic about the technological milieu. However, Ellul cannot be rightly understood unless we know that he deliberately wrote in two very separate tracks. In his theological works he offered hope and practical suggestions for Christian life in the midst of the technological milieu, but he kept those works distinct from his sociological writings, in which he painted things as starkly as he could so that his argument could not be ignored.[6] He knew that people thoroughly deafened and deadened by the surrounding ethos needed a megaphone to rouse their attention.

---

4. Jacques Ellul, "The Technological Order," trans. John Wilkinson, *Technology and Culture* 3, 4 (Fall 1962): 401–402.

5. See Jacques Ellul, *The Technological System*, trans. Joachim Neugroschel (New York: Continuum, 1980), and *The Technological Bluff*, trans. Geoffrey W. Bromiley (Grand Rapids: Wm. B. Eerdmans Publishing Co., 1990).

6. In a 1954 essay Ellul indirectly explains the brutality of his works of social criticism by emphasizing how human efficacy against the powers is impossible. He also stresses the importance of the Christian task of exposing or destroying the world's false hopes and consolations—which is one of my goals in this book. See chapter 4, "On Christian Pessimism," in Marva J. Dawn, trans. and ed., *Sources and Trajectories: Eight Early Articles by Jacques Ellul That Set the Stage* (Grand Rapids: Wm. B. Eerdmans Publishing Co., 1997).

History convinces me that Ellul was right about the nature of our milieu. Ellul's prophetic insights awaken us to the importance of learning how to put limits on technology and our employment of its devices. Consequently, in this chapter we will join Ellul in confronting boldly some of the ways that the technological world fetters us instead of freeing us.

In later chapters, then, we will look for true freedom by considering how the unfettered hope of the Christian faith empowers us to utilize what is good in our technological milieu without becoming enslaved by its values. We will see that one great gift of the Gospel is that it enables us to de-idolize, de-sacralize, de-divinize those elements of the technological milieu that begin unduly to take primary place in our lives and thereby fetter our hope. Why have churches not grasped this gift and wielded it for the sake of our own integrity, the well-being of our neighbors, and our mission to the larger world?

How Do Computers Manifest the Fettering of Hope by the Technological Milieu?

Several months ago I saw a cartoon that shows two persons on opposite sides of a computer desk. In panel after panel the one facing the computer tells his companion how he uses it to telecommute to work, to get whatever information he needs from the Internet, to find entertainment, to e-mail his friends, and recently even to shop online. During the whole conversation, he has been tapping on the computer keys. After remaining silent for all the other panels, the companion finally asks his friend what he's looking for. He responds, "A life."

When we scan the landscape, we notice that similar expressions of depression or discomfort with the ways the technological, consumerist world overwhelms us appear in a diversity of advertisements, cartoons, and journal articles. These reactions pointedly demonstrate how crucial it is that we ask better questions about the technological milieu, its commodities, and their entrapments in order to understand the hopelessness they sometimes foster.

For example, let us ask whether using computers is really good for small children. Advertisements have emphasized that home computers would change the life of children, that education could be vastly improved with computers, and that families would be left behind if they didn't buy one. Now major news journals are featuring in-depth articles on how computers aren't really good for children, how two-dimensional play does not develop their skills as thoroughly as three-dimensional play, how an increasing number of children are overweight, how pediatric optometrists are discovering an exponential escalation of younger and younger children with eye problems correlative to increased use of computers in homes.[7] Can we learn to let values from outside the technological world help us question the hype of its advertising?

A poignant warning can be found in Ellen Ullman's *Close to the Machine: Technophilia and Its Discontents*, which raises its alert from the inside vision of a computer software engineer. Ullman admits that she would prefer to believe

> that computers are neutral, a tool like any other, a hammer that can build a house or smash a skull. But there is something in the system itself, in the formal logic of programs and data, that recreates the world in its own image. . . . [I]t forms an irresistible horizontal country that obliterates the long, slow, old cultures of place and custom, law and social life.[8]

The notion of "the principalities and powers," which I described in this book's Introduction, helps us understand why the system "recreates the world in its own image." The various workings of the powers that I sketch below contribute to the obliteration of other cultures as part of the major cultural replacement which is a principal straitjacket for hope.

Before exploring that replacement in chapter 2, however, let's add more to our collage of questions about other dimensions of the hopelessness. What aspects of consumerism and its undergirding technological world cause you anything from mild frustration to severe tension or even despair?

Does the Computer Really Save Us Time and Worry?

While drafting this book I've been extremely careful to save files after every burst of writing. At one point, I had just saved a file and then decided to transfer one paragraph to another chapter. When I returned to the original file, the cursor froze, and nothing I tried could unlock the jam. I

---

7. See, for example, Kate Kelly, "False Promise: Parking Your Child in Front of the Computer May Seem like a Good Idea, but Think Again," *U.S. News and World Report* 129, 12, September 25, 2000, 48–55.

8. Ellen Ullman, *Close to the Machine: Technophilia and Its Discontents* (San Francisco: City Lights Books, 1997), 89.

had no choice but to turn off the computer, wait a while, and begin again. But when I called up the file, it was gone. Totally gone! I would guess you might have had similar experiences.

I called several computer-literate friends to ask for help. No one knew how to locate the missing document. We tried every tool in their extensive repertoire; nothing worked. One teenage friend suggested a few things I hadn't yet attempted and finally said, "Well, that's technology. It likes to do that." But why?

Then today we discovered that the zip codes on about ninety-five prayer-letter envelopes were all wrong—for the second time, even though two people had worked a long while to fix the problem after it happened the first time. Some addresses had the zip code for the next name on the list, but in other sections of the file all the codes were scrambled with no rhyme or reason to it, as far as the person who'd printed the labels could tell. That's technology. It likes to do that.

So we feel ensnared. We "need" these machines to do our work, but often we lose more time than we save as we try to correct scrambled zip codes or to remember what we wrote so that we can recapture the way we crafted it. It is a strange bondage, and whenever a glitch occurs it deepens our fear of technology or steals our time, which in turn deepens our frustration or despair. We will never understand why *these things* happen, and they leave us frightened and/or overworked.

Does All This Information Help Us Think?

Almost everyone I know feels overwhelmed by the information glut of the technological milieu. We're shackled in many ways—for example, by the impossibility of discerning what information is useful, the danger of idolizing information for its own sake, or the confusions of contextless information. Jacques Ellul particularly emphasized that "people . . . deluged by information become incapable of making decisions. An excess of information . . . results in total paralysis of the process of decision[-making]."[9]

Neil Postman traces one root of the modern info-glut to the telegraph because it first

> gave a form of legitimacy to the idea of context-free information; that is, to the idea that the value of information need not be tied to any function it might serve in social and political decision-making and

---

9. Ellul, *Technological Bluff*, 278.

action, but may attach merely to its novelty, interest, and curiosity. The telegraph made information into a commodity, a "thing" that could be bought and sold irrespective of its uses or meaning.[10]

As Henry David Thoreau observed when the first telegraph messages were sent, suddenly there was an abundant flow of information that might not really be *related* to those who received it (67). We experience this now in our reading of the daily "news," which consists largely of information that we can discuss with others, but that does not result in much meaningful action and thus dramatically reduces what Postman calls the "information-action ratio" (68). Perhaps we should ask (as does Jacques Ellul) whether the "daily news" really helps us understand and serve our world better. Might in-depth weekly journals provide less of a catastrophic and fragmentary perspective? How much of the news really relates to us?

What do we do with all the information we possess? Postman answers that we invent contexts for it, such as crossword puzzles (a "pseudo-context"), cocktail parties, radio quiz shows, television game shows, and *Trivial Pursuits*. These all supply some sort of answer to the question "'What am I to do with all these disconnected facts?' And in one form or another, the answer is the same: Why not use them for diversion? for entertainment? to amuse yourself, in a game?" (76) This leads to ever greater (and continually new forms of) consumerism.

According to Postman, one of the chief culprits in overloading us with useless information is television, which fosters an impotent passivity and produces what he calls a "Low Information-Action Ratio." The acronym LIAR reminds us that it makes liars of us if we learn from television news about hungry people throughout the globe, for example, and do nothing about it or change nothing in our lives for the sake of world justice.

What Postman says about television info-glut is multiplied boundlessly by the plethora of information on the Internet. Data from the wired world, too, "is altering the meaning of 'being informed' by creating a species of information that might properly be called *disinformation*." By that term Postman does not mean false information, but rather "misleading information—misplaced, irrelevant, fragmented or superficial information—information that creates the illusion of knowing something but

---

10. Neil Postman, *Amusing Ourselves to Death: Public Discourse in the Age of Show Business* (New York: Viking Penguin, 1985), 65. Page references to this book in the following paragraphs will be given parenthetically in the text. See also his *Technopoly: The Surrender of Culture to Technology* (New York: Alfred A. Knopf, 1992).

which in fact leads one away from knowing." He insists that, in saying this, he does not intend to imply that television news [or "Webbed" information] "deliberately aims to deprive Americans of a coherent, contextual understanding of their world." Rather, he proposes "that when news is packaged as entertainment [as is most information on the Web], that is the inevitable result" (107).

Postman quotes Terence Moran, who shows that the very structure of media fosters fragmentation and furnishes isolated images. Without continuity and context, we can't integrate information bits into any sort of whole. Thus, the media render us "unfit to remember." An emphasis on images and instantaneous news is "silent about yesterday," so with today's media "we vault ourselves into a continuous, incoherent present" (137).

Consequently, information actually keeps us from thinking.

Besides depriving us of continuity and context, the overload of information causes some people to become preoccupied with it, to become "unbalanced and addictive in their response" to information. According to Hugh Mackay, a prominent social commentator in Australia, addiction can take primarily three forms. Information can be used

> [as] a *distraction from thinking* (as long as I keep absorbing this information, I won't have to make sense of it); or as an *insulation from reality* (as long as I'm immersed in information, I don't have to confront what is actually going on around me); or as a form of *constant stimulation* to create the illusion that something is always happening (I'm never bored . . . there's always the TV or the Internet, or the latest CD-ROM).[11]

Mackay emphasizes that these addictions to a constant flow of information effectively guarantee that our ability to make sound judgments about it will be dulled. The third form, the need for constant stimulation, is perhaps the most dangerously binding and destructive to finding larger meaning in life, because people formed into that addiction by the wired world want hope also to be a constant stimulation, something exciting or splendorous, rather than recognizing it in its more subtle, silent, ordinary forms.[12]

---

11. Hugh Mackay, *Turning Point: Australians Choosing Their Future* (Sydney: Pan Macmillan Australia, 1999), 104–105. Mackay's insights concerning the major issues faced by people in Australia are also remarkably applicable to our situation in the Northern Hemisphere.

12. An excellent book that critiques the destructive habits of our info-glutted world and offers better alternatives is Quentin Schultze's *Habits of the High-Tech Heart: Living Virtuously in the Information Age* (Grand Rapids: Baker Book House, 2002).

Do I Really Need All This Stuff?

At times we are unable to make sensible judgments because we become unwilling junkies of accumulations. Our house, for example, seems incapable of building any immunities to the onslaught of infestations of mugs (which are harder to get rid of than swarms of bugs!).

Today I counted 27 mugs on the mug rack and in our kitchen cabinet—that includes 15 Christmas mugs, but does not include the 4 soup mugs and the 4 plastic huge coffee thermal mugs. After the season, when we put the Christmas mugs back into another cabinet, we will find there 24 other mugs from which to choose some to put on the rack. Besides that, we have given away *several dozen* mugs to church coffee hours, Goodwill Industries, and Christian camps. Yet my husband and I can think of only seven that we have actually bought ourselves in the past thirty years. All the rest have been given to us—Christmas presents from Myron's fifth-grade students (3 this year) or gifts from places where I speak or from friends (which we keep to be mindful of them). There is hardly any way to avoid the glut of mugs.

We can say the same about T-shirts (from many events), calendars and return-address labels (from charity organizations seeking donations), or CDs. We've collected about 160 of the last group, of which we bought only a very few. But frequently at my speaking engagements someone hands me a CD and says, "My daughter/son made this, and I think you'll like it." From where could I get the courage to say, "To be honest, I don't think I'll ever listen to it; I haven't listened yet to the last 10 CDs given to me at conferences"? Even when someone gives a CD that interests me, it is difficult to find the time to pay it due attention.

Perhaps you struggle with the same sort of unintentional accumulations. What sorts of deluges flood your house when you're not looking? Suddenly there are piles of debris for which we cannot give account, and we find ourselves in bondage to a stack of stuff. We can't limit its flow into our house even if we are trying to live more plainly. We express our hopelessness by wishing, "If only I could simplify my life . . ."

Let's realize that the technological world has made possible these mass productions of possibilities. Before the technology became available for everyone to make her own recordings, we didn't receive so many samples and purchased them more deliberately. Before mugs were mass-produced, they were the gifts of potters' artistry (I have some of those, too). But in our technologized, commodified world, we are no longer as closely engaged with artisans as was possible in simpler societies; we are, instead, frequently fettered by a mound of goods (should we instead call them "bads," or at least "less desirables"?) which we cannot manage or escape.

Are the Commodities of the Wired World Useful for Education?

I raise this question because many elementary teachers (my husband is one) struggle with the same sort of "mound"—in this case, of educational programs. School districts add new programs, such as keyboarding on computers, without taking anything out of the curriculum. Teachers are overwhelmed by all the subjects they are supposed to fit into the day. Meanwhile, many of the children are not even able to read at grade level, and school budgets have no money for assistants to help with the students slipping through the cracks. What kinds of questions should we be asking about the commodities of the wired world in relation to elementary education?

On higher levels, we might ask if mass production is good for education. How useful are all the options from the enormous range of possibilities made possible with electronic media?

Just as Neil Postman has shown how *Sesame Street* encourages children to love school only if it is entertaining and non-sequential like *Sesame Street*,[13] so various scholars now comment on destructive effects of electronic information on the university. Eli M. Noam, economics professor and director of an institute for Tele-Information at the Graduate School of Business, Columbia University, in New York City, observes that the system of higher education, which has remained notably stable for over 2,500 years, is now in the process of breaking down. The fundamental reason, he insists (and he is echoed by David Noble of Toronto), is not primarily technology (a point this book will repeatedly emphasize), but the resultant changes in the volume, production, and distribution of information, its increasing commodification, and its relation to commercial vendors, which undermines "the traditional flow of information and with it the university structure."[14] It is important to note these comments about the

---

13. See Postman, *Amusing Ourselves to Death*, 143–151.

14. Eli Noam, "Electronics and the Dim Future of the University," *Science: The Global Weekly of Research*, 270, October 13, 1995, 247–249, reprinted in *Council of Societies for the Study of Religion Bulletin* 30, 4 (November 2001): 78. Similarly, David Noble, a professor in the social sciences division of the Faculty of Arts at York University in Toronto, bemoans the commodification of education. See David F. Noble, "Digital Diploma Mills: The Automation of Higher Education," *First Monday* [an online, peer-reviewed journal] 3 (January 5, 1998), reprinted in *Council of Societies for the Study of Religion Bulletin* 30, 4 (November 2001): 81–85.

relationship of technology to commodification, for we will explore this more deeply in chapter 2.

Vivian-Lee Nyitray, a religious studies professor at the University of California in Riverside, responds to the "grim assessments" of Eli Noam and David Noble by looking more closely at the highly vaunted possibilities of "Distance Education." She worries that, in the midst of its positive potential (already discovered long ago through such endeavors as the education of youth in remote areas in Alaska), it threatens community.[15] Raymond B. Williams elaborates that threat by showing how distance electronic education changes the character of interpersonal relations, the kinds of interaction between the students and their professors.[16] Relationships become less tangible; the key element of personal mentoring for character formation is usually displaced.

David Stewart of Princeton Seminary distinguishes between the library and the "info-quagmire" and the problem that the presence of so much data on the Web obscures its source. In contrast, generally "[i]n the print environment, publishers evaluate manuscripts, then painstakingly edit and review them before sending them to press. Likewise, libraries scrutinize items carefully according to standards and policy before adding them to their collection."[17] Because there is no similar possibility for such vigilance on the Web, the result is a "treasures-to-trash disparity."[18] How much trash do we imbibe in daily life from our wired world? How will we learn to sort it and to search for genuine treasure?

By these comments I do not reject unilaterally the gifts of the wired world for education. Rather, their many possibilities add to our collage of various commodifications that make us feel overwhelmed by our technological milieu. For many people, they are another of the multiple sources of anxiety and hopeless dissatisfaction.

---

15. Vivian-Lee Nyitray, "Distance Learning: Proceed with Caution," *Council of Societies for the Study of Religion Bulletin* 30, 4 (November 2001): 87.

16. Raymond B. Williams, "Getting Technical: Information Technology in Seminaries," *Christian Century* 118, 5, February 7–14, 2001, 14–17.

17. Ellen Ullman makes much the same point in a footnote, stating that because there is so much information, "the search engines themselves are beginning to incorporate biases and strategies that could be characterized as ordering sensibilities. However, these strategies are not in the public domain, in a sense making each search engine a private card catalog, a personal collection" (Ullman, *Close to the Machine*, 78).

18. David Stewart, "Nurturing Curiosity: A Librarian's View," *Christian Century* 118, 5, February 7–14, 2001, 18.

How Do I Cope with Being Left Behind?

When we are overwhelmed by all the possibilities available to us from the wired world's latest developments, we find ourselves asking if it is necessary to "keep up" with this onslaught of new technologies. It might be quite astonishing to us that a person in the thick of software engineering would also raise the issue of the impossibility of keeping up, but Ellen Ullman, herself a skilled technical expert, admits this:

> It had to happen to me sometime: sooner or later I would have to lose sight of the cutting edge. That moment every technical person fears—the fall into knowledge exhaustion, obsolescence, techno-fuddy-duddyism—there is no reason to think I could escape it forever. Still, I didn't expect it so soon.[19]

If a person whose life specialty is technological can't keep up, it deepens our fears. How could all the rest of us ordinary people hope to keep pace in utilizing the best tools of the wired world?

As with all the products of our present milieu, such as the fashion changes and brand labeling with which teenagers try to cope,[20] technology creates numerous instances of new bondages in the processes of change. As a visually impaired person who can't use Windows or a mouse, I've been impossibly left behind by the dependence of most software programs on that operating system instead of the DOS that enables me to do word processing. Sometimes, however, when colleagues keep telling me about all the things I "could do," I wonder how valuable it really would be for me to do them. How can one discern what truly is necessary or important?

Do We Recognize the "Bluff"?

Why is it that so many of us have bought into this technological revolution? We have to recognize the big "bluff" of the encompassing technological milieu—that we are misled by its bold (and often false) promises,

---

19. Ullman, *Close to the Machine*, 95.
20. See Thomas M. Beaudoin, "Celebrity Deathmatch: The Church Versus Capitalism?" and "After Purity: Contesting Theocapitalism," in *Proclaiming the Gospel in a Wired World: The 2001 Princeton Lectures on Youth, Church, and Culture*, ed. Amy Scott Vaughn (Princeton, N.J.: The Institute for Youth Ministry of Princeton Theological Seminary, 2001), 1–29.

which disguise the negative aspects of whatever is being endorsed. Do we see how the advertising world bluffs us into thinking that more technology or more implementation of the wired world's possibilities is the only solution to world problems in economics and politics; to such church problems as the decline in worship attendance, the reduction of membership numbers, or the lack of interest in "church"; and to personal or family problems?

Jacques Ellul urges us to be more alert to the "gigantic bluff" in which the technological world "envelops us, making us believe anything and, far worse, changing our whole attitude to techniques." Ellul uses the word *techniques* to summarize all the intertwining methods of various technologies and to underscore how these methods have created in us a "quick fix" mentality. In our society, we are bluffed by politicians, the media, publicity, economic models, and other agencies into accepting their techniques for fixing things. We need to be aware of these bluffs

> because so many successes and exploits are ascribed to techniques (without regard for the cost or utility or risk), because technique is regarded in advance as the only solution to collective problems (unemployment, Third World misery, pollution, war) or individual problems (health, family life, even the meaning of life), and because at the same time it is seen as the only chance for progress and development in every society. There is bluff here because the effective possibilities are multiplied a hundredfold in such discussions and the negative aspects are radically concealed.

How often we hear of the great advantages of technologically "progressive" societies—but do we comparably hear about their disadvantages? Ellul concludes that this bluff "causes us to live in a world of diversion and illusion. . . . It finally sucks us into this world by banishing all our ancient reservations and fears."[21] That is perhaps why the bursting of the illusion that North America was "secure" on September 11, 2001, has led to such despair.

How Does Language Hide Our Enslavements?

One main reason that we do not realize the extent of our fettering is that we are bluffed by our culture's misuse of words. The technological milieu

---

21. Ellul, *Technological Bluff*, xvi.

corrupts the content of words we value when it incorporates them into its bluffs.[22] The media world has robbed numerous words of their former weight.

For example, advertisers employ terms like *stupendous* and *extraordinary* to sell laundry soap, but never have I found a detergent that truly matches up to such expectations. If we waste our words in this way, what words do we have left to talk about what really matters in life? Moreover, how do we choose which commodity to purchase when we are barraged by commercials that tell us nothing about the product, but only about our market-researched dreams and (puny) hopes?

Jacques Ellul urged us to consider how our language is cheapened as words are distorted, abused, turned from their customary meaning, and, especially in a wired world, fragmented. For example, to avert an insulin reaction I just picked up a package of "Fun Size M&M's" and wonder why this particular Size is necessarily Fun!

Australian Hugh Mackay notes the danger of the phrase *mass communication*. It is a lie—and often we fail to recognize its deception, for it is "easy to be seduced by the dazzling performance of the electronic media and to ascribe almost magical powers to them." However, all machines can really do is move information around. Though they do that well, "data transfer is their one trick." Even if they do it brilliantly, we shouldn't use the phrase *mass communication*, since the process is only "the mass dissemination of information."[23] Genuine person-to-person communication is much more complex and subtle; it involves facial expressions, a certain tempo of speech, finely nuanced tones of voice, careful choices of words. True communication is not merely an exchange of information, but the embedding of whatever is discussed within a rich personal relationship. We communicate *with* someone else and develop meaning together.

One of the worst misnomers is the term *user-friendly* as an attribute of machines. I have never yet met a machine that was my friend! We should delete the phrase from our vocabulary. Equipment might be more or less difficult to use, but machines are neither friendly nor unfriendly. As Mackay notes, they may be "quick, accurate and convenient, but they do not possess such qualities as courage, integrity, fidelity or moral sensitivity. Machines are not patient, generous or tolerant" (242). Those are the

---

22. See Jacques Ellul, *The Humiliation of the Word*, trans. Joyce Main Hanks (Grand Rapids: Wm. B. Eerdmans Publishing Company, 1985).

23. Mackay, *Turning Point*, 101. Page references to this book in the following paragraphs will be given parenthetically in the text.

qualities needed in friendship and essential for genuine human communication, and only people can possess them.

The question is whether *we* are friends. By calling elements of our wired world "user-friendly," we hide from ourselves our lessened ability to make friends or sustain friendship. With the rapidly escalating technicization of our culture, more and more people are discovering within themselves an inability to nurture, or even a lack of interest in, friendship.

One word frequently used these days that hints at freedom or an unfettering, but ultimately denies it, is the verb *to simplify*. A good friend listened to a speaker at a retreat center who told about simplifying her life—their family had "downsized" from a three thousand-square-foot home to one that has two thousand square feet, but still there were three cars in their garage! Simplifying our lives seems to be the leisure (or sometimes frenzied) occupation of the wealthy of the world (in which category I include myself). Could we simplify them enough to join the homeless? At least, could we simplify them by escaping the control of the technological world and our dependence on money?

Another misleading term, which falsely scripts our society, is the word *exciting*. Overuse of this word has fostered the notion that we can be freed from the fettering pressures we feel if we can put more excitement into our lives. If life isn't always so sensational, advertisements tell us, then we should purchase some new commodity to make it so.

Is Faster Always Better?

No doubt we all have experienced (or at least recognize as true) another bluff sketched by Jacques Ellul—the notion that the faster anything is, the better. The result is that we find ourselves as *L'homme pressé*, the pushed and pressured person.[24] We ask people, "How are you?" and they answer, "Busy," as if that were a badge of honor.

We are so immersed in this busy-ness that it is hard to step back from it and assess whether all our work frees or fetters us. Perhaps the comic relief of a children's tale can give us a new perspective. Through one adventure in his brilliant story about a boy named Milo, architect and design critic Norton Juster illustrates the hopelessness that arises in our culture because we have placed our hopes in how much better things will be if they are faster.

---

24. Ellul, *Technological Bluff*, 258. Page references to this book throughout this section and the next will be given parenthetically in the text.

Milo and two friends were walking in the Forest of Sight with Alec, a resident, and looking for the city of Reality. Suddenly, they saw in the distance a magnificently shining metropolis, with walls glistening from embedded jewels and wide silver thoroughfares. Milo hoped that wondrous city was Reality, but it was another called Illusions.

They were already standing in the midst of Reality, Alec reported, but no one could see any buildings or streets at all. However, they noticed many people rushing about as if they knew where and how they were going, even though their heads were bowed.

When Milo murmured that he saw no city, Alec replied that the people there saw none either, though it didn't matter since they didn't miss it.

This, Alec explained, was how it came about: Reality had been a beautiful city where nobody hurried, where the people dallied to see the lovely places and things. Even when they had somewhere to go, they understood that "the most important reason for going from one place to another is to see what's in between, and they took great pleasure in doing just that."

This was changed by someone discovering that walking quickly and looking at nothing enabled one to reach a place more speedily. Others began hurrying, too, and failing meanwhile to notice the loveliness around them. (Milo recognized the same habit in himself and couldn't even remember his surroundings at home.)

As the people of Reality continued to ignore their city and to rush increasingly faster, things grew "uglier and dirtier," and so the citizens hurried all the more. Eventually, since no one minded, the town gradually faded.

Finally, it disappeared completely, but the people continued living there just as before—without noticing that there was nothing to see. To live in Illusions wouldn't help, Alec said, for "it's just as bad to live in a place where what you do see isn't there as it is to live in one where what you don't see is."

Both situations could be remedied, he concluded, only by the return of the princesses Rhyme and Reason.[25]

In Juster's book, Rhyme and Reason had been banished by their feuding brothers, but why are they so often banished from our society? What has caused us to believe the bluff that faster is intrinsically better when that falsity hides from us our loss of vision and of contentment with what surrounds us. Often, however, our concentration on being faster is a symptom of our fear that we won't have enough time.

---

25. Norton Juster, *The Phantom Tollbooth* (New York: Random House, 1964), 115–119.

What Are Some of the Other Bluffs That Hide Hope's Fettering?

A second, inextricably intertwined bluff is the notion that "faster" will actually save time. Ellul asked people taking the speed train from Paris to Lyons what they were doing with the time they saved, but reported that no one could ever give him an answer. Ellul observed,

> The time saved is empty time. I am not denying that on rare occasions speed might be of use, for example, to save an injured person. . . . But how few are the times when it is really necessary to save time. The truth is that going fast has become a value on its own. . . . [T]he media extol every gain in speed as a success, and the public accepts it as such. But experience shows that the more time we save, the less we have. The faster we go, the more harassed we are. What use is it? Fundamentally, none. I know that I will be told that we need to have all these means at our disposal and to go as fast as we can because modern life is harried. But there is a mistake here, for modern life is harried just because we have the telephone, the telex, the plane, etc. Without these devices it would be no more harried than it was a century ago when we could all walk at the same pace. "You are denying progress then?" Not at all; what I am denying is that *this* is progress! (258)

The discontent (hidden by the first bluff that says faster is better) and then the lack of saving time (the second bluff) lead together to a third— that more commodities will solve the problems of both non-contentment and not enough time. Moreover, advertising especially points our accelerated consumerism toward more gadgets that "save time." In a book called *Faster: The Acceleration of Just About Everything*, James Gleick discerns that even the difficulty with our attention spans is not so much that they are shortened as that they are focused on commodities and turned into a commodity themselves by advertising.[26] Thus, we are deprived of the skill to pay deeper attention to, and to engage more deeply with, others that could arise if we slowed down and mused expansively, if we "wasted" time with others, if we learned to be content within ourselves and within companionship.

A fourth, correlative bluff then arises—that we must have the newest gadget or we will be hopelessly outdated. Keep in mind that I am not

---

26. James Gleick, *Faster: The Acceleration of Just About Everything* (New York: Pantheon, 1999).

opposed to technology and its developments. If objects are truly useful and correspond to true and original needs, they are not mere gadgets. Some developments do make it impossible for us to stay with the status quo, but it is a bluff that the upgrades are always improvements or that being outdated is necessarily bad. The ludicrousness of this bluff strikes me as I begin to work afresh on this project today. Though earlier I bemoaned that some word processing applications are not possible because my visual impairment keeps me from effectively landing an arrow on the right icon in Windows, yet with only two typed words I can move from my DOS operating system into the appropriate file and start working on this chapter immediately, while Windows users are still playing with their mice.

Neil Postman suggested in a lecture that we should always ask about the newest technology, "What problem do I have that this technology solves?" He illustrated his point with an amusing story about trying to buy a car without cruise control and automatic windows. "Why should I pay the cost of including them?" he asked the salesman. "I live in New York City! There are no *freeways*, and I *need* the exercise" of cranking the windows.[27] Yet it is difficult to buy a car without the gadgets, so we often pay for them whether we need them or not. Similarly, a friend said he found it impossible to buy a CD player that can rotate among five CDs without also getting a DVD player—and then his hopes of more ease in connection with entertainment were fettered when he couldn't figure out how the various elements worked. Maybe he needs the exercise of switching one CD himself?

The result of all the bluffs described in this section is what Ellul calls "empty time"—an artificial world that dislodges time and space, that causes people "to lose their sense of reality and to abandon their search for truth" (337). Many people in our society find it traumatic to try to fill empty time with conversation, contemplation, reading, or friendship and its activities (338). As a result, many escape into more and more diversions, and the whole situation spirals into ever-expanding consumerism.[28]

---

27. Postman made these comments at the conference "Education and Technology: Asking the Right Questions," September 17–20, 1997, at Pennsylvania State University, State College, Pennsylvania.

28. On the increasing overlapping of consumption communities, see Otto Selles, "What's Cooking When Martha Stewart Meets the VeggieTales?" *Books and Culture* 7, 4 (July–August 2001): 8–11.

My husband discovers the truth of Ellul's analysis every year when he urges his fifth-grade students to observe "National Turn Off the TV Week" and they complain raucously about then having nothing to do. Many go shopping.[29]

As Ellul warned, by means of the wired world and its fascinations "we take a giant stride along the path of abstraction and addiction." He is referring to diversions not just in the sense of amusement but in the sense Blaise Pascal meant, that we are "diverted from thinking about ourselves and our human condition, and also from our high aspirations, from the meaning of life, and from loftier goals" (358).[30] Pascal also recognized that another diversion quickly has to replace the previous one. We jump endlessly from one amusement to another, one distraction to the next, and never step aside to assess what we are doing. We fly off in all directions. Moreover, contemporary diversions are universally available—even when we are alone, before our own screen. Ellul concludes,

> [A]s in the case of all our base, vile, and dangerous pursuits, we have to cast a large veil of idealism, grandeur, and seriousness over them. . . . Conversely, we have a poor, foolish, mediocre idea of freedom if we call all these exploits freedom! For diversions are always against freedom inasmuch as they are against conscience and reflection. (359)

Because our society has been so good at inventing diversions, because the wired world is inundated with them, the media have to bluff us into the fettered thinking that consumption is our absolute duty—for if we do not consume, the pace of the economy will slow down, money will not circulate, and people will be forced out of work. Consequently, we are also bombarded with the bluff that we should follow the opinions and styles propagated by the advertising media (406). Thus we are always directed toward enslavement by self-concern and the various idolatries of possessions and the "Mammon" that purchases them.

---

29. See the story "Brenda" in Jerry Spinelli's *The Library Card* (New York: Scholastic, 1997), 55–83. This delightful book offers four stories of children, two of them impoverished and two incipient juvenile delinquents, whose lives are radically turned around when they discover and use a library card.

30. Blaise Pascal, *Pensées*, trans. A. J. Krailsheimer (New York: Penguin, 1966), pensée #764, warned that "[a]ll the major forms of diversion are dangerous for the Christian life." This is cited in Ellul, *Technological Bluff*, 358.

How Does Our Communication Fetter Our Hope?

Part of the difficulty with the various fetterings we experience is that we do earnestly want and try to escape them. Yet our very efforts sometimes ensnare us in other bondages, often caused by other people's responses to our efforts.

One example that combines many of the bluffs in the previous sections and thus hides from us how other people's actions fetter us is the illusion that e-mail is a necessary form of communication. The frustration that many experience with it, however, is exposed by an ad that you, too, might have seen in news journals. It depicts a country road with trees, peaceful fields, and the shadow of a man with a bike. Beneath the alluring picture are these words:

> 18 speed bike: $1,225
>   shipping bike to Italy: $235
>   map of Tuscany: 9,000 lira
>   seven days without e-mail:
>   priceless

In connection with speaking engagements I am usually asked for my e-mail address. When I answer that I have deliberately chosen not to have one, almost always the response is "Wise woman," "How did you manage that?" or "I can understand."

Of course, I recognize that for many people e-mail is essential—for example, for the tasks of a missionary whom I met yesterday who supervises from a central city field workers throughout Eastern Europe and Asia. But the question is how to avoid its fettering and overburdening and how to prevent the amassment of too many messages, which often leads to superficiality in our responses.

Analysts think the amount of e-mail this year will be up 45 percent over last year. Many companies are inventing programs to help people deal with unwanted e-mail—programs such as Spam Buster and Spam Killer. A company monitoring "spam" recorded 28,000 such unwanted messages on *one day*, as opposed to 2000 last year.

Of course, we have always dealt with junk mail in the surface postal system, but the ease of e-mail has multiplied the problem exponentially. Also, junk mail in our boxes didn't usually infect our other work (with the exception of anthrax-laden letters), but e-mail attachments often contain viruses that can destroy our files. One person who assists me with correspondence and administration said that she spent about five hours downloading a patch kit to fix one such problem, run that repair, and reinstall her anti-virus program. But think of the problems caused when "patches" have not already been developed. News commentators report that one virus developed recently by a young hacker in the Philippines cost U.S. corporations billions of dollars in lost business and recovery expenses.

In *Close to the Machine*, Ellen Ullman describes her work in designing a system for a collaboration of groups ministering to AIDS victims. While trying to fix some bugs in the software (and descrying that all systems have bugs of some sort), she discovered that she had "passed through a membrane where the real world and its uses no longer matter."[31] She admits, "I'd like to claim a sudden sense of real-world responsibility. But that would be lying. What I really thought was this: I must save the system." As a result,

> The image of patients with AIDS recedes. . . . We give ourselves over to the sheer fun of the technical, to the nearly sexual pleasure of the clicking thought-stream.
>
> Some part of me mourns, but I know there is no other way· human needs must cross the line into code. They must pass through this semipermeable membrane where urgency, fear, and hope are filtered out, and only reason travels across. (15)

Later, when she returned to assess how well her system was working with the AIDS project, she found the workers in the organizations making comments such as these:

> "I worry that e-mail is breaking down our system of care."
> "We relied on knowing each other. Now we don't." (82)

Perhaps you know business staffs that function in the same way. Sometimes large staffs, in the face of the difficulty of scheduling being together, no longer meet face to face but simply send e-mails. There is nothing inherently wrong with e-mail, of course, unless we forget that it is not genuine *communication*, since it is at least three steps removed by no longer involving real-time interaction (usually), facial expressions, tone of voice, and touch.

---

31. Ullman, *Close to the Machine*, 3. Page references to this book in the following paragraphs will be given parenthetically in the text.

How Does This Changed Communication Contribute to Society's Loss of Civility?

The brevity, acceleration, tonal absence, and ease of sending multiple e-mails can contribute (though, of course, it doesn't have to) to a loss of messages that are genuine, true, selfless, just. Moreover, other aspects of society's commodification make these characteristics harder to find in a culture that has lost its civility.[32] Today's endless diversions can form people consumed with self-indulgence and cause them to forget the obligations of common civility. The incessant advertisements of the wired world foster insatiability by constantly promoting more commodities to please ourselves rather than suggesting what we might be and do and possess for the sake of the common good.

Philosopher Albert Borgmann suggests that the extended network of possibilities—such as telephoning, listening to music on the Web, doing research via the Internet, shopping electronically—actually diminishes our communication because it disconnects us from people we might meet incidentally at various social events. By being attached (and thus immobile) to the web of communication, our lives are deprived in two ways. First, we are cut off from the pleasure of seeing people in the thicker world of context and, as Borgmann notes, "from the instruction of being seen and judged by them. It robs us of the social resonance that invigorates our concentration and acumen when we listen to music or watch a play" in a social group.[33]

Second, we lose civility because the hyper-world of communications changes the way we inhabit our own bodies. As the communications network grows and thickens, it has "begun to transform the social fabric, our commerce with reality, and the sense we have of our place in the world" (108). This happens primarily because we receive information about the entire world with just our eyes and ears, while the rest of our body is rendered "immobile and irrelevant. The symmetry of world and body falls to the level of a shallow if glamorous world and a hyperinformed yet disembodied person" (106).

Third, some people lose civility because the communications network has caused a decline in their ability to remember. Who we are in the world

---

32. Two analyses of this cultural problem are Stephen L. Carter's *Civility: Manners, Morals, and the Etiquette of Democracy* (New York: HarperPerennial, 1998) and Richard J. Mouw's *Uncommon Decency: Christian Civility in an Uncivil World* (Downers Grove, Ill.: InterVarsity Press, 1992).

33. Albert Borgmann, *Crossing the Postmodern Divide* (Chicago: University of Chicago Press, 1992), 106. Page references to this book in the following paragraphs will be given parenthetically in the text.

is formed by how we comprehend the world and store what we have gathered in our memory. Yet today many people store their schedules, appointments, tasks, and relationships on their watches or palm computers and are helpless if the battery runs down and the data evaporate (107). Many of the practices by which societies formerly trained their minds to remember are no longer necessary, since our wired world offers many possibilities for memory storage, but perhaps without that training we lose some of our ability to retrieve aspects of the world for deeper pondering, new revelations, and retention of what we discover in the process.

Fourth, civility is lost if people think that television or other entertainments simply fill empty slots in their lives. Borgmann calls such an assumption absurd, for "life is always and already full; it is a total fabric. It may contain empty spaces for inconsequential additions. But if anything is added to life that takes time, the web of life is torn and rewoven; a hole is made by the new device" (112). This is the true source of our irritation if a dining partner talks on a cell phone while sitting with us. The fabric of life is being torn by the lack of an embodied relationship present to us. Thus, as people use more and more of the numerous commodities our wired world offers, the fabric of life is more frequently torn, and time is taken away from simple civility, extended courtesy, and long-term compassion.

Furthermore, many of the factors I've already posted on this collage contribute to the fact that U.S.ers are working more than ever (which, in turn, leads to such things as the loss of relationships, which we will consider next). A research study by the United Nations, under the supervision of economist Lawrence Jeff Johnson, reported that U.S.ers added nearly a full week to their work year during the 1990s by working an average of 1,979 hours per year. In 1995 the United States surpassed Japan and it has increased its lead ever since, so that by now U.S. workers spend 3.5 more weeks at their job than do Japanese workers, 6.5 more weeks than British workers, and 12.5 more weeks than German workers.[34]

Why Does the Technological, Commodified World Lead to Hyperactivity?

The loss of civility noted above is often goaded by our national propensity to hyperactivity, both as a culture and as individuals. Albert Borgmann stresses that this hurried busy-ness evolves for some people from the loss of reality (mocked so piercingly in the excerpt above from Milo's story).

34. This was detailed in a study paper on stress sent to professional educators in the Evergreen School District, Vancouver, Washington, on December 12, 2001.

If we lack the skill to notice the grandeur and subtlety of nature, art, and religion, we try to compensate because our lives start to seem one-dimensional, banal, or boring. Meanwhile, that very hyperactivity heightens our fears of not having enough time.

I know I'm guilty of hyperactive work habits. I claim that it's because I have a limited lifespan and want to get as much done as possible before I die. But might it also be due to what Borgmann recognizes, that hyperactivity "provides direction in the face of idleness and doubt and serves as the warrant of individual accomplishment and collective salvation"?[35] If so, then it is simply idolatry (see chapter 4) and is thereby destructive to my relationships with both God and others.

What Other Factors Contribute to Our Society's Loss of Relationships?

The various fettering bluffs and overwhelming overloads already sketched are some of the factors contributing to our hopelessness about relationships. I was struck by the yearning expressed in a fraternal insurance magazine column bemoaning the lack in homes not of the latest technology but of genuine relationships, symbolized by a place for the family to gather "to learn we are all in this together." The columnist also lamented, "No one has time to confess—and to forgive."

The article acknowledged that our homes are finer even than those in our parents' dreams, that by technological sophistication we have worlds of information within easy reach. We have more mobility, freedoms, and wealth than ever before. But at the same time, we are "poorer, more broken and less able to be a family because somewhere we lost . . . [the] center of our lives—our meeting place; our altar; our laughing, praying and being place."[36]

Notice that these yearnings involve both place and time, the true embodiment/body-ness of genuine relationships. Since I hear the same sort of desires from many people (on airplanes and at conferences), I add them to this chapter's collage as a fettering that many feel. In the face of our society's glut of advertising for all the things that the technological world enables us to possess, our deepest longings are left unanswered.

Contemporary film makers have recognized this cultural anguish. In the last year I have seen at least half a dozen movies in which the main char-

---

35. Borgmann, *Crossing the Postmodern Divide*, 16.
36. Rev. Ted Schroeder, "A Place to Come Together," Aid Association for Lutherans *Correspondent* (March–April 2001): 29.

acters at the beginning of the film have everything money can buy and somehow come to realize by the end that their lightning-paced, super-affluent, non-relational, self-centered lives are not what they really want.

Ellen Ullman amplifies the sense of emptiness from lack of relationships when she describes her connection to the workers in her business and with another software engineer. Once when she took her "company" out for a celebrative lunch, she admits, "[W]e were careful not to say too much about ourselves, careful not to make assumptions about the future. We were all practiced virtuals. We knew better than to get involved." Later, when she went home to her silent computers, "I had a rush of affection for the machines. They had a presence, a solidity, that made the empty [home] office feel occupied." So she gave her four computers names.[37]

Ullman also discovered that even in her romantic relationships she "had stopped expecting much. . . . It was too easy to live in these discrete, free-roaming capsules, a life like particles from an atom smasher, exploding into spectacular existence—for an instant—then gone." She felt sorry for both herself and her partner and bemoaned their lack of bravery. "Surely we were missing something essential if our idea of other people was a program downloaded from the Internet."[38] These are heartbreaking examples of the turnabout I learned from Ellul's work, that when technicization[39] reduces our skills, time, and social fabric for intimacy, we reverse the poles and technologize our intimacy while we intimize our technology.[40]

What Other Losses Do We Suffer Due to the Technologized, Commodified World?

School teachers frequently comment on how the technological milieu and its commodifications seem to be causing many young children to lose their sense of wonder. They see all kinds of techno-dazzle, but it is immediately outshined by the next spectacle and the next. In such a milieu, how can we

---

37. Ullman, *Close to the Machine*, 147.

38. Ibid., 180–181.

39. This word seems to have been coined by Jacques Ellul or his English translators to mean the onslaught of *techniques*. The word is to be differentiated from the problem of "technologization," which is the rapid proliferation of technologies, for it denotes instead a dependence upon quick-fix techniques that may or may not utilize technological gadgets or tools.

40. See chapter 2, "The True Source of the Pain," in Marva J. Dawn, *Sexual Character: Beyond Technique to Intimacy* (Grand Rapids: Wm. B. Eerdmans Publishing Co., 1993).

help our youth recapture genuinely freeing wonder? Many school programs try to match the culture's excitement and hype—but such a strategy fails in the end because we can never keep up with the Web's luster. Nor is this tactic desirable, since it merely contributes to the escalation of commodification.

Correlatively, Mitchell Kalpakgian comments on our present society's divorce of play from the natural world and its inexhaustible sources of "good old-fashioned fun."[41] As a result, even play is not lived by some people in an authentic way. For example, individuals might play chess with the computer instead of with a live person with whom they might converse, as part of a relationship in a natural world. Of course, there is nothing inherently wrong with entertainment, but we must learn to ask better questions about our amusements to ascertain whether they fetter our relationships and genuine play.

Kalpakgian is concerned for children who do most of their playing by means of the video culture; he insists that immersion in its diversions can lead to a "spiritual condition, an emptiness in the soul." If they become addicted to the excitement of the wired world, that often leads to passivity and apathy, lethargy and despondence when the stimulation is absent. In turn, they might actually become slothful and unwilling to exert themselves or unable to exercise any will power.[42] All these characteristics rob their lives of depth, action, truth. Perhaps the popularity of the magic and goodness and friendship evidenced in the Harry Potter stories and films expresses a yearning for these lost virtues.

English teacher and moral essayist Alan Jacobs has recognized that what J. K. Rowling has accomplished in the Harry Potter books is to create an alternative world (of the sort fabricated by J. R. R. Tolkien in *The Hobbit* and *Lord of the Rings* trilogy). He invokes Lynn Thorndike's eight-volumed *A History of Magic and Experimental Science* to show that magic and experimental science once shared the same path as efforts to control the natural environment. Science, of course, triumphed in history, but in Rowling's world the magic works as effectively as technology. Thus, Jacobs insists, "the fundamental moral framework" of her books is "the problem of technology."[43] He responds to those who don't recog-

---

41. Mitchell Kalpakgian, "Why the Entertainment Industry Is Bad for Children," *New Oxford Review* 63, 2 (March 1996): 13.
42. Ibid., 15.
43. Alan Jacobs, *Vanity Fair: Moral Essays on the Present Age* (Grand Rapids: Brazos Press, 2001), 143–145.

nize Rowling's moral carefulness about the magical world with these questions:

> Is your concern about the portrayal of this imaginary magical technology matched by a concern for the effects of the technology that in our world displaced magic? The technocrats of this world hold in their hands powers almost infinitely greater than those of Albus Dumbledore and Voldemort [the books' strongest characters of good and evil, respectively]. How worried are we about them, and about their influence over our children? Not worried enough, I would say.[44]

Jacobs asks questions somewhat as I am urging in this book, so that we look more carefully at the ways the technological world fetters us and sometimes steals our sense of wonder and play.

Closely related to the loss of wonder and concord with the natural world is the constricting of beauty in society's hyperactivity, sounds, landscapes, architecture, overcrowding, advertising. Perhaps we can best see this loss through architect Norton Juster's jesting description of Milo's encounter with Kakofonous A. Dischord, Doctor of Dissonance, whose specialization was all sorts and levels of noise—"from the slightly annoying to the terribly unpleasant."

He demonstrated some of his specialities, such as the sound of "a square-wheeled steam roller [driving] over a street full of hard-boiled eggs," but Milo couldn't imagine why anyone would want to hear such disagreeable sounds.

Yet they were popular. The doctor couldn't keep up with pleas for "noise pills, racket lotion, clamor salve, and hubbub tonic."

It hadn't been so in the past, he complained, when people had usually requested pleasurable sounds (except for times of war or earthquakes). His business started booming, however, when large cities were constructed—necessitating such sounds as "honking horns, screeching trains, clanging bells, deafening shouts, piercing shrieks, [and] gurgling drains."

The doctor offered Milo medicine to ensure that he would never hear lovely sounds again, but Milo insisted he didn't want that cure.[45]

A few adventures later, Milo and his friends entered the Valley of Sound, where everything had been silenced. The people there had been wisely ruled by a dearly loved Sound-keeper, who generously supplied

---

44. Ibid., 148.
45. Juster, *Phantom Tollbooth*, 137–138.

them with lovely sounds of raindrops and hoot owls, with songs in their stew pots and their hearts.

People got busy, though, and soon they had no time to listen. Then, "as you know, a sound which is not heard disappears forever and is not to be found again."

Laughter and songs decreased, grumbling and shouting increased, and everything got "louder and uglier." When hearing birdsong or breezes became too demanding, people quit listening.

Most people thought the tragedy started when Rhyme and Reason were exiled, but nobody could figure out what to do about it.[46]

By the end of Milo's adventure—visiting the Doldrums, Dictionopolis, the Island of Conclusions (to which one can only jump!), Digitopolis, the Foothills of Confusion, and the Mountains of Ignorance—he was able, with the help of a great community of people, to bring back the sisters Rhyme and Reason from their captivity at the Castle in the Air.

What will bring back Rhyme and Reason and their parent Hope to our world, drowning as it is in its various Sloughs of Despair?

What Fetters Prevent the Development of True Culture?

Noise displacing beauty, dazzle supplanting wonder, bluff and illusion superseding reality, speed shifting engagement, information replacing communication—all these might be summed up as the strangling of culture in North America. In *Faded Mosaic: The Emergence of Postcultural America*, Christopher Clausen, professor at Penn State, describes the word *culture* as signifying a morally demanding setting for one's life. A culture defines our existence in comparison with that of other groups and, by means of its own traditions, differentiates good and evil.[47]

What, then, should a culture supply? Christian culture, for example, offers its participants habits (such as praying before meals, hospitality), customs (like Advent wreaths), manners or a way of being (such as reconciling, being generous), traditions (for holidays, worship services), practices (like Sabbath keeping), even its own language about aspects of life (such as time, money, meaning in life, hope). Christianity also provides rules for behavior in certain settings, not in an oppressive or legalistic sense but as directives that actually free us to behave appropriately for the sake of relationships and communal well-being. The

---

46. Ibid., 147–149.
47. Christopher Clausen, *Faded Mosaic: The Emergence of Postcultural America* (Chicago: Ivan R. Dee, 2000).

absence of such a culture in general (and sometimes also in churches) is evident in our society's lack of conversation about sacrifice or the common good.

In 21st-century North America we experience a denuded non-culture. Canadians and U.S.ers no longer have shared values by which to assess good and evil and by which character is formed and focused, and this contributes to the personal de-centering that characterizes postmodernity. This leads, Clausen suggests, to a loss of identity, loss of direction or certainty as to who one is and to what one does in life.

If we do not participate in any community's culture and its authority or ideals, then we are more liable to become enslaved by conformity to the latest fads, to the media's bluffs, to the theology of capitalism, to the technological paradigm (explored in chapter 2). We become pseudo-individualists, dominated by narcissistic consumerism.

What Amplifies Our Loss of a Guiding Culture?

Closely attendant to an enfolding culture is a "guiding story," the meta-narrative that provides a framework for understanding how aspects of our individual and corporate lives connect. We need such a larger story to encompass our own and to link us to history and people, to provide cogent and unified beliefs, principles and goals, and reflection tools for making sound judgments about life and for living it wisely (see chapter 5).

U.S.ers in the past have had a guiding story—couched not only in economic, but also in religious, familial, philosophical, idealistic terms. However, that guiding story also carried political implications that were significantly onerous to minority peoples, certain ethnic or religious groups. We were ready to dispense with that story when postmodern philosophers insisted that any meta-narrative is intrinsically oppressive.

Nevertheless, we can't really live without an overarching outlook by which to steer our course as persons and a people. Consequently, into the resulting vacuum sped the technological, consumerist story, which I analyze in chapter 2 as the "technological paradigm."

Has Virtual Reality Overtaken More than Entertainments?

As various facets of this chapter's collage suggest, increasingly we live in a virtual reality, not merely as the result of certain technological tools and toys, but also because the commodification of everything hides from us the true nature of the globe and its inhabitants. The more the world is hidden from us, the more virtual reality becomes our reality. Tony Jones, who is a minister to youth and young adults in a wealthy suburb, warns of the danger that loss of culture poses to the users of technological toys: "As virtual reality becomes less virtual and more real, more and more people—especially youth—will choose this kind of ignorance: a life lived inside movies and games rather than in families and schools and relationships and jobs."[48]

The most poignant of all Ellen Ullman's technophile revelations concerns this "virtual life" and its bluffs. The word *virtual*, she comments, once meant "the sense of the false note, something missing, an ineffable quality of not-quite-happy,"[49] and while it still connotes "the missing, the not real . . . somehow this not-ness has become a good thing." It is considered grand to "be ephemerally existent, to float in some indefinable plane now known as cyberspace." Whereas companies once functioned like families, now those ideas of long-term commitment and fidelity to others have passed away (127).

She describes her own company like this:

> [A]ssemble a group of people to do a job, get it done, then disassemble. . . . The skill-set changes before the person possibly can, so it's always simpler just to change the person. Take out a component, put in a zippier one. The postmodern company as PC—a shell, a plastic cabinet. Let the people come and go; plug them in, then pull them out. (129)

She recognizes that as family life has changed and divorce has increased, workplaces seemed to remain stable as places for people still to gather. She suggests that this might be

> why the decline of industrial work and the downsizing of corporations have produced such anxiety: the final village is dissolving, and those of us without real jobs or fakes—where will we meet each other now?
> On line, I suppose. As virtualized creatures swimming alone in private pools of time. (145)

Recognizing her own deep sadnesses and writing about them so poetically, Ullman compares herself to the birds sent down first into the mine

---

48. Tony Jones, "Liberated by Reality," *Books and Culture* (September–October 1999): 27.

49. Ullman, *Close to the Machine*, 126. Page references to this book in the following paragraphs will be given parenthetically in the text.

shafts to determine whether the air in the cavern is toxic. She warns that "virtual workers are everyone's future" because

> [o]ur job commitments are contractual, contingent, impermanent, and this model of insecure life is spreading outward from us. I may be wrong, but I have this idea that we programmers are the world's canaries. We spend our time alone in front of monitors; now look up at any office building, look into living-room windows at night: so many people sitting alone in front of monitors. We lead machine-centered lives; now everyone's life is full of automated tellers, portable phones, pagers, keyboards, mice. We live in a contest of the fittest, where the most knowledgeable and skillful win and the rest are discarded; and this is the working life that waits for everybody. Everyone agrees: be a knowledge worker or be left behind. Technical people, consultants, contract programmers: we are going first. We fly down and down, closer and closer to the virtualized life, and where we go the world is following. (146)

Do we want to follow, down and closer to the virtualized life, in our society? Is there any choice, any chance to be freed from the mass of various fetters sketched in this chapter's collage? Can people in our society find a way out of this bondage? (The rest of this book will suggest how we might find hope and freedom.)

Ullman's descriptions raise critical and urgent questions for a society filled with despair as it faces the future she exhibits. The technological world's bluffs hide the fact that "virtual" reality has become so much our reality that we are virtually or really in bondage to the way it enslaves our hopes. The enslavement is all the more disturbing because it hides from one smaller part of the world the desperate reality of the larger proportion of the globe.

How Does the Technological, Commodified World Lead to Irresponsibility?

Furthermore, our society's inability to stop the slide into virtual reality afflicts us on the national landscape. Philosopher Albert Borgmann suggests that the United States is afflicted with the "sullenness" that characterizes many technologically advanced countries. Among other ways, the sullenness is manifested in indolence, which, he points out, is not simply laziness but a passivity that "is at bottom the incapacity to be pained by things undone and challenges unmet . . . a sort of paralyzed irresponsibility."[50] We see this irresponsibility in individuals (sometimes ourselves) and in the government.

Borgmann notes that this is strikingly apparent in connection with the foreign debt and federal budget deficits of the United States. Both illustrate our nation's inability to "tighten its belt," to call for self-discipline on the part of the people.[51] For a few years at the end of the 20th century the federal budget was balanced, but with tax rebates, a strong push by the government to lower taxes, the cost of the war against terrorism, the price of new security measures, and enormous fears about recession, it seems unlikely that the nation will live within its budget for the foreseeable future. Some people feel our country is fettered by the national debt, but they are often similarly indebted themselves and remain eager to have government benefits, such as lower taxes and better roads (a contradiction!), as well as the lower prices of foreign-made goods that continue to cause deficits in the nation's trade balance. Thus, the fettering caused by the country's economics continues to be amplified by the bondage of our inability as individuals and as a nation to deal with money resourcefully and stringently.

Is the Answer Always More?

Meanwhile, we ignore the real situation of the world. While one small part of the world eases its pain by producing and consuming more non-edible commodities, the rest of the world suffers an opposite kind of hopelessness—when persons are not able to secure the nourishment necessary to live. Let us add to the statistics already mentioned in the Introduction to see the picture of the world's financial discrepancies more clearly:

- One-half of the world's population of 6 billion live on less than $2 a day; 1.3 billion people live on less than $1 a day. Over 1 billion have no access to clean water; 3 billion have no access to sanitation. ("The Politics of Hunger," *Le Monde*, November 1998; and James Wolfenson, "The Other Crisis," World Bank, October 1998)
- The wealth of the 3 most well-to-do individuals now exceeds the combined GDP (gross domestic product) of the 48 least developed countries. (*Economic Apartheid in America*; and "The Politics of Hunger," *Le Monde*, November 1998)

---

50. Borgmann, *Crossing the Postmodern Divide*, 7.
51. Ibid.

- The world's 200 richest people have a combined wealth of $1 trillion. This is equal to the combined wealth of the world's 2.5 billion poorest people. (United Nations Development Program 2000 report)
- An analysis of long-term trends shows the distance between the richest and poorest countries was about
  3 to 1 in 1820
  11 to 1 in 1913
  35 to 1 in 1950
  44 to 1 in 1973
  72 to 1 in 1992 (1999 Human Development Report,
    United Nations Development Program).
- The wealthiest fifth of the world's people consume 86% of all goods and services; the poorest fifth, 1%. (Bread for the World)
- The wealthiest fifth of the world's people consume 45% of all meat and fish; the poorest fifth, 5%. (1998 Human Development Report, United Nations Development Program)
- In the two decades 1980–2000, the current form of globalization has caused marked declines in progress as compared with 1960–1980. Progress in life expectancy was *reduced* for every group of countries, except the one with the highest life expectancy. Progress in reducing infant mortality was also considerably slower. (Mark Weinbrot, Dean Baker, Egor Kraev, and Judy Chen, "The Scorecard on Globalization 1980–2000: Twenty Years of Diminished Progress," Center for Economic Policy and Research, August 2001)[52]
- The external debt of all developing countries has grown from $277 billion in 1971 to $2,171 billion in 1997. The cost to developing countries of servicing these debts has grown from $32 billion in 1971 to $269 billion in 1997. (World Bank, *Global Development Finance 1998*)
- In 1998 in developing countries, about 130 million eligible children out of a total 625 million did not attend primary school; 73 million of these children are girls. A 10% increase in girls' primary enrollment could be expected to decrease infant mortality by 4.1 per 1,000 babies. (UNICEF)

---

52. For perspectives from inside the opposition movement to the World Trade Organization, the World Bank, and the International Monetary Fund and their role in global poverty, see Kevin Danaher and Roger Burbach, eds., *Globalize This! The Battle Against the World Trade Organization and Corporate Rule* (Monroe, Maine: Common Courage Press, 2000).

- Around the globe, 250 million children are working; 600 million children live in extreme poverty. In the 1990s, 2 million children were killed in armed conflict and 35 million displaced from their homes. Thirty million children are being bought and sold into exploitation and abuse. Half a million children have died of AIDS. (Save the Children)
- Studies by the University of Maryland and the Harris polling organization show that the average citizen believes the United States is spending 16–18% of its entire budget on foreign aid. The actual amount is about 1%, only a fraction of which goes to sustainable development assistance. Most U.S.ers think we should contribute about as much as our major trading partners. In reality, per capita we spend less than one-fifth as much as Denmark, Norway, Sweden, and the Netherlands; one-third as much as Germany, Austria, Belgium, France, and Switzerland; less than half as much as Britain, Australia, Finland, and Canada. (Organization for Economic Cooperation and Development; Bread for the World)

By the time you read these pages, the statistics will be outdated. I use them only to sketch the disparities of the world. Other statistics underscore injustice in the United States.

Do We Recognize the Gross Injustices and Racial Disparities in the United States?

- Twelve million U.S. children live in households where people have to skip meals or eat less to make ends meet. One in ten U.S. households live with hunger or are at risk of hunger. (Bread for the World)
- In 1998 the average U.S. CEO was paid as much as 419 factory workers. (*Business Week*)
- A 1989 survey of 44 major U.S. companies showed that not one of them paid any federal taxes, though they made a collective total profit of $53.6 billion. All the companies had *reduced* their work forces. Their profits went for higher stock dividends, for higher pay for CEOs (an average pay hike of 54%), and to pay for corporate mergers and acquisitions. (Citizens for Tax Justice)[53]
- As of 1998, median income for a black household was $25,351; for a white household, $40,912. Thus a black family earns $619 for

---

53. For an extensive overview, see Michael Hudson, ed., *Merchants of Misery: How Corporate America Profits from Poverty* (Monroe, Maine: Common Courage Press, 1996).

every $1,000 earned by a white family. The unemployment rate was 3.9% for whites in 1998 but 8.9% for blacks.[54]

- Black men are seven times more likely to die as murder victims than are white men, and black women four times more likely than white women.
- Black women live five years less than white women; black men live nearly seven years less than white men.
- A higher percentage of blacks than whites live in poverty at every level of educational attainment.
- Some influential, often wealthy, and trusted persons, including teachers and diplomats, have been found to be forcing immigrants, hired to work as nannies and maids in private residences, into virtual bondage with low wages, physical mistreatment and sexual abuse, denial of medical care, and chaining and other means to bar escape. (*USA Today* series of reports, beginning November 19, 2001)

Do We Know the Disastrous Consequences of AIDS for Poorer Nations?

- In Africa, 17 million have died from AIDS, 26 million are infected with HIV, and 12 million children have been orphaned.
- Cases of infection in Russia doubled in the last year, and in the Caribbean they increased by almost 20%. Epidemiologists warn that in India, where the HIV-infected population is rapidly rising above 4 million, AIDS cases by 2010 could number more than those in all Africa today.
- Worldwide, 1,800 babies are born infected with HIV each day; 42,000 children die of AIDS each month; and 3,000,000 children lose one or both parents to AIDS each year. (United Nation Security Council's 1st meeting of the 21st century; "Prescriptions for Hope," International Christian Conference on HIV/AIDS, sponsored by Samaritan's Purse)

---

54. These statistics and the next three sets are from David Gushee's manuscript of his chapter 19, "Race," in Glen M. Stassen and David P. Gushee, *Christian Ethics as Following Jesus* (Downers Grove, Ill.: InterVarsity Press, forthcoming). He adds (from Andrew Hacker, *Two Nations: Black and White, Separate, Hostile, Unequal* [New York: Ballantine Books, 1992]), that numerous studies reveal that whites get uncomfortable if the black proportion of their neighborhood reaches 8 percent; beyond that, "white flight" begins and the neighborhood rapidly turns over. Imagine the sense of humiliation and rejection the "white flight" phenomenon must inculcate in racial minorities.

Do We Understand That Violence
Is Often a Result of Economic Injustice?

The ubiquitous violence that we all fear and mourn is directly related to economic and other disparities. We can work for peace only if we are engaged in practices of justice building. However, instead of investing heavily in building justice, many put enormous reliance on guns and violence to "protect our stuff." The United States abets violence elsewhere in the world:

- In each of the ten years between 1992 and 2002, the United States has sold between $15 and $30 billion worth of arms, two or three times as much as were sold even in peak Cold War years of the 1980s. In some years, the United States sold more weapons than were sold by all the other nations of the world combined. (*Arms Trade Monitor*, Federation of American Scientists; see also Jeff Cole and Sara Lubman, "Weapons Merchants Going Great Guns in Post–Cold War Era," *Wall Street Journal*, January 26, 1994)
- The number of countries to whom the United States sells weapons has gone up, not down—150 countries in 1995, nearly twice the Cold War number. Arms sales dwarf almost anything else the United States is doing for other nations, *exceeding the combined budgets* of the Peace Corps, development assistance, the State Department, and all our embassies and their programs. ("World Military Expenditures and Arms Transfers," U.S. Arms Control and Disarmament Agency annual; Federation of American Scientists list of recipient countries)
- Despite rhetoric that U.S. arms are sold to help recipient nations defend themselves, the United States has transferred weapons or military technology to one or more participants in 45 of 50 significant conflicts in the post–Cold War world. Civilians represent 70–90% of the casualties. (William Hartung, "Weapons at War: Arms Deliveries to Regions of Conflict," World Policy Institute report, June 1995; Ruth Leger Sivard, *World Military and Social Expenditures 1996*)[55]

---

55. Further information on these issues can be found in these useful and respected overviews: William Hartung, *And Weapons for All* (New York: HarperCollins, 1994); John Tierman, *Spoils of War: The Human Costs of the Arms Trade* (New York: Free Press, 1997); and the annual yearbooks published by the Stockholm International Peace Research Institute.

What Were the Conditions in Afghanistan
When the War on Terrorism Began?

- Some 3.5 million Afghan refugees were in Pakistan and Iran. One in four Afghan children died before the age of five. Life expectancy for men and women had fallen to 46.
- Because of a three-year drought, herdsmen had lost more than two-thirds of their sheep and goats. About half of all irrigation systems had been knocked out by war or abandoned. There was little or no electricity; safe water was hard to find; and health services were scarce for men and nearly nonexistent for women. Relief agencies warned that a fourth of the population remained at risk of death from war, hunger, or poverty.
- Relief agencies estimated that 7.5 million Afghans, refugees as well as those displaced within the country, would need food assistance within a few months.
- Powerful earthquakes in 1998 collapsed roofs on sleeping families in northern villages, killing more than 7000 and destroying 53,000 homes.[56]

Do We Put a Personal Face on Poverty and Listen to Its Voice?

In *A Hand Full of Stars*, by Rafik Schami, a young boy who lives in poverty and under political oppression in Damascus, Syria, tells his story through his diary. The novel, which we will look at again in chapter 3, is true to its author's own childhood.

In the May 10 entry of his journal, Rafik mentions that his friend Mahmud was taken out of school to help his father feed the family of nine. Rafik writes, "Mahmud cursed, for, just like me, he enjoyed going to school. Mahmud's fondest hope was to become a pilot and see the world. Poverty smothers our dreams even before we have finished dreaming them."[57]

Besides the quenching of their dreams, the boys and their families experience political oppression (which is often correlative with situations of

---

56. These statistics were compiled by the National Geographic Society at the beginning of the U.S.-led war in Afghanistan and reported in "Afghanistan: Land in Crisis" (National Geographic Maps, December 2001).

57. Rafik Schami, *A Hand Full of Stars*, trans. Rika Lesser (New York: Dutton Children's Books, 1990), 95. Page references to this book in the following paragraphs will be given parenthetically in the text.

poverty).[58] On June 24, Rafik writes of a sudden police appearance at his father's bakery. Officers jumped out of a car, "stationed themselves at the door, and barred it with their machine guns." When Rafik's father was arrested, the soldiers pushed customers with the butts of their guns as his father looked on, horrified and pale (101). After his father was taken away, Rafik writes about how the police worked him over—threatening him with a pistol pointed at his head, pulling the trigger when he repeatedly declared that he didn't know whatever "truth" they wanted.

> The pistol was not loaded, but my father fainted. . . . Four days the scoundrels beat my father, until they discovered they had confused him with a lawyer who had worked against the government and who happened to have the same name.

When Rafik confides his hatred to an old friend, the latter says, "Whoever forgives injustice, gets more injustice" (103). Could Rafik's diary rouse us all to ask ourselves whether our passivity about the injustices in the world has simply allowed them to multiply faster?

On October 20, Rafik writes that he is composing an article about beggars. He tells how the new mayor in Damascus was sending the police to hunt beggars because upon taking office he pledged to get rid of them within half a year, since they "make the city look bad to tourists." Rafik's comments are enormously insightful:

> I found the new mayor genuinely stupid for persecuting the poor and not poverty. If tourists stay away because of them, then a monument to beggars ought to be erected. . . . The mayor comes from one of the wealthiest families in the north. His grandparents owned whole villages, including the inhabitants. His father has a bank, and now the son wants to persecute the very people his parents and grandparents put out of work. For many beggars were once craftsmen or farmers who lost everything and came to Damascus in the hope of finding

---

58. For a fascinating account of methods of resistance and weapons of self-preservation used by oppressed working-class people, whose hopes are continually fettered by new technologies and supposed "developments" that restrict them further—such tenacious efforts as ridicule, truculence, irony, petty acts of non-compliance, foot-dragging, dissimulation, resistant mutuality, the disbelief in elite homilies, and other such "steady, grinding efforts to hold one's own against overwhelming odds" (350)—see James C. Scott, *Weapons of the Weak: Everyday Forms of Peasant Resistance* (New Haven, Conn.: Yale University Press, 1985).

work. The beggars, I wrote, understand more about people and their souls than many schoolteachers. All they need do is look at someone, and instantly they know how to address that person. Does the mayor know how to do this? (125)

Rafik's reflections ask us to consider whether our wealth puts people out of work, if we comprehend how their dreams are smothered, if we understand the kinds of oppressions they suffer, if we know how to listen to them in order to partner with them. Do we know how great the world's tragedies are?

Can We Expand Our Grief at Tragedy to Encompass the World?

We began this book with the 2,800[59] people who died because hijackers flew planes into the Trade Center towers and the Pentagon. That woke us up to larger afflictions than the constant fetterings we experience in the technological, commodified milieu. May we continue to be made more alert to the huge tragedies of our glaringly unjust world!

The disparity of the world is shown clearly by this adaptation of a report from the United Nations Food and Agriculture Organization comparing the deaths caused by terrorists on September 11, 2001, and the statistics of deaths by starvation and other preventable conditions on that same day:

STATISTICS FOR 9/11/01
- Victims: 35,615 children
- Where: poor countries
- Newspaper articles: none
- Special TV programs: none
- Messages from the president: none
- Bills before Congress to deal with the crisis: none
- Military alert level: unchanged
- Minutes of silence: none

---

59. I leave this number inexact because commentators continue to report the extensive psychological toll the tragedy is taking on the families of those who died and on children in New York City. At least one survivor has died by suicide and some from other anxiety-induced causes.

Chapter 2

Why Does the Technological Society Overwhelm Us?

How has the world become so unbalanced that part of the world struggles to cope with all the stuff it possesses while the larger part of the world scrambles to find enough? How have citizens of the richer nations lost the ability to choose, to limit their consumption, to question the commodities and technologies of their milieu? Why does the technological society overwhelm us with its speed of change, its tempo of activity, its plethora of possibilities, its glut of information? Why, with all our technological and consumer capabilities, do we feel more burdened than ever?

In this chapter, Albert Borgmann, philosophy professor at the University of Montana in Missoula, will help us discern more clearly the underlying nature of the technological milieu so that we can become more liberated from its control. Moreover, Borgmann offers suggestions so that we will be able to move more positively toward reform—for our own sake and for the sake of others and the world.

The Technological Paradigm

Borgmann first asks whether technology, at this stage in history, is able to be truly liberating, whether emancipation in one location doesn't usually impose another new kind of burden somewhere else.[1] To pursue the question of whether "technology can make good its promise in a socially just way, nationally and internationally" (39), Borgmann develops an account

---

1. Albert Borgmann, *Technology and the Character of Contemporary Life: A Philosophical Inquiry* (Chicago: University of Chicago Press, 1984), 38. Page references to this book throughout this chapter will be given parenthetically in the text.

of the character of technology which acknowledges that the problem is not technology per se, but its "device paradigm."

To begin to understand Borgmann's idea of the device paradigm, let us ponder short sections of his description of the ease that technology promises.

> As a first step let us note that the notions of liberation and enrichment are joined in that of availability. Goods that are available to us enrich our lives and, if they are technologically available, they do so without imposing burdens on us. Something is available in this sense if it has been rendered instantaneous, ubiquitous, safe, and easy. (41)

Borgmann uses the example of warmth to demonstrate what he means by this kind of availability. One hundred years ago in Montana (or much longer ago in the eastern United States), the kind of warmth we now can produce in our homes was not available according to the definition above. At that time heat

> was not *instantaneous* because in the morning a fire first had to be built in the stove or the fireplace. And before it could be built, trees had to be felled, logs had to be sawed and split, the wood had to be hauled and stacked. Warmth was not *ubiquitous* because some rooms remained unheated, and none was heated evenly. The coaches and sleighs were not heated, nor were the boardwalks or all of the shops and stores. It was not entirely *safe* because one could get burned or set the house on fire. It was not *easy* because work, some skills, and attention were constantly required to build and sustain a fire. (41, emphasis mine)

We might think that these four characteristics are adequate for understanding availability's distinctiveness, but that is because we tend to think that technological progress is

> a more or less gradual and straightforward succession of lesser by better implements. The wood-burning stove yields to the coal-fired central plant with heat distribution by convection, which in turn gives way to a plant fueled by natural gas and heating through forced air, and so on. (41)

But Borgmann shows that technological progress involves much more than increasingly better tools. He demonstrates this by distinguishing between *things* and *devices*. In the sense in which he uses the word, a *thing* cannot be separated from its context—the whole world of tasks and skills that are related to it—and from the way we become engaged with the thing and its world. When we experience a thing such as a fireplace, we also become bodily and socially engaged with its world of preparing wood and other tasks. Because of that complex engagement, "a thing necessarily provides more than one commodity." For example, a fireplace or stove

> used to furnish more than mere warmth. It was a *focus*, a hearth, a place that gathered the work and leisure of a family and gave the house a center. Its coldness marked the morning and the spreading of its warmth the beginning of the day. It assigned to the different family members tasks that defined their place in the household. The mother built the fire, the children kept the firebox filled, and the father cut the firewood. It provided for the entire family a regular and bodily engagement with the rhythm of the seasons that was woven together of the threat of cold and the solace of warmth, the smell of wood smoke, the exertion of sawing and of carrying, the teaching of skills, and the fidelity to daily tasks. (41–42)

So far we have discovered that the world of a thing (the fireplace or stove) includes such aspects as its location and the meaning of that location in people's lives, the tasks that had to be undertaken for the thing to do its work, the skills that those tasks required, the ways in which different people related to the thing or worked for its use. But these aspects of bodily engagement and of relationships, according to Borgmann, are just part of all that the thing's world entails.

Even physical engagement is more than simply our actual bodily contact with the thing. It also includes the way the thing's entire world is experienced through every bodily sensibility—seeing, hearing, smelling, tasting, touching, feeling, thinking, imagining. Moreover,

> That sensibility is sharpened and strengthened in skill. Skill is intensive and refined world engagement. Skill, in turn, is bound up with social engagement. It molds the person and gives the person character. Limitations of skill confine any one person's primary engagement with the world to a small area. With the other areas one is mediately engaged through one's acquaintance with the characteristic demeanor and habits of the practitioners of the other skills. That

> acquaintance is importantly enriched through one's use of their prod-
> ucts and the observation of their working. (42)

I can understand more deeply what Borgmann means by engagement with all one's bodily sensibilities when I compare my husband's experience of the garden with my own. His skills are extremely refined, whereas mine are not. Consequently, when we walk in the garden, he notices plants more minutely, smells the combination of soil and plants more thor-oughly, tastes the air, touches the amount of moisture in the soil, imag-ines what a plant will be like in a few weeks or months, recognizes where we are in the seasons by the level of growth, and so forth. These skills are a large part of the patience and gentleness of his character.

Since my skills are minimal in the area of gardening, I am only "medi-ately engaged" through my acquaintance with Myron, but as I have watched him and learned from him, my knowledge of both gardens (the *thing* and its world) and him is deepened. I taste corn differently since I married him.

Borgmann now expands our background still more, for work

> is only one example of the social context that sustains and comes to
> be focused in a thing. If we broaden our focus to include other prac-
> tices, we can see similar social contexts in entertainment, in meals, in
> the celebration of the great events of birth, marriage, and death. And
> in these wider horizons of social engagement we can see how the cul-
> tural and natural dimensions of the world open up. (42)

With this background in seeing how each thing focuses an entire social context or world, we can now look at Borgmann's notion of the *device*. We have learned from Borgmann that a *thing* like the fireplace not only sup-plies warmth, but also invariably provides numerous other experiences and relationships and skills that are part of the fireplace's entire world. In many cases those other elements were burdensome. In contrast,

> [a] device such as a central heating plant procures mere warmth and
> disburdens us of all other elements. These are taken over by the
> machinery of the device. The machinery makes no demands on our
> skill, strength, or attention, and it is less demanding the less it makes
> its presence felt. (42)

An important key for understanding Borgmann's notion of the device is our recognition of the *machinery* that removes from us the burdens we experience with a thing. The best machinery doesn't require us to have any skill at all. As a result, as technology develops, we notice the machinery less and less. It becomes hidden because we don't have to do anything about it.

Therefore, the only physical aspect of a device we pay attention to is the commodity which it produces or procures. A commodity, then, is "what a device is there for." The device of a furnace produces warmth. A cell phone gives us communication; a car, transportation; frozen food, a meal; a CD player, music (42). In most cases we know very little or nothing about the machinery that makes it possible for the devices to give us these commodities—and we are very glad if we don't have to find out.

Let us look practically at Borgmann's insights to note what troublesome dimensions of contemporary life his descriptions have already illuminated. First of all, we recognize, though we appreciate the great gift of central heating, that many other gifts have been lost by the displacing of the fireplace's "world."

Please note that I do not intend to romanticize these gifts; throughout the following listing, I am very conscious of the burden of work and discomfort that the aspects I enumerate generated. My concern is for how we have compensated or will try to compensate for these treasures which have been displaced by central heating (to use Borgmann's example): children's chores to keep the firebox filled, their responsibility to fulfill that chore, their resultant self-discipline, their accountability (experiencing cold) when the responsibility was not met; the rhythm of the day marked by morning's lighting of the fire, the gathering of the family in the evening by the fire, and the day's conclusion with the banking of the coals; the possibility for a fabric of intimacy when parents and children worked side by side to produce the heat for their home; and the practice of adults mentoring their children in skills essential for living. What in contemporary society replaces these jewels?

Many parents bemoan their experience that their children don't need them or respect them. What skills essential for living (such as how to know which trees to fell, to fell them, to cure the wood, to lay a fire) do parents actually have to teach their offspring presently? What natural opportunities are there for them to mentor their descendants these days in a way that builds the same intrinsic connections that were developed when children *had* to learn skills from their parents to be able to survive in the wilderness? In fact, computers have reversed the mentoring, since many adults depend on their children to master them faster and then teach their parents how to work computers.

Thus, Borgmann includes in the present-day plight of the family the fact that technology has taken over many of the family's shared tasks (such as dishwashing) and the world of family relationships. Small nuclear families no longer require the help of extended households with grandparents and other relatives, and the reduction in shared tasks and the consequent

> growing emptiness of family life leave the parents bewildered and the children without guidance. Since less and less of vital significance remains entrusted to the family, the parents have ceased to embody rightful authority and a tradition of competence, and correspondingly there is less and less legitimate reason to hold children to any kind of discipline. Parental love is deprived of tangible and serious circumstances in which to realize itself. (226)

Technological devices develop so rapidly that the competencies parents might hold are quickly outdated, so these do not provide the same kind of mentoring possibilities demonstrated with the illustration of the fireplace and wood preparation. Correlatively, many of the aspects of "vital significance" which were formerly taught by parents to their children are now, lamentably, turned over by many parents to the schools and churches.

Changes in family relationships are not the only major alteration caused by technological devices. Borgmann also highlights three ways in which devices change the relationship of means and ends. First, many kinds of means (e.g., all sorts of heating devices or watches) can produce the same ends (the commodities of warmth or a way to keep time). As a result, those many kinds of devices compete on the market and both create, and provide the means to fill, the constant consumerist requirement to "upgrade" one's devices.

Closely related is a second feature, "the concealment and unfamiliarity of the means and the simultaneous prominence and availability of the ends" (43–44). This second dimension leads to many of our frustrations and anxieties in this technological age. Of course, we need (or simply want) our furnaces and cars, VCRs and computers, but we don't know how the means work, so we are unable to fix our furnaces or word processing problems by ourselves (as in the case of my lost file reported in chapter 1). Moreover, many of us do not know our mechanics or repair workers personally because of the "social anonymity of the technological universe," as Borgmann describes it, so our interaction with them is based entirely on money and signed contracts, rather than on trust and fidelity in the work. When we know the furnace builders and shopkeepers as members of our community, they will be held responsible for their present business by the possibility of our future shopping and trust in their labor. Perhaps most of us no longer experience in our present milieu a web of relations that knits a local community together and that inherently involves morality of relations, faithfulness and honesty in craftsmanship.

Third, the relation of work to nature is thwarted. Borgmann cites George Sturt's *The Wheelwright's Shop* (first published in 1923), which described the care and mastery by which a wheelwright watched for certain curves in wood suitable for particular farm implements and the way his knowledge of the neighborhood made him aware of which tools were needed. In contrast, technologically driven manufacturing can force itself against the natural grains of wood (or instead construct tools with artificial materials), and commodities are produced without relation to the genuine needs of the consumers (44–47) but simply because a certain factory produces only this commodity. As a result, sometimes inventories of manufactured products far outpace or lag behind real need.

Borgmann thus encourages us to learn to see

> how the presence of things is replaced with the availability of commodities and how availability is procured through devices. Devices . . . dissolve the coherent and engaging character of the pretechnological world of things. In a device, the relatedness of the world is replaced by a machinery, but the machinery is concealed, and the commodities, which are made available by a device, are enjoyed without the encumbrance of or the engagement with a context.

This leads to other aspects of commodities, such as that they are carefree (like unbreakable dishes) or increasingly disposable (since repair is impossible or more costly than replacement). These factors make us inattentive to anything but the commodity itself; it has no context (47).

Borgmann's descriptions keep ringing true in my experience, as I would surmise they do for you. I think, for example, of the rush of some plastic-dished meals on ordinary days, in contrast to festival gatherings when I use my grandmother's china. Then I handle the plates with immense care (since only one has been broken in the eighty years the china's been in the family), gratitude (for grandmother's precious and beautiful gift to me), and love (both for her and for my guests whom I want to honor with these treasures of cherished dishes). An immense web of relations is part of the world the china introduces.

To expand this illustration, let us think about the food that we might put on china. Is it made ready as part of the world of "bountiful harvests, careful preparations, and festive meals," or is it a frozen dinner which we merely nuke in the microwave and consume as "an isolated entity without preparation, resonance, and consequence" (51)? Another way that Borgmann names the difference is whether I view my cooking as a distraction (from my primary work of writing this book) or engagement for the sake of my relationships (with my husband or with guests).

Once we understand Borgmann's idea of the device paradigm, we start to recognize how that pattern has also taken over in many aspects of life not related to technological tools or toys, but nonetheless important components of the consumer society. One prominent example my husband and I discuss concerns what is happening in education because of the national programs that require students to pass certain tests to be promoted. In many cases, this leads to the loss of the arts in the curriculum, because such instruction is not a useful device for producing the commodity of passing grades on the exams. Teachers find themselves having to teach to the test, with the result that the classroom becomes merely the device for a certain commodity of proficiency rather than a place where students engage in the discipline of learning in relationship with each other and their teachers.

Of course, it is necessary for students to reach certain levels of skill, and schools need ways to ascertain whether or not they are reaching those levels. My point is simply that this particular means for accomplishing that end can endanger true learning, stifle eager curiosity, and take away the delight of discovery, replacing it with the fetters of a test that ignores the many other kinds of intelligence children have. It can eventually produce the kind of consumers of education (found on university campuses) who see their years in college merely as a device to produce the commodity of a high-paying job.

It is important for us to remember Borgmann's distinction between distraction and engagement—illustrated above by whether cooking is a distraction from my work or the opportunity for deeper engagement in my relationships—for in many instances we can't do anything about the advances of the technological milieu. In general, we can hardly return to horses instead of automobiles or to communal shoemakers instead of shoestores—nor would it be essentially desirable. However, Borgmann adds, sometimes we encounter situations in which we are able, if there are no economic or legal barriers, to make choices for engagement rather than distraction. When we make such decisions, we protest technology's rule, rather than confirm it (104).

Simple examples (dependent on where we live) might include such choices as supporting a local baker's shop, purchasing furniture from a wood craftsman, or obtaining fruit from a nearby orchardist. Through a wonderful chain of unlikely events, I was introduced to a highly skilled shoemaker in Minnesota, who crafts shoes to fit and support my crippled leg. Now the task of obtaining shoes, formerly a very bothersome distraction, has become an occasion for engagement with a friend. He and his wife even called me to chat yesterday while visiting their son who lives near me here in the Pacific Northwest.

Since what fetters us is not technology per se, but that its device paradigm has become the primary, though usually inconspicuous, pattern by which much of our society operates (105), the key question is how we can stay alert for opportunities in which we can choose to be engaged. For example, think of the difference between parents buying their child a CD player and three CDs or buying or renting a violin and lessons. The CD player and discs are a device to produce the commodity of music. As such, that choice will inevitably lead to the need to purchase more discs when the musical commodities of the first CDs begin to get "boring." To introduce the child instead to genuine engagement with music, in contrast, is to acquaint her with an entire world of relationships—with teachers, fellow students, orchestra members, model performers, composers—and with endless possibilities for music to play.

However, parents are often inclined to choose only the former because it is a "quick fix," and that is precisely why the device paradigm is such a dangerous pattern for our society. The quick fix is easy—and usually what both parents and child prefer—but it does not lead to lasting engagement. To enable a child to listen to CDs does not require much parental involvement; the child becomes easily entertained with only one simple lesson in how to turn the player on.

Violin lessons, in contrast, require enormous endurance through the first months (years?) of screeching sounds and complaints about practicing. The parent might attend plenty of student recitals and some professional concerts so that the child can be exposed to superb playing in order to have the patience to continue. Such patience might not even be possible if the child's character has not been so formed by other experiences in which hard work "pays off" in the end. The great benefit of this process, though, is that the child's character will be formed, in turn, by the disciplines of listening, practicing, performing, and relating to the musical world, and her character will affect other dimensions of her life.

One other point about remaining alert for occasions when we can make decisions and evade the control of the device paradigm is all the more crucial because of the inextricable connection that Borgmann identifies between this rule of technology and world economic inequality. Since democracy advocates and claims to foster a notion of equality, he asks why inequality seems to be so much accepted that the machinery of government (and, we might add, of religion) is not employed fully to eradicate it. This is a crucial question for us and helps us realize why we must understand the device paradigm in order to work for justice in the world.

Borgmann considers several unsatisfactory answers but finally concludes that the questions are why inequality persists and, "more precisely, how technology has put its stamp on it." His perceptive answer is "that inequality favors the advancement and stability of the reign of technology" (112). Since the wealthy will always want new products for the sake of greater ease and fresh entertainments, technological advances will continue to be fostered by the inequality.

There is not space in this book to delineate Borgmann's entire (and entirely persuasive) argument, but there can be no doubt that, as he notes, the distinctive connection of technology and inequality in industrially advanced Western democracies leads to a societal stability that will be preserved only if technology keeps on advancing (113). Later in this book we shall have to ask whether that equilibrium needs to be upset and how it might be done.

How Does the Device Paradigm Enable Us to Understand Our Fetters?

Borgmann's description of the "device paradigm" as the controlling rule of societal consumption and economic growth helps us see that the issues exposed in chapter 1 are not merely a simplistic matter of "values." The reduction of many dimensions of our lives to "devices producing commodities" limits or fetters our ability to be engaged in life with genuine hope.

For example, when the devices of a factory and a microwave produce instantly available "freshly baked" cookies, we lose not only the opportunity to engage in baking cookies together with our children but also the surrounding social fabric that makes possible the development of intimacy. I do not romanticize the past and claim that intimacy created by shared tasks and pleasures was always good intimacy, but at least the social fabric presented the opportunity for healthy engagement in relational work, leisure activities, or shared silence. In our present society, parents and children have far fewer tasks in which they can or must be engaged together.

Borgmann's exposing of the prevailing device paradigm enables us to see that the cultural info-glut is also a commodity tied in with this controlling societal rule. We are burdened by the info-glut not only because of the immensity of the piles of data that cross our desks but because the information is not connected to the matters that engage us and give our life meaning and purpose. Instead of giving us satisfying work because of our engagement in good labor, information serves as a distraction that societal pressures prevent us from escaping.

Even news is hardly ever really news; it is merely a commodity produced by the devices of cameras and tape recorders, broadcasting studios and relay stations. Most of us receive more than enough so-called communications, which are merely commodities not grounded in a relational world.

Borgmann's paradigm also helps us begin to understand the almost inescapable correlation of technological advance, media hype, and consumption. We cannot very easily evade the influence of advertising when it is so intricately interwoven with the fundamental fabric of society. In North America, the economy "must grow" because technology has become the foreground of existence instead of its background. Consequently, in the weeks after September 11, 2001, citizens were urged to "spend" to fulfill their patriotic duty.

This cultural mindset leads to the economic strangulation that many families experience. When they are no longer able to be engaged in their primary interests because of the control of the device paradigm, they become caught by the tugs and lures of advertising and the tangle of needs (1) to earn enough money to give their children every technological advantage, (2) for novelty to replace engagement in order to escape the demands of work, and (3) for an endless accumulation of consumer gadgets to save time.

As an example, consider parents who are themselves being turned into a device at their jobs because their bosses expect them, or their situations require them, to produce more and more commodities of work. Since they have to labor increasingly longer hours to accomplish that work, they are no longer able to spend the kind of time they would like with their children. They can't afford to quit that job and find one less demanding because they need the money, but often they need the money to buy gadgets to save time or for entertainments for their children because they themselves can't devote time to them. The whole cycle seems inescapable.

The result of the device paradigm's operation is a variety of kinds of violence—not only of the rich over the poor, as more and more resources become devoted to the technological advancement of the few rather than to the alleviation of the poverty of the many, but also against our own personhood when we are ensnared in the way of life precipitated by the technological milieu and its rule. Thus, our world is characterized by the despairs of the hopelessly enmeshed.

Why Do We Not Notice What the Device Paradigm Does to Our Sense of Work?

Borgmann identifies several key dimensions of work and labor in relation to technology that apply to our reflections here. As a quotation above from Borgmann noted, early technologies genuinely liberated workers from arduous tasks. However, he has observed that over time "liberation has gradually given way to disengagement, and distraction has displaced enrichment." If hard work is still supposedly valued as the primary activity that bestows dignity, why is it being increasingly "degraded and disliked"? Why haven't we noticed that increasingly those who are the technological leaders have the most interesting, the most respected, and the best paying jobs, while many unskilled laborers are left with stultifying work and little respect? In many areas of the work force, what was originally the work of artisans is largely being done by machines and what remains is divided into repetitive labors (118)—so, for example, skilled chefs who can enjoy creative work are vastly outnumbered by the factory workers who oversee machines that produce hamburger patties or package them and the fast-food workers who fry endless mounds of them.

Several factors have kept us from noticing this dissonance between society's praise for hard work and our actual disrespect for it. First, we don't readily distinguish genuine liberation from disengagement. For example, in spite of the drudgery of carrying water and the merit of plumbing systems, the biblical Rebecca, in "going to the well, not only found water there but also companionship, news of the village, and her fiancé" (119).[2] Because in a technological society we really view labor

---

2. Borgmann credits Daniel Boorstin's *Democracy and Its Discontents: Reflections on Everyday America* (New York: Random House, 1975), 112–114, for this idea.

merely as the means to an end, we overstate how much technology really liberates us when it transforms our work. As a result, we don't notice how much we actually lose culturally and socially. Thinking that liberation from drudgery is possible only if we degrade the work, we sanction the debasement even if maintaining the work would not cause unacceptable difficulty.

Second, hard work's degradation is hidden because we assume that the sophistication of the technology correlates with the sophistication of the worker's skill. As a result, farmers who carefully steward and tend their family's land and housewives, whose work involves immense but primarily pretechnological craft, are considered unskilled. Compare how homemaking mothers and CEOs of major corporations are valued in U.S. society (yet which is ultimately crucial to human flourishing?).

A third factor that conceals the degradation of labor is the assumption that common technological work increasingly requires us to gain larger amounts of education. Borgmann, however, questions that assumption in two ways: (1) Is education in this country increasing in quality? and (2) Does typical labor in the technological milieu actually allow us to use more knowledge and training? He suggests that both questions should be answered negatively and then presents these frank convictions:

> To avoid the consequent embarrassment of finding that much of our education is irrelevant to labor, length of education has been put to new purposes which are really foreign to its nature. Since desirable work is scarce, education is used as an obstacle course which is lengthened as such work becomes scarcer. Educational requirements are used as a device to screen applicants. And finally, educational credentials serve to solidify the privileges of professions and the stratification of society. (119)

Why Do We Need to Be Entertained?

Obtaining a certain privileged position, or a large amount of money, or a high level of busy-ness, or increasing consumption of more (and more varied) commodities has become the driving force in people's lives because the technological milieu has trained us to despise common labors, has stolen from us the inherent enjoyment of work, and has hidden from us the degradation of labor. We have learned to desire only the final *product*, the commodity, and not to value the *process* of work, which has instead become merely the device. (An example of this constant temptation is my struggle not to value only the finished product when I have completed the writing of this book, but instead to appreciate the process of thinking these things through and the labor of crafting progressions of thought into sentences and chapters.)

Our disdain for labor and process leads to the despairing boredom so prevalent in our present society. Once again, Borgmann's analysis is very enlightening:

> [T]he great defensive devices that protect us from hunger, cold, disease, darkness, confinement, and exertion have been in place [for the wealthy] for at least a generation now; they constitute the inconspicuous periphery of normalcy that we take for granted, especially so since most of us have been born into this setting. Technology now mimics the great breakthroughs of the past, assuring us that it is an imposition to have to open a garage door, walk behind a lawn mower, or wait twenty minutes for a frozen dinner to be ready. Being given riding lawn mowers, garage door openers, and microwave ovens, we feel for a moment the power of wielding the magic wand. The remembrance of strain and impatience, of relative powerlessness, yields to a sentiment of ease and competence. We seem to move with the effortlessness of youth, with the vigor of an athlete, with the quickness of the great chef. (140)

We also don't stop to realize that those who make technological tools such as lawn mowers are stuck for the most part in repetitive and boring work that doesn't offer them the possibility to be creative or to develop new skills. Moreover, our sensation of ease and vigor

> is an entirely parasitic feeling that feeds off the disappearance of [our] toil; it is not animated by the full-bodied exercise of skill, gained through discipline and renewed through intimate commerce with the world. On the contrary, our contact with reality has been attenuated to the pushing of buttons and the turning of handles. The results are guaranteed by a machinery that is not of our design and often beyond our understanding. Hence the feelings of liberation and enrichment quickly fade; the new devices lose their glamour and meld into the inconspicuous periphery of normalcy; boredom replaces exhilaration. (140)

If we are still captivated by the bluff (as explained in chapter 1) that technology will free us from our burdens (including boredom), we will continue to look for extant hardships and for devices that will release us from them.

However, as Borgmann emphasizes, there are two kinds of limits to such a pursuit. On a larger scale, with regard to time and space, growth has social and physical limits, and these make it impossible for everyone to own one or two vacation homes or to take holiday trips to exotic destinations. More personally, "regarding the daily and domestic sphere, disburdenment leads to more and more frivolity and clutter and to a worsening balance between means and ends where a sophisticated machinery is required to procure a commodity which is as quickly attained by a simple mechanical tool" (140). Examples Borgmann offers include electric pencil sharpeners and doors that open by voice command, both of which eliminate only the turning of a crank or handle. Of course, we haven't reached either kind of limit in our search for liberation and enrichment. But because our society remains infatuated with technology, we will keep on inventing new technologies that approach those limits, even though there will be diminishing returns. In this way, the bluffs of our technological milieu continue to hide from us how thoroughly we are fettered (also by boredom) and kept from finding true delight and hope in life.

To keep technological boredom at bay, then, we have to find some unlimited, unending means for enriching our lives.

> It is available under the heading of entertainment and comes in the shape of commodities that we ingest, that we eat, see, or hear. These constitute the final and central commodities and the foremost foreground of technology. The procurement of such commodities . . . is largely free of social and physical limits. . . . Interest is maintained not through the extension of the consumption activity but through the novelty and diversity of the entertaining commodities. (140–141)

Because entertainment has become the primary foreground of technology, we must recognize the destructive forms entertainments such as television begin to take. Borgmann mentions how history and nature are mined for television specials that "terrify or amuse us." But we don't seriously understand history (for once again, it is removed from its context) and do not become "engaged" in nature other than as voyeurs.

Another source of entertainment is the violation of social, moral, and sexual taboos: "The unmentionable is said, the strictly private is exhibited, and the forbidden is done." Eventually, as traditional taboos are exploited, usually to the worst extreme, the level of amusement dwindles. Borgmann explains that "[t]he contravention of taboos is entertaining only to the extent that there are residues of traditional morality which are pleasantly irritated when the taboos are violated. As these moral sensibilities fade, the 'immoral' first becomes bizarre, then ridiculous, and finally boring" (141).

Even as Borgmann turns his attention to television as one site for the violation of taboos, he sees that television is far more debilitating because of what and how it displaces—it tends "to prevent an idyllic childhood and a vigorous adolescence, to suffocate conversation, reduce common meals, supersede reading, to crowd out games, walks, and social occasions. And this irresistible displacement effect rests in turn on the incredible attractiveness" of television; consequently, it becomes addictive (141). Borgmann suggests that these factors combined help explain "why technological leisure keeps us both enthralled and unhappy" (142). I'm sure we can also apply this description to the addictive leisure of the Internet, of the games and combats of computer software—though the unhappiness finally frees some people from their addictions.

What happens when something causes families to do without television—because the set breaks down or the local school tries to enforce "National Turn Off the Television Week"? Borgmann claims (and the experience of those I've interviewed confirms this) that in such situations "almost all families experience a restoration of vigor and depth. They recall with fondness and a wistful pride life without television" (143). But are they able to keep it up?

Throughout my years of traveling to teach, I have met perhaps about 75 families who have succeeded in giving up television for good in a principled way. None of them has regretted it. But to ask that of everyone, Borgmann admits, is both too much and not enough. Because our society is characterized by the device paradigm, it seems excessively demanding to take away the device that produces the commodity of entertainment. Moreover, it is actually not enough to discard or restrict television. Instead, we must deal with the larger pattern of technological consumption, the entire device paradigm in all its applications (more of which will be sketched in chapter 4).

How, Then, Can We Begin to Break Free?

Technology in its best sense releases us from burdens. Most of the life-endangering or onerous burdens, however, have already been lifted from a large proportion of North Americans, so for the past half century or so technology continues to be developed in the form of what Ellul calls "gadgets"—not corresponding to genuine needs but for the sake of diversion. Borgmann recognizes that now we are getting rid of burdens that perhaps we should not eliminate, such as those that require sophisticated machinery to replace a simple mechanical tool or those that provide chores for children.

Technology has thus moved beyond its proper vocation[3] to create an orientation that has shifted away from engagement in practices that relate to what is most important to us. Instead, society is characterized by the proliferation of devices that produce an endless stream of commodities unrelated to any context and thereby leaving consumers without a world of relationships.

The paradigm of the technological milieu, of devices producing commodities, is supported by businesses' barrage of advertisements urging us to acquire more commodities. Meanwhile, the accumulation of more and more merely deepens our insatiable appetites.

The problem is not the commodities, nor the technological devices that produce them. The problem is the paradigm. Therefore, my purpose here is not to disparage the consumerist world or its technologies. Instead, to be released from the various fetters sketched in chapter 1, we must reform the paradigm and the theology that accompanies it.

Borgmann recognizes that in our society it is impossible to enclose technology in boundaries. Thus, we can only limit it and employ it appropriately by relating it to a center (168). Consequently, he offers the beginnings of reform by urging us to engage in practices related to our "focal concerns" or those central dimensions of life to which we are most committed.[4] By the term *engagement*, Borgmann refers to more than commitment. True engagement in work or craft or other practices also requires "the acquisition of skills, the fidelity to a daily discipline, the broadening of sensibility, the profound interaction of human beings, and the preservation and development of tradition" (214).

By this kind of engagement we deepen relationships and use the devices and commodities of the technological world with skilled selectivity. Borgmann elaborates this rehabilitation thus:

---

3. For a deeper understanding of this language of vocation in terms of biblical insights into the nature of the principalities and powers, see Dawn, *Powers, Weakness, and the Tabernacling of God*.

4. In *Crossing the Postmodern Divide* (119), Borgmann defines "focal reality" as the "encounters each of us has with things that of themselves have engaged mind and body and centered our lives."

A reform of the paradigm is even less, of course, a dismantling of technology or of the technological universe. It is rather *the recognition and the restraint* of the paradigm. To restrain the paradigm is to restrict it to its proper sphere . . . the background or periphery of focal things and practices. Technology so reformed is no longer the characteristic and dominant way in which we take up with reality; rather it is a way of proceeding that we follow at certain times and up to a point, one that is left behind when we reach the threshold of our focal and final concerns. The concerns that move us to undertake a reform of the paradigm lead to reforms within the paradigm as well. Since a focal practice discloses the significance of things and the dignity of humans, it engenders a concern for the safety and well-being of things and persons. (220, emphasis Borgmann's)

Both of these reforms—restricting the paradigm to the background and reforming *within* the paradigm to care more deeply for people when we can't escape technological dominance—are important for our efforts in this book to combat the technological society's tendency to foster global injustice. In chapter 3, I outline a few of the focal concerns that help people restrict the technological paradigm (though the literary characters involved do not have Borgmann's understanding of what is at issue). Chapter 5 explores more thoroughly the specific focal concerns of the Christian community and how those focal concerns can enable us to respond more profoundly to the imbalances and confusions of our world and thereby both restrict the paradigm and contribute to reforms within the paradigm.

How Might We Begin to Reform the Technological Milieu?

Borgmann identifies three steps by which our focal commitments limit technology and its paradigm—when we clear space for our focal concern, simplify its context, and extend that same engagement to wider areas of our lives (220–222). As examples of the first step, clearing a central space for whatever is our focal concern, Borgmann suggests the way people establish an inviolate time for running or develop the space, time, and skills for "the culture of the table." The latter is an especially good case to illustrate Borgmann's emphasis that the skills accentuated by clearing our lives for our focal concern enable us freshly to discriminate in our use of technology. For example, if we are interested in the culture of the table, we would use certain technologies such as a stove or oven but refrain from using those, such as a microwave and prepackaged food commodities, that prevent us from enjoying the process of cooking and its fragrances.

When I was discussing this first step in a lecture at the Princeton Divinity School chapel, I couldn't help but use the example of the chapel's stunning organ to consider how its builder, Paul Fritts, cleared a central space for his focal concern. He learned many skills—of design, of pouring molten metal and rolling pipes, of building tracker connections—even as his sister Judy learned to carve the beautiful artworks that grace organ facades. The more their skills developed, the more they could carefully select which technologies to use (such as a special computer for drawing plans) for the sake of genuine, breathtaking craftsmanship.

The second step for reform is to simplify the surrounding context of our focal concern so that the context can truly support the concern. If we have truly cleared a space for focal things and practices, technology will be returned to its proper role in the background (as means to serve the focal ends).

This is essential because technological devices change the relationship of means and ends in the three ways we saw above. In contrast, in this second reforming step we return means and ends to their broader relationship. In the view of our technological society, both means and ends are *within* the device paradigm and basically match the distinction between machinery (means) and commodities (ends). As a result, technology's role stays hidden and remains unchallenged. But if we restrict the entire paradigm, then both the machinery and the commodities are returned to their proper status as means contributing to our true ends, our focal practices and concerns.

Clearly to put the various issues we noted in chapter 1's collage—information, e-mail, money, computers, new technologies—all in the category of means and to ask more pointedly what ends they serve enables us to practice skills of discernment in order that we might simplify the surrounding context that supports our focal concerns.

E-mail offers a good example of this second step. Considering its use both for our professions and for communication with friends and family, we could ask how well this technology serves in the background. What matters—the focal concern—is the relationship. Consequently, we can discern whether our friendship or business relationship is fostered by the use of the technology of e-mail or whether it is lessened.

Many people have never thought about *whether* to use e-mail, but often when I ask they express frustration with how much time it wastes or how superficial "communication" becomes. Could our focal concerns enable us to ask more carefully whether to use the tool? I have chosen not to have e-mail; it would fill up my time with so many messages that I would not have adequate time truly to care for my friends or those I serve in ministry. Of course, there are disadvantages in this choice, but so far they are vastly outweighed by the advantages.

I'm not expecting you to make the same choice. I'm merely suggesting that it is important to ponder it and to decide more painstakingly whether this tool of the wired world contributes to your focal concerns or whether the context surrounding your priorities could be simplified by eliminating e-mail or reducing your use of it.

The third step of reform extends what we have gained in the first two steps to other areas of our lives. The more we are able to clear space for our focal concerns (our true ends) and then are able to limit technology and other consumerist products to their proper place in the background (as means), the more we will want to extend the sphere of engagement as far as possible. When we experience *things* (as opposed to devices) in their full depth, and when we discover the delight of our own fully embodied competence in relation to our priorities, then we will long to experience the same excellence from the center to the margins of our lives. Our focal concern starts to become incorporated into every dimension of life—how we spend our time, our money, our energy, our love. All our practices become more centered in our focal concern. That is why it is so important to choose our focal concerns carefully, lest they be selfish or destructive.

When we understand the device paradigm undergirding our technological milieu and its consumerism, then we can, in contrast, clear a space for our focal commitments and thereby use the commodities of the technological milieu wisely. What kind of focal concerns are worthy of our commitment? What can continue our deliverance from our bondage to the technological paradigm? To that we turn in chapter 3, where we will see examples of focal concerns and the three steps of reform.

What Focal Concerns Are Worthy?

You might wonder why, thus far, I have not mentioned much that is particularly religious. Perhaps readers who both are and are not persons of faith might agree on the first chapter's collage of various kinds of fetterings and also find helpful the second chapter's emphasis on focal concerns as a way to find an exit from those fetterings.

I don't claim thereby to establish common principles for thinking upon which all persons, no matter their orientation of belief, can agree. Rather, I think our understanding of the crucial need for hope in this 21st century is widened and deepened if we recognize the ubiquity of fettering experiences and the universality of some of our basic tools for coping with, and perhaps for shattering, those bonds.

However, the diversity of human beings' focal concerns annihilates any pretense of unity, for the principles that give "life" to some people (such as Osama bin Laden) bring death to others. Individuals' focal concerns will conflict, and our personal and societal ways of letting them guide our choices for consumption and participation in the globalized, technologized, commodified, unfairly distributed world will also clash with those of other people and nations.

In this chapter we will look at some focal concerns as they are manifested in daily life and in literature in order to learn to choose better focal concerns ourselves and to understand more deeply the three steps of reform proposed by Borgmann. I will utilize books that I found simply in reading fifth-grade stories to assist my husband as he chooses fiction appropriate for his classroom. Another book, which had been described on the radio, I found in an airport while stranded there.

These books demonstrate that focal concerns can be found anywhere. They make good stories because they influence the development of good character—which hints to us that they also make a good life.

Why Are Focal Concerns So Important?

The Latin word *focus* means "hearth." For the Romans the *focus* was holy; marriages were sanctified at the hearth. Albert Borgmann's employment of the fireplace to illustrate what has been lost under the technological milieu's device paradigm is especially felicitous, since before central heating was developed the fireplace was the center where the family found warmth and light and where they joined together in activities. The hearth ordered their days, sustained their relationships, and centered their life together.[1] In this chapter, then, we are asking about the center of our lives. What are the "things," the activities, the places, the persons that give them warmth?

Madeleine L'Engle demonstrates such a "hearth" when she tells in *Walking on Water* of her husband's criterion for turning down a lead role in a cheap play: "Do we want the children to see it?" Then she explains:

> It is a criterion of love. In moments of decision, we are to try to make what seems to be the most loving, the most creative decision. We are not to play safe, to draw back out of fear. Love may well lead us into danger. It may lead us to die for our friend. In a day when we are taught to look for easy solutions, it is not always easy to hold on to that most difficult one of all, love.[2]

What are our foremost loves by which everything else is judged? In what do we place our hopes?

In wealthier societies, those who possess plenty desperately need this kind of centering, for in our first chapter we saw that lives and hopes are fettered by various accumulations—of information, belongings, jobs on our to-do lists, aspects of society that stifle relationships. In the second chapter, we discovered that much of that fettering is due to the paradigm that controls our society: that the development of the technological milieu has moved us away from engaging in practices that are related to our focal

---

1. Borgmann, *Technology and the Character of Contemporary Life*, 196.
2. Madeleine L'Engle, *Walking on Water: Reflections on Faith and Art*, commemorative ed. (Wheaton, Ill.: Harold Shaw Publishers, 1998), 174.

concerns, the center of our lives, and instead toward a way of life cluttered with commodities (objects, data, achievements, even persons) produced by devices (physical machinery, networked communications machinery, or more hidden machineries such as that of advertising or the pressures at our jobs to accomplish certain levels of performance).

The Diversity of Focal Concerns

The athletic club two blocks from my home displays vividly the great diversity of focal concerns that drive people's lives. For some exercisers the focal concern seems to be solely physical strength and/or appearance. Swimmers whose only concern is their supreme fitness seem not to care if they knock into other people as they jet through their laps. A few women spend many hours on the workout machines and use weights in front of the mirrors to tone every muscle into perfect form and a gorgeous figure; they discuss body-building methods and are often also dressed in the most exquisite outfits. Still others seem to have interest in exercise primarily to keep them healthy enough to engage in other, more important concerns. That is why I am there.

At the side of the pool while putting on my leg brace after my own workout, I enjoy watching the elderly men and women who gather for the water aerobics class. Some are there primarily for the fellowship, and it is charming to watch their faces light up as they interact with others before class begins and during their warm-ups. Others exercise to speed their recovery from recent surgeries or to deal with arthritis or other afflictions; their diligent movements are often paired with grimaces of pain or scowls of impatience at their uncooperative bodies.

For a while it was also possible to see at the club the influence of society's device paradigm in the behavior of two women who seemed to consider the club their own personal device to produce commodities of pleasure and convenience only for themselves. Rather than engaging with others in conversation, one screamed at those (including me on crutches at the shower) who got in her way. Rather than practice communal sharing, the other one spread her belongings all over the available counter space in the locker room and thereby frequently made it difficult for older, less agile women to use the locker room. She also was selfish about lanes in the pool. Other swimmers would warn each other, "The monster is here today!" Everyone else was a means for these women's ends.

What are our cardinal focal concerns? How do they help us maneuver in an overloaded world? I confess that sometimes I let my own concern for sustaining bodily health get in the way of what should be my primary focus of caring for my neighbors. When that happens, I turn people into devices for my own convenience, too, and join the world's monsters.

In the following samples from literature, my goal is to deepen our insight into the idea and importance of focal concerns and the steps by which those priorities can enable us to restrict the operation of the device paradigm in our lives. I ache acutely to stir us to pay more constant attention to, and to wrestle more deeply with, our focal concerns so that they might free us from cultural fetters and enable us to discern and choose how best to engage in just practices in spite of our commodified, technologized world. We will eventually discover that hope is not only our goal; it also provides our means for faithfully attending to our focal concerns.

Clearing Space and Time for Our Focal Concerns

In a series of books detailing the life of a girl named Betsy, Maud Hart Lovelace invites young readers to discover what really matters to them. Betsy, who longs to be a writer, got tangled in other activities and in her various confusions did not prepare for the high school's annual essay writing contest. Betsy's subsequent reflections and actions offer excellent commentary on the importance of knowing and living by one's focal concerns:

> "What makes me feel bad is that I didn't give myself a chance."
>
> When Julia had a part in a home talent play, her social life went by the board. If she had a solo to sing, she practiced it, even though she neglected everything else.
>
> "That's the way my writing ought to be treated," Betsy thought.
>
> She looked back over the crowded winter. . . . [S]he should not have let its fun, its troubles, its excitements squeeze her writing out.
>
> "If I treat my writing like that," she told herself, "it may go away entirely."
>
> The thought appalled her. What would life be like without her writing? Writing filled her life with beauty and mystery, gave it purpose . . . and promise.
>
> "Everyone has something, probably. With Julia it's singing, with Anna, it's cooking, with Carney and Bonnie, it's keeping house and having families . . . something that's most important of all because it's theirs to do."

She jumped up and went down the steps and started walking.

She walked down High Street, past the high school, and on and on, trying to beat out on the sidewalk her angry self reproach.

"Help me to straighten this thing out!" she said to God. "Please, please, help me to straighten this thing out!"[3]

As we will discover in chapters 4 and 5, the kind of God we have will have a direct bearing on how we straighten it out when we have lost sight of our focal concerns (as we frequently do in our present technological milieu). What arrests me in this excerpt is how strongly it encourages its readers to think about what might be most important to them because "it's theirs to do." Betsy also illustrates Borgmann's first step for deliverance from the bondage of the consumerist society's rule: clear a central space for the focal thing. As Betsy tried to "straighten this thing out," she was reorganizing her life so that she would not ever let her writing get crowded out again.

Developing a Discriminating Use of Commodities

In Kate Seredy's *The Good Master*, a beautiful account of farming life on the Hungarian plains before World War I, she tells of the ranch owner (called Father) and Kate, his city niece, meeting Pista, a sheepherder. Humble Pista takes Kate into his hut to show her the finely crafted contents of his painted chest—all of which he had made.

There were hundreds of trinkets in the chest. Rings, chains, bracelets, little square and round boxes, carved spoons, forks, cups, salt cellars—everything under the sun. All were beautifully inlaid and painted.

"But what are they made of? They're beautiful," cried Kate, handling a delicate necklace.

"Ram's horns, wood, bones, roots—anything I find. I make my paints from herbs and roots, too. The Lord gave us everything to use; I just find them and use them."

"But why don't you sell them? They're more beautiful than any jewelry I ever saw in stores. You could make a lot of money."

3. Maud Hart Lovelace, *Heaven to Betsy* (New York: HarperTrophy, 1980; originally published in 1945), 258.

"That's what I always tell him," said Father, stepping closer. "He's an artist, a great one, and doesn't know it. He should earn money and study in schools."

Pista turned to him seriously.

"What would a shepherd be doing with money, Mister Nagy? I have everything here. I am happy. Look," he said stretching his arms wide, turning to the open doorway. "Look. The sky gives me sunshine and rain. The ground gives me food. The spring gives me water. The sheep give me shelter and clothes. The beautiful flowers, the animals, the birds, show me what to carve with my knife. Can money and schools give me better things?" He turned to Kate. "I don't sell these things for money, little lady. I give them to my friends."

Then he let her choose her own gift, whatever she wanted from the laden chest. After selecting the necklace, Kate also promised that in the winter when he did not have much to do she would help Pista fulfill his goal to learn to read and write so that he could sign his artwork.[4]

Pista offers us an excellent model of Borgmann's principle that closely connected with the central clearing of space and time for our focal concerns is a discriminating use of technology or other commodities. In Pista's case, he has no need for money or schools, but it would be valuable to learn to read and write.

Those caught in our society's paradigm would think Pista crazy for not wanting his art to be sold in stores so he could become rich and famous. Others may admire his deep sense that having gifts to present to friends is more important. That focal concern, correlative with his practice of making beautiful art, enables him to discern what knowledge and resources do or don't contribute to his craft.

The Danger of Ill-Chosen Focal Concerns

To explain and reinforce his point against money, Pista tells the Hungarian tale of a greedy rich man who owned everything and treated people and animals cruelly. He and one hundred soldiers went to rob a poor shepherd, who had always been kind to both creatures and neighbors. The birds and rabbits, who had been wounded by the avaricious man, sent a nightingale to get a good fairy to deliver the poor shepherd. She came

---

4. Kate Seredy, *The Good Master* (New York: Viking Press, 1935), 74–75. Page references to this book in the following paragraphs will be given parenthetically in the text.

dressed as an old hag but produced from her pocket a shiny gold piece, which she gave to the soldiers in exchange for some of the lamb they were cooking (from the shepherd's little flock). They greedily asked if she had more gold.

She replied, "I have lots of gold. I'm so rich all my houses are full of gold. My village is over there, beyond the poppyfield. The houses are so heavy with gold, the weight turned them upside down. I was just looking for some good strong men to turn them back again."

Of course, the soldiers were interested in this and immediately set out for the village, even though she wouldn't let them take their horses since the poppyfields would offer them nothing to eat (78). Bit by bit they dropped pieces of their armor as they trudged on, seeing the village always not too far away, but never getting any closer to it. After a long time walking, the disguised good fairy asked to take a rest, but the covetous man and soldiers insisted they would go on without her. The rich man said:

> "You rest, old woman; we will walk to your village and start working on your houses. Don't you worry, by the time we are through, they'll be so light they will float in the air. Ha-ha!"
>
> They walked off, leaving the fairy behind. She lifted her arms and spoke a charm: "Follow the mirage of wealth until you perish, and may it remain there forever out of reach, to warn men against greed and cruelty!"
>
> The rich man and his soldiers walked on and on. The village of gold seemed always just a little farther away, shimmering in the hot, still air. They stumbled on and on all afternoon, through the red poppyfields, until it grew dark. Then they threw themselves among the poppies to sleep. They never woke up again, the heavy scent of the poppies killed them all. But the village appears, floating in the air around midday ever since. Nobody can ever come close to it. It's just a mirage. (80–81)

Some focal concerns do not liberate us, but bind and enslave us. These mirages—"wealth, power, pleasure," which many people "follow blindly" (81)—bring not life but death.

Communal Focal Concerns

In a sequel to *The Good Master*, Kate Seredy offers us a glimpse into the kind of focal concerns that could be held generations ago by a people together, a commitment that forged them into a community or nation. Kate and her cousin Jancsi, guided by Kate's schoolteacher father, discover a post inscribed "liberty . . . equality . . . fraternity. . . . The month of March 1848," followed by a list of names, beginning with Márton Nagy, the largest landowner, and ending with Moses Mandelbaum, the local Jewish merchant. Kate's father explains,

> "Between those two lies the past and the future of Hungary. As long as these two work together in peace and understanding, little harm can come to the country. We are all dependent on these two: the farmer who grows food and the small merchant, the Jewish merchant who knows through centuries of scrimping and saving how to buy and sell wisely.
>
> "The month of March in 1848 meant the beginning of this partnership, the dawn of a happy new era in Hungary. Feudal estates were divided into farms; peasants, who had been little more than slaves, were made into free men with the right to vote, marry, and travel as they pleased. People of the Jewish religion, who had been shamefully persecuted and oppressed for centuries, were once more free to trade and barter openly or to pursue any occupation they chose.
>
> "Your great-grandfather Márton Nagy was one of the last great feudal landlords. Moses Mandelbaum, grandfather of Uncle Moses [the present, kindhearted and generous shopkeeper], was one of the first Jews who opened a store under the new laws. And this avenue of trees"—he pointed ahead into the green lane—"had been planted in March 1848, one tree by every one of those whose names you have just read. The former master, who was one of his people now, all the peasants, who now were his equal in rights, and Moses Mandelbaum, they each planted a tree. A green, living thing to grow and remind them always that they were brother Hungarians, first and last."
>
> He paused, looking ahead. The trees whispered in the light breeze; otherwise there was no sound. "Whispering trees," he went on gently as if speaking to them, "they have weathered many storms. Some of them are broken and almost dead, but new shoots are springing up from their roots every year. Those roots grow deep in the soil, deeper than the trees are tall. No one could kill them without destroying the very soil they grow in; what they stand for

lives in the hearts of all Hungarians. Nothing could kill that without destroying the country."[5]

Seredy's narrative displays many severe tests of the people's rooted commitment that the community endured throughout World War I. The reader wonders what might be left of that communal commitment now, after Nazi destructions and Soviet oppressions.

We also wonder if such a focal concern for community is possible anymore under the rule of the technological milieu. The accumulation of commodities not produced by friends is inherently more conducive to competition than to concord.

Simplifying the Context of Focal Concerns

Borgmann's second step for reform of the device paradigm is to simplify the surrounding and supporting context so that both the hidden machineries and their commodities are confined to being means and are therefore not able to obstruct the focal goals. Though the context in Martin Goldsmith's *The Inextinguishable Symphony* is not the rule of technology but the tyranny of Nazi rule, this non-fiction account gives us a dramatic example of how a profound focal commitment can restrict the rise of other ends—even fear. Even Nazi machineries could not keep the central characters from their focal commitments.

In this narrative, former National Public Radio host Goldsmith tells the story of how music literally saved his parents' lives. We grasp how crucial to our sense of values and priorities are our focal concerns when Goldsmith asserts, "As I heard my father tell me his story, I came to realize that somehow I had inherited the knowledge that music can not only enrich your life, it is also something worth risking your life for."[6]

After telling of his parents' beginnings as musicians, Goldsmith reports what happened when the Nazis began their escalating assault on the Jews. The "Law for the Restoration of Tenure for the Civil Service" enacted on April 7, 1933, forced every state theater, orchestra, and opera company to fire all its non-Aryan workers. In response, Dr. Kurt Singer, a charismatic

---

5. Kate Seredy, *The Singing Tree* (New York: Puffin Books, 1939), 36 and 39.

6. Martin Goldsmith, *The Inextinguishable Symphony: A True Story of Music and Love in Nazi Germany* (New York: John Wiley & Sons, 2000), 4. Page references to this book in the following paragraphs will be given parenthetically in the text.

Jewish conductor and administrator, had the extraordinarily bold idea to approach Nazi officer Hans Hinkel with a thoroughly organized plan to create a "Jüdischer Kulturbund" (Jewish cultural association), which gave jobs to actors, musicians, dancers, and operating personnel who had been thrown out of work by the law (49–60).

Through an amazing combination of political infighting, personal self-aggrandizement, and the recognition by the Nazi Ministry of Propaganda that the existence of the all-Jewish organizations could be used "as a shield to blunt international disapproval of the still-new Reich" (66), the plan was approved. The first Kulturbund in Berlin sponsored its first dramatic performance on October 1, 1933.

Eager to participate in the association's concerts, plays, cabarets, and lectures, the members also knew that more than shared culture was involved. Jewish philosopher Martin Buber wrote in an essay entitled "The Name Obliges" that "[a] federation means that the members are bound not by interest or activities alone but by life-giving principles and are inextricably bound together" (63).

Those life-giving principles—what I call "focal concerns"—are demonstrated poignantly by narrator Goldsmith's parents, Rosemarie and Günther. In order to play chamber music and participate in the community life of musicians, they risked going home from evening musical gatherings after the Nazi curfew. Their son writes,

> My heart goes out to them as fools, fools for love, fools for the love of music—music that could cost them their lives, but music they cannot live without. As moviegoers cry out uselessly to the screen to warn the celluloid hero and heroine of imminent danger, I beg my mother and father to be careful, please be careful, as they navigate their way. . . . And I am so proud of them and so grateful to them for showing me what is truly important, for showing me that you must love the people and things that are important to you and that you must sometimes risk everything for that love. There is no finer lesson for parents to teach their children. (247–248)

What focal concerns do we have for which we would risk everything? Do we have commitments profound enough that they enable us to return everything else to the status of means, to keep technology and its commodifications in the background?

Goldsmith quotes composer Gustav Mahler, who compels us to ask ourselves, too, "And now there arise the great questions: Why did you live?

Why did you suffer? We must answer these questions some way if we are to continue living—yes, even if we are only to continue dying" (259).

Extending the Sphere of Engagement

Though not a book I would recommend for children because of its sexual content, *A Hand Full of Stars*, by Rafik Schami (cited at the end of chapter 1), is a stirring account of its author's own childhood and displays compellingly the fighting spirit of the persecuted. Through his journal comments, Rafik demonstrates Borgmann's third step in reform—that the more we clear space for our focal concerns and thereby limit our consumption, the more we become able to extend the sphere of engagement to include other people and other areas of life.

Rafik's first focal concerns, revealed in diary entries, are his attempts to make money and his various friendships. In one betting incident, however, one of his friends betrayed him, so he remarks to his old friend, whom he calls "Uncle" Salim, that he "felt like examining every would-be friend with a magnifying glass" before calling him a "real friend." Uncle Salim disagrees and urges him instead to seek out new friends but not to be suspicious.

Salim suggests that "it's the poor in this world who invented friendship. The powerful have no need of it. They have their power. Seek out friends, and let the magnifying glass alone. Using it could be the biggest mistake of your life: You will be alone."[7]

These twin concerns of friendship and trying to overcome poverty when one lacks power are combined when Rafik is forced to quit school to work in his father's bakery. When he wants to run away, Uncle Salim persuades him to try to imagine how his situation could provide him with the opportunities he needs. Eventually developing his own bread-delivery route, he meets a journalist, Habib, from whom (at age sixteen) he begins to learn the craft. As a result, he develops a larger focal concern: to free others from poverty and oppression.

Together with another young friend, Mahmud, the two writers Rafik and Habib begin to produce an underground newspaper, which the younger two distribute by stuffing cheap socks with it and selling them in the markets. Then the boys invent hot air balloons which carry a basket

---

7. Rafik Schami, *A Hand Full of Stars*, trans. Rika Lesser (New York: Dutton Children's Books, 1990), 44. Page references to this book in the following paragraphs will be given parenthetically in the text.

of newspapers that tips over in the breezes so that the papers can float to the ground. Meanwhile, Habib leaves papers at churches and mosques. Having previously worked for the government, however, he is arrested. The book's final two journal entries show the intensity of Rafik's focal commitments of fighting poverty and friendship and how they have intertwined and been extended into all of his life.

> *July 13*—Today I was in the cemetery, at Uncle Salim's modest grave. It does not distinguish itself from the earth that bore him and to which he has returned. I set five red roses on it.
>
> My sadness for Habib is nearly choking me, but I want to live and laugh. I don't want to give up hope. My old friend Salim taught me this.
>
> "Everything grows," he said to me one day. "Everything grows, except for catastrophe. It is largest at birth, and then it shrinks from day to day." (194)

> *July 14*—We spoke for a long time together. Mahmud also became pensive when Nadia asked him, "What do you think Habib would most like to do now?"
>
> "Make another newspaper," we whispered as if with one voice.
>
> "Exactly, the newspaper. These murderers ought to know that if they kill Habib, many Habibs will spring up in his place."
>
> Nadia wants to collaborate. She wants to report on the women of Damascus; Mahmud is writing about some of the secrets of the last coup. I am writing an article about Habib, the bravest journalist in Syria. . . .
>
> [The youth spent their savings on a typewriter, mimeograph machine, paper, ink, and balloons. Someone else contributed rent money for an attic room in which to produce the paper.]
>
> Habib needs the newspaper. We will show the military just how many Habibs the imprisoned journalist has brought into the world. (195)

Rafik's concern for his own freedom from oppression and poverty has evolved into a focal concern for the entire community. We remember from the previous chapter Borgmann's advice that we stretch the sphere of our engagement with people and practices as far as possible because the experience of competence at the center motivates us to extend the same excellence to the edges of our lives. When this happens, all our practices become more centered in our focal concern, and our commitment to our focal concern defines all our other priorities.

Is This Possible in Present-Day North America?

It is one of the strange mysteries of life that we comprehend life most deeply and live it most fully under the shadow of death. The most intense focal concerns in the literature sketched above came to life under the threat of political, military, and economic tyrannies. Perhaps in North America we are not so centered because we don't know who or what the enemy is.

As I mentioned in the Introduction, the tragic events of September 11, 2001, spurred many people to rethink their priorities and renew their focal concern for their families. However, as much as commentators say that it takes a war to unite a nation, the "war on terrorism" that followed the hijackers' attacks has not knit people together into a national focal concern, because many people recognize that evil isn't located only in militant terrorists and that the United States also sponsors terrorism in the world (as the statistics on weapons sales at the end of chapter 1 show). Almost every person I've talked with in frequent airplane trips and conferences has been troubled by the violence and suffering that has been unleashed in the world through the U.S. pummeling of Afghanistan. The war itself was undertaken according to the prevailing rule of the device paradigm, since it has been executed with super-technology for the purpose of achieving the commodity of ending terrorism—without much engagement with world partners or aid organizations, without much understanding that violence begets more violence, without clear plans for how all the terrorists in the world could ever be found and convinced not to vent their anger, without much recognition of the ways in which our nation's wealth and its exportation of immoral and culturally insensitive commodities agitates that anger.[8]

On a smaller scale, the Christmas season seems to cause many individuals and families to rethink their focal commitments. Nothing in secularized North America offers a better example of focal concerns than

---

8. Benjamin R. Barber, director of the Walt Whitman Center for the Culture and Politics of Democracy at Rutgers University, critiques this exportation of U.S. culture and the resulting escalation of a world "monoculture" to the detriment of social institutions and cultural folkways in *Jihad vs. McWorld: How Globalism and Tribalism Are Reshaping the World* (New York: Ballantine Books, 1996).

Christmas, for the celebration seems to promise that it will make people feel knit to their families, that it will give them security and happiness. Yet the Christmas holidays often leave us feeling empty, depressed, disappointed, even angry. Churches react against the holy day's secularization (beyond the commercial) and scold their members about keeping Christmas focused on its true meaning, but the fact is that Christians and particular churches can be just as misfocused as the rest of society in their celebration of the festival.

I don't intend to offer here another diatribe against the commercialization of the holiday. It seems that almost everyone acknowledges that, because the commercialization has become so blatantly obnoxious—especially in 2001, when panic about a recession dominated the news and shopping was urged as a patriotic duty.

I am far more interested in the sorts of expectations people bring to their holiday celebrations and the device paradigms or focal concerns that those expectations might reflect. For example, some might insist on cooking and baking exactly the same foods and desserts they had as a child—not because they enjoy their engagement in the preparations but because that specific meal has become the device or means to produce the commodity of certain sentimental feelings. Nostalgia is not a very beneficial goal toward which to aim because the means employed rarely succeed in resurrecting the feelings we remember.

It is extraordinary how often we (I definitely include myself) seek the goal of various feelings—excitement, surprise, coziness, even devotion or adoration. These expectations are most evidenced by those who are not in the habit of attending worship services and who show up for the midnight candlelight service on Christmas Eve. Not knowing how to become engaged in the practice of worshiping, they perhaps expect the candlelight experience itself to be the device that will produce some sort of religious feelings in them.

Why do we do the things we do for holidays? Totally apart from the question of commercialization, what is it we want to accomplish with our cards, parties, presents, decorations, meals? How many people whom you know come away from the season refreshed because their practices accorded with their deepest commitments and reinvigorated them for the new year?

Since some of this book is being written during Advent, it is causing me to ask whether my focal concerns are being duly attended to in this season. My preparations for Christmas are usually quite extensive during Advent—putting up a manger scene and a display of angels on the first

Sunday of Waiting; making an Advent wreath and having family devotions every day; writing a long, duplicated letter to family and friends and adding extensive personal notes on each; arranging and practicing music for worship services or planning sermons for the Advent Sundays when I preach to give local pastors more time to prepare for Christmas; decorating for and preparing a holiday meal for family and friends; attending numerous Advent and Christmas concerts and worship services. This year is somewhat different.

This season's new questions led me to do much less than usual of the usual. Instead, my focal concern to honor the Child Who is born has led me to believe that I do that best by writing this book. It is a passion that is extending into every dimension of my life. It has inspired my behavior at my daily workouts in the swimming pool, such as spending more time today checking on the health concerns of a few people who exercise at the same time. I write lines in my dreams and hear Advent concerts differently (see chapter 7). This book's emphasis on focal concerns also influenced my decision to accept a pastor's request for me to sing a solo—and which piece to sing—on Christmas Day. It even made me tenacious enough to start over this evening with the backup file when, for some really impenetrable reason, my computer lost the whole file of this chapter's new editings.

It is not to my credit that this Advent is different. Rather, the question is, why haven't I been so focused in the past? It is to my great shame that to live each moment in light of my focal concerns has not in the past (or present) been a habit of my character.

Focal Concerns Worthy of the Eternity in Our Minds

A top hit song in the '60s asked, "Is that all there is?" and responded to the absurdity of life's emptiness with the notion that then we might as well keep partying. Somehow we all know intuitively that we should be able to find meaning in life. Unless we do, we have no hope.

Focal concerns orient us toward meaning and hope, but only if they are large enough, worthy enough.

How large do they have to be?

After a decided turn toward secularization in the middle of the 20th century, North Americans have returned to new interest in spirituality. Why is that?

Again, somehow we all know intuitively that the meanings and hope we find have to be larger than ourselves, somehow connected with the transcendent that the technologized, commodifying world seems frequently to deny.

The preacher, *Qohelet*, said that long ago. After the prolonged set of "a time fors" in Ecclesiastes 3:1–8, he recognizes that God has put "eternity" into our hearts (v. 11). The Hebrew word is *ha-olam*—the forever, everlastingness, perpetuity.

It is demonstrated by God: "I know that whatever God does endures forever [to *olam*]; nothing can be added to it, nor anything taken from it; God has done this, so that all should stand in awe before Him"[9] (v. 14).

If God has put eternity into our hearts, then our focal concerns, to be worthy, must be eternal, God's. But how do we fittingly stand in awe before God? More important, how do we live that awe—especially when the same preacher keeps telling us in Ecclesiastes that "all is vanity" (1:2, 14; 2:17; 3:19; 12:8)?

Focal Concerns Worthy of Our Lives

It is my primary thesis in this book that Christianity provides focal concerns worthy of our creation as human beings and efficacious for dealing with the encroachments and fetterings of our technologized, commodified milieu.

I believe that the focal concerns of Christianity (and Judaism, as will be seen in chapter 5) are these two: the love of God and the love of the neighbor.

---

9. More and more I think that our difficulty with masculine pronouns for God commenced not when we first realized that they oppressed women, but when we stopped capitalizing them and thereby lost the mystery that transcendence could also be personal. Though I try to avoid pronouns for the other persons of the Trinity (when it is possible without violating speakable English), I find no problem with using them for Jesus, who came to earth as a man. However, I have returned to capitalizing the pronouns to emphasize that they are meant to signify not gender, but surprising relational intimacy. Though I grew up in a somewhat patriarchal denomination, still I have always recognized the words *He, Him, His*, and *Himself* not to signify God's maleness, but to carry a sense of the ineffable, the secret yet revealed wonder of God's immanence. Consequently, when male pronouns for God appear in biblical texts cited in this book, I will capitalize them. For further discussion, see my *Corrupted Words Reclaimed* (Grand Rapids: Brazos Press, forthcoming). On the importance of Jesus' maleness in order to model servanthood—one can't dismiss it as a typical female role when a strong male (carpenter) and respected rabbi exhibits tenderness and compassion, the servanthood of God's infinite mercy—see William C. Placher, *Jesus the Savior: The Meaning of Jesus Christ for Christian Faith* (Louisville, Ky.: Westminster John Knox Press, 2001), 44–45.

These focal concerns are given us in the commandments of the First Testament[10] and the sayings of Jesus in the New Testament. They are also repeated throughout the ages of Christian history. For example, one of the legends concerning John, the beloved apostle, is that when he was old and feeble and failing in all his senses, he would ask to be borne into the presence of the assembled congregation where he spoke "but these words: 'Little children, love one another!' And when asked why he always said this, and only this, his answer was: 'It is the command of the Lord, *and if this only were done, enough were done.*'"[11] Thus, to love our Lord by fulfilling His commandment is to love our neighbor; our dual focal concerns are inextricably intertwined.

These two loves are to be the central and controlling commitments of a Christian's personal and home life, working life, corporate life in the Christian community. These twin focal concerns change the way we spend our money, time, energy, and love. They also enable us to follow Borgmann's three steps for handling our overloaded, overwhelming times by keeping the device paradigm and its technologized commodifications in check.

Christianity's dual focal concerns enable us to limit technology and make use of only those commodities that genuinely contribute to our commitments. These concerns equip us to clear more space for the ways in which we love God and love our neighbors, as we will see in chapter 6.

As noted in my comments above about changes this Advent, living Christianity's focal concerns also enables us to follow Borgmann's second step for reform in simplifying the context surrounding and supporting our focal domain. The dual call to love God and our neighbor is so strong that technology and its commodities can be returned to their proper sphere in the background as only usable means for serving the focal ends. We will see the crucial need for this step in chapter 4, when we consider how churches frequently fail to surmount the device paradigm and

---

10. I join many other scholars and pastors in calling the first three-quarters of the Bible the First Testament or the Hebrew Scriptures, to avoid our culture's negative connotations of the name *Old* Testament and to emphasize both the consistency of God's grace for all God's people and also the continuity of the LORD's covenants in the Bible first with Israel and then, in addition, with Christians.

11. W. Frank Scott, *A Homiletical Commentary on the Gospel According to St. John* of 1896, emphasis Scott's, quoted in *For All the Saints: A Prayer Book For and By the Church*, vol. 3: *Year 2: Advent to the Day of Pentecost*, compiled and edited by Frederick J. Schumacher, with Dorothy A. Zelenko (Delhi, N.Y.: American Lutheran Publicity Bureau, 1995), 146.

falsely let aspects of the commodified life be the foreground instead of our twin loves.

Third, Christianity's focal concerns enable us continually to extend the sphere of engagement as far as possible, to be constantly learning new ways to love God and the neighbor and unceasingly discovering elements of our lives that are not yet centered in those commitments. Our focal concerns are worthy to control every dimension of life. When our practices are so ordered, we will know the fullness of hope without any fetters.

Chapter 4

Do We and Our Churches
Live by Our Focal Concerns?

A s chapter 1 mentioned, in response to the crises of September 11, 2001, many people, in grief, turned to family, home, and communities of worship. The question is whether churches were ready.

I don't mean simply whether their doors were open on that day and for the following weeks. All sorts of news reports have stressed the extraordinarily compassionate responses of churches to those who suffered from the tragedies.

My concern in this chapter is with churches over the long haul. The question is, are churches ready to help people—members and seekers and even non-interested neighbors—ask deeper questions about what overwhelms them, about the nature of our society, about who God is and who we are in response to God at this place and this time in history?

My reason for writing this book is that many churches seem to me to be too caught up themselves in the technological milieu's paradigm to be effective in helping people break free of the technological world's fetters. The hopes that many churches convey to members and seekers are not genuinely liberating hopes, but come with attachments that cause further shackling.

At the end of chapter 3, I mentioned that churches frequently fail to surmount the device paradigm and mistakenly let aspects of its commodifications be the foreground instead of merely the background for Christianity's twin loves of God and neighbor. In this chapter we will look more closely at some of those false moves—often taken without biblical consideration and adequate deliberation—in order to challenge all of us who claim to be Christian to rethink our focal concerns and how those should enable us to follow Borgmann's steps for reform, to keep our lives and church life focused, to restrict the device paradigm and its technological commodifications, to simplify the context for our focal concerns, and continually to extend the sphere of our loving engagement as far as possible, especially for the sake of justice in the world.

Christian Realism

With such a strong critique in chapters 1 and 2 of the tendencies of the technological milieu and its displacing or distorting of relationships, and with a critique in this chapter of churches' failures to rise above the captivating and entangling paradigm ("arresting" in both senses of the term), you might object that these chapters are much too pessimistic. A little digression is essential, then, to emphasize the vital truth that Christians are not, by definition and doctrine, pessimistic.

Christians can't be pessimists because we know the future and its connections to the character of God (to be explored in the next chapter). Moreover, that future aeon has already broken into this present age, and God's kingly reign has already begun.

On the other hand, however, Christians cannot be optimists either, because we know that this aeon is still in severe trouble. This time and this world are still characterized by sinfulness, brokenness, evil, idolatries, overwhelming fetters.

Instead of being either pessimists or optimists, Christians are hopeful realists. We have to be realistic about the fettering nature of our present society. Nevertheless, because we have a deep and abiding hope (see chapter 5), we are able, as Jacques Ellul says, to get outside ourselves through faith and thereby to have objectivity in studying the cultural forces that alienate us, as we have done in chapters 1 and 2. Ellul insists that Christian freedom makes him "able to hold at arm's length these powers which condition and crush me . . . [and to] view them with an objective eye that freezes and externalizes and measures them."[1] We as Christians can likewise scrutinize our concrete world and call it into question prophetically.

The biblical disciple Thomas shows us the importance of both components of being hopeful and a realist. Poor Thomas has gotten "bad

---

1. Jacques Ellul, *The Ethics of Freedom*, trans. Geoffrey W. Bromiley (Grand Rapids: Wm. B. Eerdmans Publishing Company, 1976), 233 and 235. See also chapters 3 and 4, "Political Realism (Problems of Civilization III)" (from 1947) and "On Christian Pessimism" (from 1954), in Dawn, *Sources and Trajectories*.

press"—undeservedly, since he certainly wasn't any more "doubting" than any of the other disciples. He was, indeed, a realist and was the first actually to face Jesus' death—as evidenced by his comment (when Jesus, tardily from a human perspective, determined to go to Lazarus), "Let us also go, that we may die with him" (John 11:16). Thomas's problem was that his realism was not coupled with the hope he could have had if he had believed Jesus' words about His own resurrection. That is why, in chapter 5, we will look more closely at the nature of resurrection hope, so that our realism does not leave us in despair.

In this chapter we have to be bluntly realistic about the fetters and dangers of the technologized, consumerist world that stifle or shackle the genuinely *Good* News our churches could be offering, the proclamation of vital resurrection hope. We need to be as explicitly and unambiguously realistic as possible, so that people can be freed from their false and fettering hopes, their idolatries, the techno-dazzling wonders that hide our culture's deceptions and bluffs.

Cultural Elements That Prevent Churches from Implementing Their Focal Concerns

We have to be realistic about how difficult it is for congregations to take Borgmann's first reforming step of clearing space for our focal concerns. Several cultural factors make this especially difficult, but they are subjects too large for our space here, so I will only briefly introduce them for your further reflection and research.

The Death of Culture

In *Faded Mosaic* (mentioned in chapter 1), Christopher Clausen insists that traditional cultures exerted power over their members by instructing them and determining boundaries for thinking and behavior. In that sense of unified boundaries and values, the United States no longer has a single, dominant culture.[2] Meanwhile, the various local or ethnic subcultures that make up U.S. diversity tend to decline, perhaps by media-induced homogenization or especially if the community fails to pass on its traditions to younger generations. Have we noticed how much the United States waters down regional and ancestral cultures?

---

2. Clausen, *Faded Mosaic*, 7. Page references to this book in the following paragraphs will be given parenthetically in the text.

I have often cited our society's loss of truth, beauty, and goodness as aspects of declining culture. This loss is due to a great extent to the device paradigm's transformation of "commerce" primarily into commercialization and the resulting need for our present media barrage of hyped slogans to continue fueling economic growth. When the arts became, in response, simply individualized efforts to "express myself," then they no longer exhibited the kind of genuine creativity that discloses transcendence, whether in relation to deity or to a larger community in which one is rooted.

Clausen identifies this "extreme emphasis on personal feelings and self-gratification" as the root of the losses of truth, beauty, and goodness (13), and he links this individualism with the enormous mass of commodities available to suit each person's taste (119–155).

This combination of fetters—the bondage to self and the enslavement of too much for that self—makes it difficult for churches to keep the love of God and of neighbor as their members' focal concerns. As one example (which we will develop further below), consider the many battles over musical style in worship that arise because of members' desires for self-gratification, at the expense of love for their neighbors and a consequent willingness to sing songs they don't like for the sake of the community.

Can we learn in our churches that worship is for God and not to please our own tastes or express ourselves? Can we learn to be genuine communities in our churches so that we are willing to forego our musical preferences at times for the sake of our brothers and sisters in faith?[3]

Postmodern Pluralism

Part of the problem for many Christians in our pluralistic world is that they have never seriously inhabited the "culture" of Christianity and learned its faith language. Consequently, they do not have confidence in Christianity's gifts or their ability to verbalize them.

At the same time, many churches, not knowing how to deal with or respond to pluralism, think they must water down their own uniqueness for the sake of welcoming the outsider. The result is a reduction of God; then their focal concern to love God (in this diminished conception) is not worthy of the outsider's adoration.

---

3. See Marva J. Dawn, *Reaching Out without Dumbing Down: A Theology of Worship for This Urgent Time* (Grand Rapids: Wm. B. Eerdmans Publishing Co., 1995) and *A Royal "Waste" of Time: The Splendor of Worshiping God and Being Church for the World* (Grand Rapids: Wm. B. Eerdmans Publishing Co., 1999).

We can offer the gifts of our faith most generously if we enter into the pluralism of the neighborhood not afraid of who we are and thereby free to receive who the other is. When we understand our faith as gift, we have no need to pressure others into accepting it. Meanwhile, we can more gladly learn from them the gifts their faiths have to offer.

The Loss of Truth in Postmodern Times

The loss of truth takes especially two forms in churches. The first lies in the postmodern philosophical judgment that any claim to truth is a bid for power and in the prevailing societal notion that faith is merely another commodity that some people choose rather than a complete orientation for life. In response, Christians are often afraid to tell the truth they know and live for fear they will be seen as oppressive. However, if our faith teaches that Truth is not a What but a Who (and a very counterideological, unpowerful One at that), then to speak of Christ is to introduce people to a great delight, a true gift.

Second, in a society rife with myriads of "commodities" in the religious sphere, including the world's chief religions, major Christian denominations, minute "churches" of all sorts, New Age faiths, Internet rituals, and a great diversity of gurus, the notion that "truth is whatever you make it" leads to the intermingling and incoherence that characterizes many persons' faith. This is the "Sheila-ism" of which Robert Bellah wrote[4] and the "Spirituality of the Inner Self" in Robert Wuthnow's terms.[5] This spirituality has no objective truth, but it is composed of elements of the practitioner's psychological polytheism which are unified by attention to the present moment.

Wuthnow observes several inadequacies of such spirituality. One is that it lacks a cohesive interpretive structure, which is necessary for faith to become the center by means of which everything else is understood (188). Another is that because it lacks a "more orderly, disciplined, and focused approach to the sacred" (196), people are overly influenced by moods, circumstances, or exposure to constantly changing ideas. In chapter 5 we will

---

4. Robert Bellah, Richard Madsen, William M. Sullivan, Ann Swidler, and Steven M. Tipton, *Habits of the Heart: Individualism and Commitment in American Life* (Berkeley: University of California Press, 1985).

5. Robert Wuthnow, *After Heaven: Spirituality in America since the 1950s* (Berkeley: University of California Press, 1998), 142–167. Page references to this book in the following paragraphs will be given parenthetically in the text.

see the importance of adequate doctrinal bones and ecclesiological muscles for sustaining the spiritual body, but for now it is sufficient to recognize that without an undergirding sense of truth, Christians are deprived of the depth and confidence with which they can remain committed to their faith's focal concerns and be buoyed by its hope.

The Loss of Authority and Mentoring in Postmodern Times

In keeping with society's rightful rejection of empty authoritarianism, some churches have developed a false fear of authority. This ties in with our societal move away from adults mentoring their children (see chapter 1). The results for churches and their members have been a loss of rooting in traditions of care, the failure to pass the faith's wisdom on from generation to generation or from experienced believer to new believer, and even a fear on the part of church leaders to teach "with authority."

I am certainly not proposing here the kind of religious authority that is centered in the self or in an idolatrous biblicism, but I seek to recover the authority that is rooted in an entire community—a community of people who, by eagerly living the traditions of faith that have existed for thousands of years, pass them on. This is an authority much larger than we are, much larger than our local congregation or denomination.

Only recently have churches begun to rediscover the sorts of catechumenal practices by which the authority of our faith can be recovered and transmitted. Without that mentoring, however, persons cannot be trained to "live" their focal concerns.

The Loss of Community in Society

Because people in a society ruled by the device paradigm have for the most part lost the experience of communal life, they have had and still have no practice to supplement their experience of community in their church. They do not realize the hard work required to support each other, truly to care for each other. We will consider more deeply this loss of the experience of community care and support later in this chapter when we investigate Robert Putnam's *Bowling Alone*, but at this point we have to recognize how difficult it is to live the focal concern of loving our neighbors when we are not in the habit of thinking about our lives in plural terms.

The individualism of our society is especially destructive because believers are trained by the culture (and sometimes even churches) to read the Bible—the major source of our faith tradition—in singular terms, rather than as pluralized instruction to a community. Consequently, commands such as those to feed the hungry are taken to be only personal requirements instead of work we each undertake as part of an entire community together. Commitment to our focal concerns becomes a solo effort rather than a biblically communal commitment.

The Quick-Fix Mentality and the Breakdown of Disciplines and Practices

Our society's device paradigm trains us in the habit of seeking quick-fix solutions to our problems. When this pattern invades churches, two especially negative effects ensue. First, churches begin to address such problems as declining numbers by seeking short-term remedies, such as making worship more entertaining and less formative of the actual *habit* of worship, that in the long run actually lead away from our focal concerns. In the process, our commitment to loving God becomes tainted with self-concern.

Second, both the love of God and the love of the neighbor are reduced by the breakdown of Christian disciplines and practices. The arduous engagements of Bible study, prayer, meditation, worship, Sabbath keeping, generosity, service, home devotions, and the raising of children in faith are supplanted by efforts to manipulate instant gratification. Without sustained involvement in habits of faith, Christians not only do not learn the value of time investments with delayed results, but they also do not develop the kind of long-term enduring emotions and deep-seated affections that would enable them to find Joy[6] in extended service for the causes of justice and peace as concrete manifestations of love for global neighbors.

The Rejection of the Actuality of "Sin"

We live in a society of victimization, abetted in many ways by the device paradigm. One way that the paradigm fosters unhealthy victimization is by considering a single source (device) to be the cause of someone's suffering (the commodity) and thereby reducing the complexity of causes and effects. Another way is that the U.S. legal system is often turned into the

---

6. I purposefully capitalize the word *Joy* because I do not mean a simple exuberance, happiness, or excitement caused by circumstances. I use the word to signify that deep, abiding confidence, gratitude, and trust that are ours when our lives are transformed by the truths of our meta-narrative (sketched in chapter 5), especially the Resurrection.

device to procure large financial remunerations instead of into a basis for genuine justice. The most egregious example of this is the woman who successfully sued McDonald's for a large sum of money because she was burned by coffee that was too hot. People prefer not to bear the burden of blame and reject both initial responsibility and continuing accountability. This societal tendency makes it difficult for churches to insist that we need God's grace, that to love God and our neighbors is quite impossible for us on our own, that we are hopeless without Triune mercy and forgiveness.

Almost one hundred years ago, G. K. Chesterton wittily addressed this matter of the evasion of repentance. He discounted the notion that we are not guilty of sinfulness but that we simply suffer from diseased emotions or addictions caused by our childhood traumas or present environments. He protested

> that torrent of modern talk about treating crime as disease, . . . of healing sin by slow scientific methods. The fallacy of the whole thing is that evil is a matter of active choice whereas disease is not. . . . The whole point indeed is perfectly expressed in the very word which we use for a man in hospital: "patient" is in the passive mood; "sinner" is in the active. If a man is to be saved from influenza, he may be a patient. But if he is to be saved from forging, he must be not a patient but an *impatient*. He must be personally impatient with forgery. All moral reform must start in the active not the passive voice.[7]

My goal in this chapter is to spur repentance—that all of us might realize and confess ways in which we personally and in the corporate body of our churches have allowed the above characteristics of our society and its device paradigm to rule our lives and consequently have failed to know and live our focal commitments as Christians.

Living True to Our Focal Concerns

Various reactions and events in the months after the tragedies of September 11, 2001, demonstrate how crucial and constant is the need for Christians to clarify and orient our lives by our focal concerns. The need for greater clarity was especially urgent shortly after the hijackers' attacks

---

7. G. K. Chesterton, *Orthodoxy: The Classic Account of a Remarkable Christian Experience* (Wheaton, Ill.: Harold Shaw Publishers, 1994; first published in 1908), 147.

because many Christians struggled to bring coherence to their very mixed feelings. We knew that Osama bin Laden and his fellow terrorists should be brought to justice, but we also were tormented by the crushing devastation of Afghanistan, already ruined by years of fighting against the Soviets, by extreme repressions under Taliban rule, by three years of extreme drought, and by the fundamental harshness of its geography.[8]

We also grieved because the world crisis had brought many kinds of death: sudden and terrifying death to those involved in the actual hijackings and demolition of buildings, heroic death to many who were attempting to aid the victims, death to the spirits of those who mourn lost ones, death to soldiers and innocent bystanders involved in the resultant war. Meanwhile, violence escalated in other parts of the world, and the U.S.'s reactions to September 11 were sometimes cited as the model for others' actions. India massed soldiers on its border with Pakistan, and Israel and Palestine stepped up invasions and terrorist acts, respectively. Suddenly also there were new conflicts and uprisings (due both to the fight against terrorism and to the global economic crisis accelerated by the 9–11 events) in Argentina, Yemen, and other parts of the world.

Moreover, reactions to these global tragedies have caused many other kinds of death: death to true hopes as they have been fettered by our society's emphasis on materialistic consumerism as an antidote to recession, death to goodness as our nation-state relies heavily on highly technicized means of violent warfare, death to compassion as money has flowed to some victims but meanwhile has been cut back from charities that meet everyday needs on a long-term basis, death to faith as some people rely only on large military budgets and technological weapons for security, death to engagement with neighbors as many have turned inward to escape the emotional traumas and stresses by means of multiple diversions.

Meanwhile, in many places, agitated disagreements over politics have led to the deaths of conversation, true dialogue, and community life. In response to some articles others and I wrote for a church-related publication to help people think through the issues with a biblical perspective,

---

8. From the flurry of books commenting on September 11, 2001, I highly recommend Rowan Williams's *Writing in the Dust: After September 11* (Grand Rapids: Wm. B. Eerdmans Publishing Co., 2002). Williams, now Anglican archbishop of Canterbury, was trapped at Trinity Church, Wall Street—only two blocks from the World Trade Center—by the dust and debris after the attacks. His Christian reflections on the grief and shock are comforting; his wisdom for the days ahead is constructively compassionate for the sake of the whole world.

some persons showed a death of civility by sending angry, even demeaning letters berating us for our attempts.

If Christians' focal concerns are to love God and our neighbors as ourselves, how will that be fleshed out when we disagree with others, when we are confused by conflicting responsibilities (such as bringing terrorists to justice while not inflicting suffering on the poor)? How shall we be the Church in such confusing times?

Living by our focal concerns is a process that requires continued questioning, faithful prayer, and renewed reorientation to loving God and all our neighbors. Especially all of us who are leaders in churches must ask whether we are serving well as primary models of these commitments.

Leadership and Our Focal Concerns

I confessed in chapter 1 how easily the device paradigm sneaks in with my hyperactive work habits. Three dangers are especially prominent for me and perhaps for you. First is the tendency to become a "device producing many commodities" in the form of accomplishments, rather than engaging with people in the practices of studying the Bible together, discussing theology, or contemplating God's truths through written reflections. Second is the temptation of the Messiah complex, to which I'm especially prone. I'm sure I'm not the only person teaching and writing in the Church who too easily thinks that if just everyone would listen to us and read our stuff we could save the Church. A third danger, much more subtle, is the proclivity to hide my own doubts and confusions in the machinery of productivity. Perhaps the works I accomplish are false "ends" and my frenetic activity the "means" ultimately to conceal my inability to hear what God would really have me do and be.

I acknowledge these tendencies and pray that writing them here will both put a restraint on them for me and also challenge you to think about how your own life is affected by our technological, commodified society's paradigm. If we are to think about the failure of Christian churches to break free of our culture's fetters, we must begin with ourselves and repent for however much we are bound and controlled by this paradigm and its strangulations.

For the rest of this chapter, I will be discussing primarily the corporate practices and decisions of Christian communities, but these disciplines and choices also all apply to our personal lives and relationships with our neighbors. I want to concentrate on corporate activities, however, because the community helps to form our individual lives as Christians and because the potent failure of large groups of Christians to question society's operating paradigm continues to allow it to flourish and remain unchallenged.

Losing the Church's Identity

Recently, I was disappointed when a brilliant instrumentalist playing a concerto with the Oregon Symphony came on stage dressed in a dazzling but extremely revealing tank top. She hadn't dressed provocatively in past appearances, so it seemed the act of a desperate woman. Could she no longer depend on the intense power of her music to keep the audience attentive? Did she not trust her own identity as a gifted and passionate virtuoso, feeling that she had to mix in the complexion of a siren?

In a similar way, the commodities of our society are so attractively packaged and so alluringly advertized that churches sometimes don't trust their own identity and think that they have to be similarly glamorous, even seductive, to appeal to the seekers in their communities, to announce their relevance, to provide all that their members need, to make a difference in the world.[9] In the process, the churches are adopting the culture's device paradigm (which can take many forms, some of which are sketched below) and thereby enter into a spiral of weakening—becoming less and less what the Church really is and then having even less to offer. My particular concern in this book is that adopting these misplaced priorities means that congregations have no ability to equip their members to question the paradigm by which the church itself is functioning.

I have raised concerns about churches' failure to trust their identity in previous books, but these days I am increasingly convinced that critiques of the loss of our focal concerns need to be in stronger terms. Indeed, God applies severe language, asking Israel, for example, why it goes whoring after other gods. The terms *whore, whoring,* and *whorings* are employed at least 55 times in Isaiah, Jeremiah, Ezekiel, and Hosea to describe the way God's people broke their covenant with their LORD and turned to other gods, primarily Mammon. (See especially Ezekiel 16, with 15 uses.) It is not a time-bound idolatry, of course. The terms related to "whoring" in

---

9. Perhaps the best book I've ever found critiquing many nuances of this fear for churches' own identity is *Selling Out the Church: The Dangers of Church Marketing,* by Philip D. Kenneson and James L. Street (Nashville: Abingdon Press, 1997).

The Revelation refer to the same issue—that consumption had replaced covenant.[10] Some people might protest that such language is too strong to describe the weaknesses of our churches, which to them seem to have lost sight of Christianity's focal commitments "only slightly." But any spouse becomes righteously cross with even a "slight" infidelity. Why have we not taken more seriously the extreme offense to God caused by our idolatries in cooperation with society's paradigm and commodities?

Do we realize the importance of this fundamental problem profoundly enough actually to change the orientation of our churches?

Loss of Thinking

In a lecture that fanned flames which were already burning in me, theologian John Cobb Jr. asked (1) if we understand how profoundly Mammon is the god of our culture and (2) whether our Christianity really affects our daily decisions.[11] His main concern is that churches are failing to confront or contend with the current mainstream cultural-political vision in which the most important public policy is to increase personal and national wealth. [This is indeed the rhetoric most frequently heard in news reports paying so much attention to how the economy can keep growing.] Though the world is hurtling toward utter ecological disaster,[12] Christians still prefer to be engaged in the suicidal activity of worshiping Mammon.

Cobb suggested that since the Enlightenment notion of objectivity has been exposed as a myth and a greater proportion of U.S. society is now shifting to postmodern thought, perhaps it is possible for churches to

10. See Marva J. Dawn, *Joy in Our Weakness: A Gift of Hope from the Book of Revelation*, rev. ed. (Grand Rapids: Wm. B. Eerdmans Publishing Co., 2002).

11. John Cobb Jr., "Will Churches Learn to Think Again in the Twenty-First Century?" presentation for the Lutheran Professors Breakfast at the American Academy of Religion/Society of Biblical Literature annual meeting in Denver on November 19, 2001.

12. Regular reading of *National Geographic* makes ecological disaster quite clear. See also "It's Official: Humans Are Behind Most of Global Warming," *Science*, January 26, 2001, 566, which reports that hundreds of environmental scientists involved in the Intergovernmental Panel on Climate Change commissioned by the United Nations agree on the subject of that title. For documentation that human activities have altered the climate and that the results will be disastrous if this isn't changed, see Richard B. Alley, *The Two-Mile Time Machine: Ice Cores, Abrupt Climate Change, and Our Future* (Princeton, N.J.: Princeton University Press, 2000). See also Steven Bouma-Prediger, *For the Beauty of the Earth: A Christian Vision for Creation Care*, Engaging Culture Series, ed. William A. Dyrness and Robert K. Johnston (Grand Rapids: Baker Academic, 2001).

speak in a way that the world around us will hear. There is a new opening now for the Word of God by the Holy Spirit to speak. Can we help the members of our churches and the wider world hear?

Let us extend John Cobb's two questions for the sake of global justice: Can our churches wake up to all the ways that Mammon and the device paradigm of our technological, commodified milieu have captured them? Can we rediscover the power of our own narrative to give us genuine hope for combating this bondage? Can we equip and enable Christians in this society to resist the encroachment of the culture's rule and to use their own freedom and resources to liberate others for genuine hope?

In summary, can we again recover the identity of "Being Church"?

Membership or Mission?

Many of the mutations of, and manacles on, churches discussed below arise because pastors, congregational leaders, and denominations worry about declining membership numbers. The loss of members causes a panic, which tempts us to react with strategies conceived according to the device paradigm: What device should we institute in order to produce the commodity of higher numbers? We try various devices, including extreme changes in styles of worship, the initiation of multiple programs to attract the neighbors, marketing strategies, firing the present staff and hiring a more charismatic one, and so forth. Lamentably, these devices mimic our culture's behavior and thereby change the identity of the congregation so that it becomes merely a mirror of the society instead of an icon of God.[13]

What is especially tragic about these panicked moves is that leaders don't realize that churches' declining numbers are part of a larger societal pattern manifested by almost every major social group. Robert Putnam's comprehensive research, recorded in *Bowling Alone: The Collapse and Revival of American Community*, gives plenty of evidence that the trend toward civic disengagement is a broadly based and widely experienced phenomenon in the United States that is presently having negative effects on education and children's welfare, safe and productive neighborhoods, economic prosperity, health and happiness, and even democracy.[14]

---

13. I apologize that I don't know from whom I learned this image and cannot give proper credit.

14. Robert D. Putnam, *Bowling Alone: The Collapse and Revival of American Community* (New York: Simon & Schuster, 2000). Page references to this book in the following paragraphs will be given parenthetically in the text.

Putnam is concerned for the loss of the wealth of communal engagement and all the benefits public interaction brings to democracy. He acknowledges that religious communities have always been a source of community life and health. He notes, "Faith-based organizations serve civic life both directly, by providing social support to their members and social services to the wider community, and indirectly, by nurturing civic skills, inculcating moral values, encouraging altruism, and fostering civic recruitment among church people" (79).

However, the pattern of participation in such organizations matches the "broad oscillations" of trends in secular civic life—"flowering during the first six decades of the century and especially in the two decades after World War II, but then fading over the last three or four decades." Also, as is common and particularly noticeable in the sphere of politics, the disengagement seems to be connected to "generational succession." As a rule, "younger generations ('younger' here includes the boomers) are less involved both in religious and in secular social activities than were their predecessors at the same age" (79).

All in all, recognizing as do many others that U.S.ers are attending worship less frequently than three to four decades ago, Putnam also laments, "the churches we go to are less engaged with the wider community. Trends in religious life reinforce rather than counterbalance the ominous plunge in social connectedness in the secular community" (79). In numerous ways U.S.ers are less connected to community life than just twenty or thirty years ago (180). One of the most important of Putnam's observations for our purposes is that this lessening of social involvement is due to pressures of time and money, technology and mass media—elements sketched in chapter 1's collage.[15]

Correlative with the widespread fettering of hopes we've outlined, Robert Putnam offers little counsel for what could be done about this decline. Though he provides 400 pages of charts and text to demonstrate the erosion from most organizations, Putnam spends only a dozen pages offering ideas about how to build community. Moreover, those pages provide very little encouragement because his proposals are so limited and undertaken on such a small scale. In contrast, what would happen if all the churches in North America recovered their mission to their neighbors?

---

15. Several charts underscore this claim, such as "TV Watching and Volunteering Don't Go Together" (231); "TV Watchers Don't Keep in Touch" and "Watching and Club Meetings Don't Go Together" (232); and "TV Watching and Churchgoing Don't Go Together" and "TV Watching and Comity Don't Go Together" (233).

Since there are many churches, their total mission would not be small scale, and efforts would not be so limited. To recover that mission, however, churches have to get untangled from the device paradigm and its destructions.

When Worship Becomes a Device

One of the major ways that churches sacrifice their identity is with the quick-fix strategy mentioned above regarding worship. I am not advocating that they should remain stuck in the "identity" of a lifeless traditionalism. Instead, my concern centers on the large proportion of congregations that have thrown out everything that can be learned from historic worship music and liturgies and leadership in order to "attract" the unbelievers. In the process, they tend to turn the practice of engaging in worship for the sake of our focal concern to love God into the device, or means, that will produce the commodity of greater numbers. But attracting neighbors is not loving them.

Another way in which worship becomes a device is if it is designed to produce the commodity of certain feelings. This might be illustrated by Robert Farrer Capon's stunning description of a splendid dinner party in comparison with cocktail parties (which also serve as devices to produce the commodity of returned social favors). For Capon, dinner parties involve guests attentively invited and placed at the table to create a *convivium*, people clothed for a celebration, the menu planned for the greatest delectability possible within the hosts' kitchen limitations, the table splendidly set, the food tastefully and fragrantly prepared, the prayer elatedly offered, the conversation engaging and memorable.[16]

We recognize that such a dinner party is much more complex and communal than a cocktail party. As a focal event, it includes much more than can be seen in its immediate space and time. Similarly, worship has ramifications that go far beyond the specific event of a particular corporate service.

Even more important, the dinner party and a worship service ought not to be misunderstood by the thought that their real meaning consists in moving the participants into a certain emotional state. If that emotional reaction becomes decisive, then party hosts and worship planners begin to search for methods (what Albert Borgmann calls "machinery"—see

---

16. See chapter 15, "The Long Session," of Robert Farrar Capon's *The Supper of the Lamb: A Culinary Reflection* (New York: Harcourt Brace Jovanovich, 1967), 167–181.

chapter 2) that will produce that reaction more quickly and universally and with less failure and effort.[17]

Worship is SO vulnerable to this type of commodification! Several musicians have confessed to me how tempted they are to manipulate the emotions of worshipers by techniques (machineries) that have been effective in the past, for they know that then the participants will "feel good" about the worship experience. Otherwise, people might complain that the service didn't "do much for them." Consequently, it is critical that we place worship music in the full context of the entire worship service and maintain the depth and integrity of the whole, that we recognize the fullness of gifts in and from a worship service and not limit its effects to a mere emotional reaction or to that particular place and time.

For the last decades of the 20th century, perhaps the most frequently expressed desire for worship was that it be "exciting." (Evidence of this desire could be found in the proportion of church service announcements in newspapers that used the word.) I distrust the word *exciting* because it is used to describe almost everything (especially new programs in the educational system for which my husband teaches), and usually the adjective means that the subject it modifies is not. Excitement, moreover, is not the best gift for helping us to love God and our neighbors. If we need excitement or become used to it, how will we learn to discover God's presence in the rocky times, in the handicaps, in the failures? How will we love our neighbors when they require extraordinary patience, genuinely loving compassion, tedious long-term care?

God be praised: agitation for "exciting" worship waned with the tragedies of September 11, 2001, and thereafter. How long might that last in our society of spectacle and glitz?

Another way that worship follows the device paradigm involves the misuse of the term *user-friendly*, mentioned in chapter 1. Many congregations change their worship liturgies in order to make them "user-friendly." However, the liturgy is not the friend; you are!

Or are you? Do we blame liturgies or worship styles for not being user-friendly when we ourselves are inhospitable? I have been freelancing for twenty-two years and have been a guest in churches about half the Sundays of most of those years. Of all those visits to congregations, only once (once!) did the person sitting next to me offer to help me follow the order

---

17. Albert Borgmann uses Capon's dinner party to illustrate focal *things* in *Technology and the Character of Contemporary Life*, 201–205. I have adapted his reflections on p. 202 to apply them to worship.

of worship, and only once (astonishing!) did someone say, as I stood in the narthex, "You're a stranger; would you like to sit with me in worship?" If I came to your congregation, would someone invite me to sit with her? Would someone make sure I could participate with him in the words and actions of worship? Do we love God and our neighbors enough to be genuine friends to our companions in worship, to enable them to participate with us in worship's disciplines?

In chapter 1 we noted how fettering is the addiction to constant stimulation because it destroys one's ability to find larger meaning in the simpler, more subtle dimensions of life. How can churches help their young people learn that they don't need (as their boomer parents seem to) a spectacular religion, an angel awakening, some sort of exotic experience that will last them for the next thirty years to convince them that they have faith.[18] Can we instead learn together to recognize God in small things, the supposed "coincidences" of daily life, the gifts of all creation, especially the Word?

Worship and Technology

Keep remembering that my purpose here is to nurture the practice of asking better questions about what we do and how we live as Christians. Using technology is not the problem. Rather, the ideology behind it must be questioned. Its device paradigm must be exposed.

Albert Borgmann has highlighted one danger in the present-day campaign to bring multi-media technology into worship services. He writes, "The focal power of a thing is denied and mocked if the thing is secluded and surrounded entirely by hypermodern technology. A thing must draw its vitality from an underlying reality."[19] Are the high-tech accoutrements the underlying source of worship's vitality and people's enthusiasm for worship—or is God?

Another danger of bringing extraordinary technology into the worship service is, most obviously, that using the technology becomes the goal instead of the means to the goal of loving God. That idolatry is exposed by such statements as "We have to use modern multi-media so that Xers know our congregation is really 'with it.'" (I have indeed heard pastoral leaders make such statements.) Then we must ask, are we worshiping God or relevance?

---

18. See Robert Wuthnow, *After Heaven: Spirituality in America since the 1950s* (Berkeley: University of California Press, 1998), especially 114–141.

19. Borgmann, *Crossing the Postmodern Divide*, 126.

Besides, can churches really be relevant to the wired world's pleasure in exciting stimulation? Why try to keep up with the dazzle of entertainments outside our church? In a series of articles on how seminaries might use electronic mechanisms, Raymond Williams observed that seminaries frequently can't afford the best technology and the necessary training for using it, so they will always appear stodgy.[20] Stodginess is not necessarily bad, but it demonstrates the futility of the goal of relevance for which some churches choose to use technology. More deeply, is relevance a worthy goal?[21] Furthermore, is it a good use of church funds to invest heavily in expensive technological devices when Christians have other priorities, especially to feed the hungry and house the homeless? What would happen if, instead of spending money on equipment for high-tech worship, churches would invest in projects that engage them in helping poor people find a sustainable way to live?

I am not saying that new technology should not be used in worship, but we have to be scrupulously careful to keep the technology in the background. Still another problem arises. How do we reconcile the spectacle of media presentations, for example, with the character of the God we are worshiping—an unpretentious Jesus who eschewed the temptation to indulge in spectacle for the sake of winning the crowds (Matt. 4:5–7),[22] a Christ of poverty who "emptied himself, taking the form of a slave, . . . [and] humbled himself and became obedient to the point of death—even death on a cross" (Phil. 2:7–8)? How do we teach worshipers to follow the steps of the Trinity manifested in Jesus if our medium doesn't match the message? Can't we serve the poor of our world best if we humble and empty ourselves, too?

Many pastors (who believe that in order to serve the poor we first have to teach the people in our churches more effectively—with which I agree) have become "excited" about using PowerPoint in their sermons. However, Scott Cormode, who teaches at the Claremont School of Theology, has recognized that using PowerPoint for lectures at seminaries "does not create actively engaged students." He noted that instead students "can become passive, believing that the pithy summaries on the projection

20. Raymond B. Williams, "Getting Technical: Information Technology in Seminaries," *Christian Century* 118, 5, February 7–14, 2001, 17.

21. See section 1, "From Relevance to Prayer—The Temptation: To Be Relevant," in Henri J. M. Nouwen, *In the Name of Jesus: Reflections on Christian Leadership* (New York: Crossroad, 1989), 13–31.

22. See section 2, "From Popularity to Ministry—The Temptation: To Be Spectacular," in Nouwen, *In the Name of Jesus*, 33–51.

screen encapsulate what they should learn."[23] We should similarly question whether PowerPoint offers great advantages for sermons if it does not help people actually to become more deeply engaged with God.

I am not completely rejecting any use of technological tools for ministry; I'm simply urging that we ask better questions about the negative effects as well as the benefits, instead of blindly accepting contemporary fads, such as the false assumption that PowerPoint makes sermons more "attractive" to young people. One question instead could be how we help congregants, especially youth, become more actively *engaged* in the Scriptures and in worship. We already have more than enough passivity in our culture; should churches foster more? Wouldn't the increased passivity form people to be *less* likely to invest energy in caring for the poor?

David Stewart of Princeton, discussing the difference between using libraries and the Internet, asks if the "high-volume, high-speed information" of the wired world is really what a researcher needs. He concludes that "the wired environment is almost intrinsically impatient, and so doesn't always foster quiet, reflection and deliberation—the low-anxiety cast of mind which often produces the best thinking about God."[24] This is a profound consideration for our churches' ministry. Many congregations specialize in high-energy worship and hyped excitement, which are not necessarily conducive to deliberate thinking about God.

Finally, let's ask how much of the pressure to use such special effects arises from the bluffs of the media and church marketers whose focal concerns are their own businesses or the commodity of numbers, and not the worship of God? We are indeed bombarded with the bluff that we should follow the opinions and styles of the culture as propagated by the media. This directs us toward self-concern and various idolatries of instant gratification or fame or Mammon, instead of toward Christian priorities of justice building and peacemaking.

If we keep in mind what we learned in chapters 2 and 3 about focal concerns, we will continually want our central priorities of loving God and loving our neighbors to illuminate our understanding of the world. For this to happen, we need a symmetry between our human life and its setting. If we turn worship into a hyper-real (more-than-real or virtual) setting with the addition of technological spectacle, then we will lose the necessary symmetry, and the worship service will be hindered from forming in its

---

23. Scott Cormode, "Engaging Students," *Christian Century* 118, 5, February 7–14, 2001, 19.
24. Stewart, "Nurturing Curiosity," 18.

participants the necessary patience and vigor for the hard tasks of our focal concerns.[25] It seems to me that our immersion in a culture of hyper-reality is one reason why people have not been able seriously to tackle world hunger. The problems (which are perpetual) seem to interest contributors only when aid organizations use hyper-real advertisements. The global crisis of poverty, however, is too large for such piecemeal responses. It requires enormous patience and vigor—and probably immense changes in our way of life.

Worship Music

I have already dealt extensively with the subject of worship music as it is influenced by the technologized, commodified world in my two books on worship.[26] However, one new facet arises because of my emphasis in this book on the device paradigm.

I have always been an advocate of using "the music of the whole Church for the sake of the whole world," with the goal of letting the people's voices be united in all sorts of styles, faithfully used for the sake of loving God and growing as a community to love our neighbors. However, music sometimes is chosen simply as a device to produce commodities of certain, often hyped feelings or a superficial, often false intimacy with God and neighbors. When the choice involves global music, that choice can become a new form of colonialism.

A case to illustrate the latter problem occurred at a music institute a few years ago. One denomination had recently produced a new Spanish hymnal, which was going to be introduced at a workshop by Latino guests. In my keynote address I strongly urged participants to attend that workshop (though, to my dismay, I was scheduled to conduct one of the other workshops at that hour). Later that day a man from Puerto Rico came to me in tears to say, "Not one white person came to our workshop."

Do we turn our global neighbors into a device for producing the commodity of interesting music? Remember that we learned from Borgmann in chapter 2 that with a device the world of relationships is replaced by concealed machinery, and the commodities, which are made available by a device, provide pleasure without the encumbrance of, or engagement with, their context.[27] Are we letting the people behind the music become

---

25. These comments were spurred by Borgmann, *Crossing the Postmodern Divide*, 96.
26. See Dawn, *Reaching Out without Dumbing Down* and *A Royal "Waste" of Time*.
27. Borgmann, *Technology and the Character of Contemporary Life*, 47.

concealed as just another machinery that produces entertaining worship? Do we ignore their context—especially if it is one of poverty or disease or oppression? For example, if we sing South African freedom songs, do we pay attention to the struggles of apartheid that gave rise to those songs? How might that equip us to be more active against the racial discrepancies and disturbances that still characterize U.S. society?

Do we simply steal another people's music in an imperious way, instead of welcoming our Latino neighbors into our congregations to teach us how to sing Hispanic music? Since an increasingly large percentage of the U.S. population will be Hispanic in future years, could some of us learn Spanish so that the Church is more able to welcome them if our communities include many Latino people? Are we willing to share their sufferings or do we simply want to share their music?[28]

Whatever music we use must be sung or played with its own integrity and according to our focal concerns for loving God and loving our neighbors in worship. For example, African American spirituals arising from the sufferings and agonies of slavery would not be sung at fast tempos; the music's creators didn't sing them that way, and the rest of us need pondering time to hear the faith arising out of the blacks' (continuing) affliction. As Borgmann writes, "To have a focal thing radiate transformatively into its environment is not to exact some kind of service from it but to grant it its proper eloquence."[29] Can we hear, and enter into engagement with, the eloquence of the world's praise when we worship by means of global music?

Technology and Congregational Life

Let me briefly introduce for your further contemplation some issues of technology and its impact on church ministry and community life. It is essential that we learn to be reflective enough to assess the various commodities of our technological milieu more carefully so that we employ only those that contribute to our focal concerns.

As an example, think of whether pastors' work is abetted or fettered by e-mail. The issue involves more than the question of whether in the long

---

28. Benjamin R. Barber, director of the Walt Whitman Center for the Culture and Politics of Democracy at Rutgers University, criticizes the capitalistic society's escalating world "monoculture" and the disproportionate exchanges between peoples of the earth that destroy local institutions and folkways; see his *Jihad vs. McWorld*.

29. Borgman, *Technology and the Character of Contemporary Life*, 222.

run e-mail saves time. Some other questions to ask might be these: Does the use of e-mail increase the pastor's ministerial skill? Is it detrimental to the "focal depth" of the clergyperson's work? By focal depth I refer to what we learned in chapter 2 about the entire world surrounding a *thing*. Does e-mail gather together various capabilities of the pastor—such as listening, advising, and other aspects of communication? As part of the focal depth, does e-mail meet the desires of the recipient for communication? Does e-mail match the setting and its cultural traditions?[30]

Each clergyperson's answers to those questions will be different, and at different times and circumstances a pastor's answers will vary. For example, in a culture in which people visit each other's homes in the evenings, to send an e-mail would be an offense. In contrast, e-mail to college students from their pastor will definitely gather and embody their desires and match their setting. But many aspects of pastoral concern, such as voice tone and hugs, won't flow over the wires or air space.

Pastors must each weigh how much e-mail enriches their capacities and whether it sustains the focal depth of loving their neighbors. Clergy will undoubtedly come to different conclusions according to their abilities, environment, and congregational aspirations and needs.

What concerns me is that so many pastors have not ever questioned it. When raising these issues at clergy conferences, I am astounded by how frequently I get responses of confession, relief, wonder. The media and often parishioners bombard us with the rule that we have to use the devices of the technological world to increase our efficiency, so we need courage to resist that compulsion and to ask whether all kinds of efficiency are good traits in church life.

Can church leaders ask the same questions about cell phones, pagers, using videos in Sunday School, electronic announcements (instead of personal invitations)? Again, please remember that I am not rejecting the gifts of the technological milieu but simply questioning its paradigm and recognizing the dangers of thoughtless consumption. Our work requires careful nuances, courageous decisions, and the endurance to carry our resistance of the paradigm through time and trouble.

What makes that arduous struggle worthwhile is that ultimately we are choosing to live carefully in order to become more thoroughly engaged in loving God and in loving our neighbors by helping them, too, spring free from the fetters of society's paradigm. We are also thereby involved in

---

30. The questions in this paragraph were influenced by Borgmann, *Technology and the Character of Contemporary Life*, 239.

practices that, on a larger scale, question the injustices in the world because of globalization and seek to right the imbalances of provisions for life.

Again, it is crucial that church leaders ask these questions about their own immersion in the technological world's commodifications so that when we love the youth of our congregations, for example, we can help them learn to put limits on their involvement in the wired world and their employment of technological devices and commodities. This is one of the main questions we must ask in ministry in such a milieu, since one great gift of the Gospel is that it enables us to de-idolize, de-sacralize, de-divinize those elements of culture that begin unduly to take primary place in our lives. If we want our ministries to enable those we serve to keep God at the center of life, then we must find ways to equip them with skills for putting limits on their wired existence.

In the interviews of *In Season, Out of Season,* Jacques Ellul elaborated his critique that Christians seem always to be behind instead of ahead of cultural developments. He expressed immense disappointment at their "extreme incapacity . . . to intervene when situations are fluid" and urged Christians to learn to pursue their mission of thinking "before events become inevitable," at "moments when history is flexible, . . . when we must put ourselves inside to move the works."[31] So often churches simply play catch-up, jumping on fads without asking theological/biblical questions. How can our churches follow Ellul's instruction to be prophetic (instead of behind the times) concerning the nature of the technologized and commodified world, its influence on our focal concerns, and the kinds of questions we should be asking for the sake of limiting what might be destructive to genuine ministry?

My goal in this book is that we might learn more rigorously to prune the excesses of our technological milieu, to restrict technology to its proper vocation in the background, and to limit both the functioning of the device paradigm and our correlative dependence on Mammon and the entire range of attendant commodities—for the sake of world justice. I do not propose these objectives because I am hostile toward technology and money, but because I believe Christians are failing both to be as engaged as we could be in working for justice in the world and also to enjoy our own lives as fully as we could. The latter is the case because we have trouble freeing ourselves from the control of our technological milieu and so

---

31. Jacques Ellul, *In Season, Out of Season: An Introduction to the Thought of Jacques Ellul,* based on interviews with Madeleine Garrigou-Lagrange, trans. Lana K. Niles (San Francisco: Harper & Row, 1982), 106–107.

we miss the experience of the fullness of *things* and their entire world. The delights made possible by technological devices are often "parasitic and voracious," to use Borgmann's terms.[32] They seem to draw their life by destroying or displacing other life—for example, listening to music via CDs on earphones pulls us away from others and often keeps people from producing music themselves.

Borgmann insists that to emphasize our focal concerns and practices does not mean being pretechnological or antitechnological. Rather, focal concerns are meta-technological. When they are made truly central, focal concerns can "attain their proper splendor in the context of technology" and in our commodified, Mammon-controlled society. At the same time, the context of technology and the capitalist society can be brought back to the dignity of its original promise only if we keep our focal concerns at the center of that context.[33]

Can we truly make the focal concerns of faith central in our personal lives and churches?

Commodifications in Congregational Decisions

Many other dimensions of church life, such as congregational decisions, become fettered by the device paradigm. For example, how are our church council (presbytery, board) meetings run? Does the meeting become the device that produces the commodity of business decisions—or do we gather together as a community to listen to God so that we might be engaged in God's purposes in the world?[34] If our focal concerns are to love God and the neighbor, business decisions can often get in the way.

Of course, we must do the business of the church. The question is whether the means by which we do it are centered in our focal concerns or become ends in themselves.

The same might be said for our financial decisions. Since the church budgets of the majority of congregations are centered on their own needs, we have to wonder what happened to the focal concern of loving God and the neighbor. Those two commitments are always kept in dialectical tension by Jesus' words that when we serve "the least of these" we are serving Him.

---

32. My own concerns were deepened by Borgmann, *Technology and the Character of Contemporary Life*, 247.

33. Ibid., 247–248.

34. See Charles M. Olsen's book *Transforming Church Boards into Communities of Spiritual Leaders* (Bethesda, Md.: Alban Institute, 1995).

Many church budgets do not include even a line item for caring for the poor. Similarly, the statistics of actual personal giving to the needy among Christians in North America are quite depressing. Though we think we contribute a lot of money, the average percentage of incomes given for charitable purposes is much smaller here than in poorer countries of the world. The most recent figure I've seen for my own denomination was about 3 percent. Just imagine, if all Christians even tithed, how much money would be available for loving our neighbors!

Commodifications in Church Life

It is tragic that denominational reports usually concentrate on the statistics of a congregation. The more I think about the importance of measuring how a church body is doing, the more I find myself asking, "Why by numbers?" Why have we let the commodification of our society determine how we assess the health of churches?

It does serious damage to pastoral ministry when clergy and church leaders have to worry about how their congregations' numbers will look on the statistical report. Why do churches measure their success by how many souls "they" have added in the past year? Could we look instead at how deeply we have nourished discipleship, how profoundly we have helped people learn to live according to their focal concerns of loving God and their neighbors throughout the world?

The device paradigm has ruined our ability to think of quality instead of quantity. Moreover, the result of commodifying people and programs is that they are degraded. Think of how our attitudes change about other commodities. Albert Borgmann offers the example of customarily earth-bound people who are "visibly enthralled" when they take their first airplane flight. "Yet," he notes, "there is scarcely more sullen and surly, if not sober, company than one composed of people who once more are jetting from here to there." Another example he suggests is a shower, often seen merely as a chore to be accomplished. Think instead of its delight after we have come in from working in a muddy yard in the cold rain.[35]

How easily we lose the delight of someone's conversion if she becomes merely another statistic. I know my enthusiasm for leading Bible studies is dampened if I worry about how many are there. Why do I let society's numbers game so affect my attitudes? I know: I lose sight of my focal concerns. Are you guilty, too? Is the congregation of which you are a part?

---

35. Borgmann, *Technology and the Character of Contemporary Life*, 247.

Similarly, many U.S. churches become caught in a nasty spiral of needing to produce the commodities of plenty of programs in order to attract enough people to generate the income necessary to keep offering the programs. At root is the device paradigm and the undoubtedly culture-driven beginning of the attitude that delivering programs is what churches are for.

The resultant pressure to maintain the institution couples with the panic I sketched above over declining numbers to construct a frightful bondage.

I realize this is easy for me to say because my income does not depend on a flourishing congregation,[36] but the corporation under which I freelance has discovered that Jesus really has surprises in store for us when He says, "Continually seek first His kingdom and His righteousness, and all these things shall be added to you" (Matt. 6:33, my translation).

Donald E. Miller discovered by research into the "new paradigm churches"[37] (who distinguish themselves by that name from mainline churches and their old ways of running the congregation) that these churches offer powerful examples of the truth of Matthew 6:33. These movements are led by people with "immodest vision"—they are not limited by their own capacities and resources. The leaders' visions of what God plans to do through them arise with extensive prayer and fasting. He concludes that "the very visitations that are described in the Hebrew scriptures and the New Testament seem still to be happening."[38]

What glorious discoveries of God's provisions do our churches miss because we do not think ourselves dependent on them? We are so controlled by cultural forms of consumption, by the device paradigm and its implications for income, by our fears for our own futures (see chapter 5),

---

36. Instead, we live on my husband's income as a school teacher. The royalties of my books belong to various educational, reformational, and justice-building missions. To correlate with this book's topic, its royalties are designated especially for medicines and other needs at Faith Mission, a Lutheran social service agency in Columbus, Ohio, which provides a day and night shelter and related services for both men and women; a "shelter plus care program" for mentally ill single adults; a "second chance program" of transitional housing and support services for single adults in recovery; a health care clinic staffed by volunteer medical professionals for any indigent person; a three-meals-a-day program (serving over 550 meals each day); a chaplaincy program; case management services; life skills workshops; and mail service, to help the homeless secure employment. For further information, contact Faith Mission at 315 East Long Street, Columbus, Ohio 43215; 614-224-6617.

37. Donald E. Miller, "The Reinvented Church: Styles and Strategies," *Christian Century* 116, 36, December 22–29, 1999, 1250–1253.

38. Ibid., 1252.

and by our misunderstandings of what it means to "Be Church" that we think we need to do everything in our power to keep the institution fully financed.

Why is it that churches are declining in wealthy countries and flourishing in those marked by extreme poverty, intense conflict, and rampant disease? The *World Christian Encyclopedia* of 2001 reports that defections from Christianity in Europe and North America number nearly 2 million a year. Meanwhile, in the world's less developed nations, Christianity has grown from 83 million to 1,120 million in the last century.[39]

Historian Mark Noll elaborates on this dramatic shift in the center of Christianity with some surprising comparisons:

- Last Sunday it is probable that more believers attended church in China than in all of so-called Christian Europe.
- Last Sunday more Anglicans attended church in each of Kenya, South Africa, Tanzania, and Uganda than did Anglicans in Britain and Episcopalians in the United States combined—and the number of Anglicans at church in Nigeria was several times the number in these other African countries. . . .
- During the past week, there were more missionaries at work overseas (as a percentage of the nation's affiliated Christian population) from Samoa and Singapore than from Canada and the United States.[40]

Noll gives similar statistics for Presbyterians, Assemblies of God, and other denominations. He concludes with some observations from a remarkable conference in July 2001 at the University of Pretoria in South Africa, where several papers documented powerfully that poverty, disease, and conflict are absolutely central in African Christianity, even as they are central in much of the newer Christian world.[41]

How could churches in North America and Europe escape the fetters of our own society's ruling paradigm and begin to learn instead how to share the sufferings of our brothers and sisters in these other lands? How

---

39. See David B. Barrett, George T. Kurian, and Todd M. Johnson, eds., *World Christian Encyclopedia*, 2d ed. (Oxford: Oxford University Press, 2001); and also the report on this book by James Billington, "Divided We Grow," *Books and Culture* 7, 6 (November–December 2001): 20.

40. Mark A. Noll, "Who Would Have Thought?" *Books and Culture* 7, 6 (November–December 2001): 21.

41. Ibid., 22.

might we become freed from bondage to Mammon to give generously to those who do not have enough money to survive? What could we learn from them about true and unfettered hope?

A True Story to Exacerbate Our Disquietude

Pastor Gary Nelson, now General Secretary for Canadian Baptist Ministries, every two or three years teaches in Kenya an "Introduction to Urban Ministry" course for pastors. He customarily brings Canadians to participate along with the Kenyans and to learn about conditions in Nairobi. Because of his new position, on his most recent trip those involved were not members of the congregation he served and had not been formed by his previous teaching to understand poverty. Moreover, the team had not emerged from community life together and did not share a set of core values (focal concerns) for ministry and faith that would help them support each other more thoroughly as they confronted harsh realities of deprivation.

The group spent mornings in lectures, and then the students participated in afternoon site visits to some of Nairobi's slum areas. The Canadians were deeply affected by the poverty around them even before those visits, for most of them had never witnessed destitution such as that they were observing. Much later, after returning to Canada, one person said, "My visit to Nairobi caused me to understand that I lived in a bubble."

One day they visited the destitute Kibera slum—1,500,000 people living in a small, concentrated area of long, narrow, winding dirt lanes and small mud-and-stick shanties. Up the serpentine paths they trudged, into the middle of Kibera's dismal bleakness to a church run by the Africa Brotherhood Church of Kenya. There they discussed the congregation's ministry and community development against seemingly impossible odds and were served tea and bread by the church members.

Abashed by the immensity of the problems and the paucity of the congregation's resources, the Canadians were penetratingly distressed and kept asking on their way back from Kibera that night, "Where is the hope?" This one question seemed to haunt them. In response, Gary invited a young Kenyan pastor named Amos Rukuru to join them one evening to talk about his faith life and experience.

As the Canadians conversed with Amos, they raised the question again. "With all this poverty and corruption, where is the hope?" Amos eloquently described his faith and finished with the astonishingly simple remark, "Our hope is Christ!" The reply from two of the Canadians was swift and startling; immediately they cried, "That is not enough!"

"Christ . . . is not enough!" Perhaps, like Jesus' first disciples, they did not know what they were saying.

In the written report that Gary gave me of this incident and its setting, he added that much has happened to the Canadian Christians since that time, that there has been deep soul searching on their part. At that time, however, the culture of North America won out over the faith that they had espoused.[42]

How fettered is our hope by the plethora of goods we have and think we need, by the notion that we can fix problems if we just have enough stuff! How small is our picture of the Triune God manifested in Christ that we might think, under duress, that He is not enough! How could Christian theology instead move churches into the marginal world—to listen to and with it and to serve there humbly?[43]

---

42. The account from which this summary was taken was written at my request by Pastor Gary Nelson of Toronto on December 4, 2001.

43. See Robert T. Osborn (professor of religion emeritus at Duke University), "Theological Table Talk: The Possibility of Theology Today," *Theology Today* 55, 4 (January 1999): 569.

Chapter 5

How Can We Escape
from Death and Despair?

In chapter 3, I introduced the story of Günther and Rosemarie Gold-smith, told by their son in *The Inextinguishable Symphony*. The last concert they played in their small Jewish orchestra in Berlin before emigrating was a seemingly impossible performance of Gustav Mahler's massive Second Symphony, called the *Resurrection* Symphony. That piece begins with a funeral service as the composer struggles with the unsolvable problems of suffering and death. All sorts of emotions flood the movement in a range from tenderness through outrage and mockery to despair.[1] The second movement's traditional Austrian country dance suggests innocence and youthfulness and thereby causes us to reflect on the cruelty that these, too, are lost in death; the third movement raises again notes of despair and absurdity. Next, a hymnlike song contemplates our yearning for God, and then the finale annihilates the world before offering Mahler's uplifting vision of ultimate redemption—rapturous music which always floods my body with exhilaration.

The chorus sings an 18th-century poem, but Mahler wanted to disclose greater liberation, so he added sixteen lines of his own, urging "my heart" to believe that nothing is lost, everything longed and struggled for is gained; sufferings have not been in vain. "Stop trembling. Prepare to live," for penetrating pain is escaped; all-conquering Death is conquered. The extra lines conclude with the assertion that "I" will die to live, rise again, and be "borne up, through struggle, to God!" (266). Goldsmith's description of the effects of this composition on all who were in the concert hall

---

1. Goldsmith, *Inextinguishable Symphony*, 265. Page references to this book in the following paragraphs will be given parenthetically in the text.

that day is truly thrilling, just as is the music itself with its ringing chords, chiming bells, reverberating organ, and thunderous percussion.

Yet Mahler himself was not able to hold on to his visions which he painted in such beautiful music. He always felt alone in the universe, and this "kept him in a permanent state of agitation and unhappiness" (201). In spite of his conversion to Catholicism, he thought himself, ultimately, an unbeliever.

Perhaps the reason lies in Mahler's fourth last line, "With wings I have won for myself I shall soar." These words haunt me, for I know, when all is weighed in the balance, that I cannot win for myself wings to soar to God. My hope would turn to dust in my mouth, cruelly spiced with despair.

Where is there a hope large enough truly to overcome death? Where is there hope sufficiently encompassing to enable us to know that all our pain and suffering has not been in vain? How do we bring together the contrary oracles of the preacher *Qohelet* (at the end of chapter 3), concerning both the "vanity" of everything and the eternity that God has placed in our hearts?

We Need a Meta-Narrative for Hope in Postmodern Times

Part of the impetus for this book was a review that cited *How We Became Posthuman: Virtual Bodies in Cybernetics, Literature, and Informatics* as one of a growing genre of studies that "challenge secular thinking about the shape and shaping power of the technological worldview." Philip R. Meadows, the reviewer, calls for a biblical narrative strong enough for us to imagine and shape "the meaning and future of our increasingly cybernated lives." What Meadows asks for in cybernetic proficiency I cannot provide, but his insistence that "neither woeful jeremiads nor New Age optimism" are really what churches need[2] made me realize that an account of the Christian meta-narrative from the perspective of genuine Christian realism (as defined in chapter 4) could at least begin the kind of response he seeks.

Human beings need to orient their lives by means of some sort of comprehensive perspective that helps them comprehend life's particulars. I am convinced that our profound yearning can be met only by a spacious narrative, personal enough to help us find our particular place in it and endur-

---

2. Philip R. Meadows's review of N. Katherine Hayles, *How We Became Posthuman: Virtual Bodies in Cybernetics, Literature, and Informatics* (Chicago: University of Chicago Press, 1999), *Christian Century* 116, 21, July 28–August 4, 1999, 752–753.

ing enough to make that place significant. Moreover, I believe that the biblical chronicle of a Triune God is the perfect narrative to empower us to envision the meaning of our lives in this time and to shape our lives to counteract the negative effects of the device paradigm and its milieu.[3]

The Scriptures enable us to discern our most profound longings (expressed or not), to name who human beings are and what we want to be, to fathom ever more clearly who God is, and to perceive how all these things connect. It is a meta-narrative large enough, thorough enough, and promising enough to give us the hope we need to live courageously in the midst of an unbalanced, technologically driven, commodification-distorted world.

The Bible offers a grandly sweeping meta-narrative. That is one of the thrills of reading the Scriptures, for they paint an account of God's action on our behalf from the beginning of the world to the culmination of God's purposes in the recapitulation of the cosmos. Descriptions in both Testaments give us many details about ways that God has intervened in, and been revealed by, both the universe and history. The entire meta-narrative fills us with an unfettered hope, the Trinity's gracious gift of a true hope that will not disappoint us, but frees us to live our focal concerns Joyfully—to love God and our neighbors wholeheartedly.

Human Beginnings

Of course, it is not possible in one brief chapter even to sketch the main passages proclaiming the hope of the biblical meta-narrative. My goal is simply to highlight paradigmatic examples for the sake of underscoring several themes important for our purposes in this book and for grasping the grand sweep of this magisterial (but not oppressive) meta-narrative.

Our society's technological fascination and the device of science produce commodities of theories and facts and discoveries that are often

---

3. Four powerful examples of the Bible's rescripting of our lives were heard in a session of the "Character Ethics and Biblical Interpretation Group" at the American Academy of Religion/Society of Biblical Literature annual meeting in Denver on November 19, 2001. Denise M. Ackermann, from the University of Stellenbosch in South Africa, led us to see how "Tamar's Cry" in 2 Samuel 13:1–22 offers possibilities for churches to guide and encourage women affected by Africa's HIV/AIDS crisis. Other papers arose from Robert Ekblad's work with undocumented workers in Washington State through his community, Tierra Nueva del Norte, and Jose Rafael Escobar's work through the Centro Evangelical de Estudios Pastorales in postwar Guatemala. Walter Brueggemann's response to those three papers helped to spur me in writing this book.

thought to negate any possibility for believing the biblical account of human beginnings. I experience the opposite effect. Whatever science ascertains simply amplifies my wonder at all that God created. It doesn't matter to me so much *how* God did it and continues to do it.

The biblical canon begins in Genesis with a glorious liturgy celebrating the harmony and design in the cosmos. Each day's description follows a specific pattern and emphasizes that everything God designed "was so." Can we respond in any other way than to be overwhelmed with amazement and reverence when we observe that day and night always repeat their pattern; that the atmosphere hasn't fallen into the sea; that water in general keeps its boundaries so that vegetation can flourish; that plants bear seeds and fruits according to their kinds; that the earth continues to rotate around its sun, to receive the beauties of both its moon's monthly patterns and a marvelous universe full of stars; that fish continue to swim upstream to spawn and birds fly south for the winter; that cattle and creepers and wild things continue to multiply; that human beings continue to bear the image of God? This extraordinarily brilliant cosmos fills us with hope in the God whose design it is.

Furthermore, the account of God's creation of human beings makes several hopeful assertions. The Creator designs the harmony of the earth to be maintained, for human beings are given dominion *with* the creatures (the Hebrew preposition is *b*); there is no hierarchy among them (for women and men equally bear God's image); and there are enough green plants for all—human beings and creatures—to eat (Gen. 1:26–30). Soon after the canon displays this initial vision it is broken, but God immediately reveals hope for its rebirth.

Two other beginnings in Genesis 1–12 are crucial for our purposes here. They are founded on God's true promises to all human beings and to a special people. After human beings disobey—lured by common temptations of good food, lovely appearances, and the desire for wisdom (Gen. 3:6; compare seductions of our present milieu)—they are promised restoration and forgiveness, through the victory of the woman's offspring. This is symbolized by the LORD God making garments for them and removing them from the garden lest they eat of the tree of life and live forever in their brokenness.

Then Chosen People are promised that they will be graced in order to bring grace to the world. This is the unfettered hope of our faith: our being a blessing to others does not depend upon us, but upon prior mercies from the LORD, the great covenant God who keeps promises.

"The LORD Will Provide"

We look now at five texts (Genesis 12 and 22; Exodus 14, 15, and 16) that establish a primary First Testament theme that the LORD will provide for Israel's future. In Genesis 12:1–4, God called Abraham to "come out" from his culture, to found a unique nation that would be blessed for the sake of the world. In contrast to the surrounding peoples, who routinely sacrificed the first-born child in order to ensure future fertility, God dramatically taught Abraham that his descendants would be different. *YHWH* was not a god who demanded such sacrifices (except from Himself!). The crucial question for Abraham in Genesis 22 was *not* how God could ask him to sacrifice his son—all the surrounding gods asked for that—but whether God would jeopardize the covenant promise that through this son all the nations of the earth would be blessed.

Genesis 22:8 and 14 give us a key to the text when Abraham answers Isaac that God will provide the lamb and then names the place "the LORD will provide." The narrator reiterates the theme by declaring it still said, "On the mount of the LORD it shall be provided."[4] The major lesson for the Israelites to learn throughout their history was this unfettered hope: that God would provide, that they did not need to resort to violence to secure their own future.

This theme is emphasized in three distinct accounts in Exodus 14–16. Chapter 14 presents the Red Sea battle as the paradigmatic Holy War. At the sea, Israel did *nothing*. They merely watched as *YHWH* delivered them from their oppressors. They secured *no booty*. (In the wars of the Conquest all booty was to be consecrated to the LORD in the holy *herem*. What would happen in the 21st century if no one fought and there was no booty to be gained in war?)[5]

Exodus 15 presents an ancient account of worship. Notice how all the emphasis is on the LORD, "for He has triumphed gloriously" (v. 1). The entire hymn of praise is a tribute to what God has done—overthrowing adversaries, leading the people *YHWH* has redeemed in steadfast love, guiding them to the divine, holy abode. In what God has done and does is our hope; that is why it has no fetters.

---

4. Unless otherwise noted, all the biblical quotations in this chapter are taken from the New Revised Standard Version.

5. For a brief sketch of biblical Holy War as part of God's movement of Israel toward peace, see Marva J. Dawn, "What the Bible *Really* Says about War," *Other Side* 29, 2 (March–April 1993): 56–59.

The very next account in Exodus 16 tells of the miraculous daily provision of manna and the doubly miraculous preserving of it for the Sabbath day. Thereby it underscores this message once again: not by their own efforts would the Israelites furnish what they needed. Sabbath rest makes the same point as genuine Holy War—that the Israelites were to be different from the world around them in learning to rest in *YHWH*'s care, in believing that God would provide for their future, in finding their hope in the LORD.

Even the Commandments Are Preceded by Grace

By now it is no doubt apparent that the reason we find unfettered hope in the LORD is that our commitment to our focal concerns rests entirely on God's prior actions of creation and promise, rescue and provision. Even *YHWH*'s commandments, which set out clearly our focal concerns, are given *after* pronouncements of God's covenant grace.

Five texts particularly will illustrate the fullness of this interrelationship between God's action and our focal concerns. First, Exodus 20:1–21 details *YHWH*'s initial giving of the Ten Commandments. Even this Word from the LORD is surrounded by grace. God begins by reminding the people of how they had been rescued by the LORD's hand "out of the land of Egypt, out of the house of slavery" (v. 2). In response, the people "shall have no other gods before Me" (v. 3). Why would they want to? This is the covenant God who delivered them.

After the commands are given, the narrator tells us the people were quite afraid in the thunderous upheaval of the LORD's presence on the mountain. They recognize that if God spoke to them they would die (v. 19)—a perception underscored in many other biblical texts. Moses, however, urges them not to be afraid, "for God has come only to test you and to put the fear of Him upon you so that you do not sin" (v. 20). The presence of grace in this scene can be more readily recognized if we pay attention to the crucial difference between being afraid and the fear of God.

This is a distinction lost in our society—and, I believe, another reason hope is fettered there. We do not have to be afraid of being destroyed, even though, because we turn so constantly to other gods, we deserve it and therefore rightly fear God. But *YHWH* comes only to test and challenge us, in order to draw us to Himself. We can love God well only if we also fear God.

Too often in our postmodern, tolerant, technologically driven, commodified world—and usually because of those factors—we lose sight of the dialectical tension of fear and love, although the Scriptures frequently describe it. For example, the apostle Paul laments over his bondage to sin (Romans 7) just before rejoicing in the truth that nothing is able to separate us from God's love (Romans 8). We cannot really begin to know the uncommon grace of the LORD's love unless we first know how much we deserve God's righteous wrath, how we deserve the death we each must die. Otherwise, we make grace cheap and assume that it is easy for God to forgive us. We think we're not too bad—that we actually can earn God's favor. Only as we totally confront our absolute hopelessness and complete corruption can we truly discover with awe the majesty and infinity and incomprehensibility of the covenant LORD's love for us. God could at any moment destroy us; that is what we deserve. But *YHWH* does not; that is divine grace.[6] And the eternal fullness of this Triune grace is what unfetters our hope.

In between Exodus 20's beginning and ending in grace are the Ten Commandments, which outline how we love God and our neighbors. In response to grace, we commit our lives to these focal concerns. By joining the versions in Exodus 20 and Deuteronomy 5, we see that the mandate to keep the Sabbath holy is the hinge between our two loves. The Exodus account urges us to remember the Sabbath because the LORD kept it (vv. 8–11), whereas the Deuteronomy narration spurs us to observe it by freeing our neighbors (even the animals!) from the burden of work because our people's ordeals in slavery have taught us how onerous bondage is (vv. 12–15). Keeping the Sabbath, then, is a way to celebrate our unfettered hope (see chapter 6).

Deuteronomy 6 underscores these same themes. It emphasizes the LORD's promises, that the grace of *YHWH* being our God is the foundation for keeping the commandments, that they should be remembered at all times (that is, be kept as our focal concerns!), that when we violate God's commands we break the covenant which *YHWH* always keeps, that the LORD is our rescuer and so we want diligently to observe His commands, which "are not burdensome" (1 John 5:3) for reasons we will explore in chapter 6.

The crucial importance of our focal concerns to love God and the neighbor is set out in Deuteronomy 30. However, the text also, in more subtle ways, reminds us that any ability to keep these commitments is

---

6. For a more full explication of the biblical dialectical combination of fear and love, see Marva J. Dawn, *To Walk and Not Faint: A Month of Meditations on Isaiah 40*, rev. ed. (Grand Rapids: Wm. B. Eerdmans Publishing Co., 1997).

based on the LORD's work—that *YHWH* will "circumcise [our] heart . . . so that [we] will love the LORD [our] God with all [our] heart and with all [our] soul, in order that [we] may live" (v. 6). Out of covenant mercy, *YHWH* warns us that if we fail to "obey the commandments of the LORD [our] God . . . by loving the LORD [our] God, walking in His ways, and observing His commandments, decrees, and ordinances" by being "led astray to bow down to other gods and serve them," then we choose death instead of life (vv. 16–20).

God has made and continues to make it possible for us to experience life in unfettered hope. When we choose death by worshiping the gods of our society instead of living by the focal concerns created by covenant grace, we only fetter ourselves with curses such as those exhibited in the collage of chapter 1.

It is easy to get bogged down in reading the extensive lists of commands in the Torah. However, if we keep thinking of them in terms of how following them enables us to love God and our neighbor,[7] then we will be overwhelmed by how the LORD's commands to the Chosen People (particularly in the Jubilee ordinances of Leviticus 25) are designed to insure economic stability through generosity. I am supremely grateful, for the sake of working to change the gross economic imbalances of our globalized world, that the Torah's command for Jubilee is again being taken seriously.[8] Could the grand narrative of our hope in the covenant LORD free us to bring economic justice according to the biblical vision?

Throughout History *YHWH* Is Both a Judge and Rescuer

By means of a continually repeated cycle, the book of Judges displays how Israel kept losing track of its covenant freedom and its concomitant focal concerns. When, as a result, the people are conquered time and again by enemies, they eventually respond with repentance, returning to *YHWH*, and enjoying again their covenant relationship with their LORD.

Similarly, the historical books of Samuel, Kings, and Chronicles show the recurrent pattern of failures, repentance, restoration, covenant rela-

---

7. I was greatly helped to understand this from a Jewish perspective by Jacob Neusner's *Invitation to the Talmud: A Teaching Book*, rev. ed. (San Francisco: Harper & Row, 1984).

8. See, for example, Maria Harris, *Proclaim Jubilee! A Spirituality for the Twenty-first Century* (Louisville, Ky.: Westminster John Knox Press, 1995); and, on the prophetic use of the Jubilee vision, John Howard Yoder, *The Politics of Jesus: Behold the Man! Our Victorious Lamb*, 2d ed. (Grand Rapids: Wm. B. Eerdmans Publishing Co., 1994).

tionship. The dominance of this pattern might cause us to think that *YHWH*'s favor rested on the people only if they were good, that their hope was indeed fettered by the obligation to obey first before blessings could be given. However, the creedal texts of the First Testament, such as Deuteronomy 26 and Joshua 24, repeatedly emphasize that the whole pattern begins with the LORD's rescue and promises.

Because *YHWH* never fails to be faithful to God's side of the covenant, Israel can always know, as the prophet Isaiah declares, that

> Therefore the LORD waits to be gracious to you;
>   therefore He will rise up to show mercy to you.
> For the LORD is a God of justice;
>   blessed are all those who wait for Him.
>   (Isa. 30:18)

I especially love the word *wait* in that text. Because Israel kept trying to solve their problems with enemies by themselves, therefore *YHWH* keeps waiting (imperfect continuing verb) to be gracious (a Hebrew word used only for God). The LORD longs to show us "womb compassion" (*racham*). How blessed we are if we wait for Him!

> For thus said the Lord GOD, the Holy One of Israel:
> In returning and rest you shall be saved;
>   in quietness and in trust shall be your strength.
>   (30:15)

Our hope is in the LORD. When we place it in ourselves, we only reap failure and fetters.

This is the meaning of the Holy War imagery throughout the First Testament. God will be the Divine Warrior for the covenant people and thus provide for their future.[9] They are not to fight for themselves. Thus, Samuel warns the Children of Israel against having a king because he would establish a standing army (1 Sam. 8:11–12 and 19–20). In contrast to the nations that surrounded them, Israel was *not* to prepare material or personnel for war. When the kings began to develop professional armies,

---

9. See Thomas R. Yoder Neufeld, '*Put on the Armour of God*': *The Divine Warrior from Isaiah to Ephesians*, Journal for the Study of the New Testament Supplement Series 140 (Sheffield, England: Sheffield Academic Press, 1997) and *Ephesians*, Believers Church Bible Commentary (Scottdale, Pa.: Herald Press, 2001).

the actual period of Holy War came to an end, though its cultic methods were never totally practiced even in the time of the judges.[10]

Consequently, I think it is more significant than we usually notice when 1 Chronicles 28:3 tells us that David was not permitted to build a house for *YHWH* because he was a man of war. Worship of, and trust in, God does not correlate with violence. Instead, Solomon (notice the relation to *shalom*) built the temple. Similarly, the capital city for the Israelites was Jeru-salem (-*shalom*), to remind them (and us) that the center of their life as God's people was to be the peace and wholeness found in *YHWH*. They should turn to their LORD for their hope, not trust in themselves or their own power.

Even so, today our hopes are fettered because we trust in our scientific knowledge and technological expertise, our military might and economic power. Though people of faith can't expect our nation-state to have a peace city for our capital, of course, yet it is astonishing (but typical for human beings) how much we Christians turn elsewhere than God for our hope.

Historical and Prophetic Visions of God's Wrath

Some who trust in military weapons believe that violence is justified because God acts violently in the historical and prophetic books of the Bible. But is that what those books are teaching? Others who read the Bible are troubled by biblical history and the prophets because they seem to show a different sort of God—a God not of grace and mercy but of wrath and violence. Is that apparent contradiction a strong argument against my belief that the biblical meta-narrative pictures a God Who is the true source and foundation of our hope?

We can answer those two questions best with the help of a probing essay on the topic, "The Wrath of God," by professor Terence Fretheim of Luther Seminary in St. Paul, Minnesota. He reflects on God's wrath in the First Testament in a way that enables us to understand how this aspect of the narratives about *YHWH* actually deepens our hope.[11] He

---

10. See Gerhard von Rad, *Holy War in Ancient Israel*, trans. and ed. Marva J. Dawn (Grand Rapids: Wm. B. Eerdmans Publishing Co., 1991).

11. I heard Dr. Terence E. Fretheim present his paper "Reflections on the Wrath of God in the Old Testament" at the American Academy of Religion/Society of Biblical Literature annual meeting in Denver on November 18, 2001. My notes from that presentation are slightly expanded and corrected because of his gracious kindness in sending me his entire manuscript. I regret that his paper will be published too late (in a slightly abbreviated form in *Horizons in Biblical Theology* 24 [2002]) for me to cite published page numbers for the ideas and few quotations I am including here.

begins by quoting Augustine's dictum that "Hope has two beautiful daughters, anger and courage; anger at the ways things are, and courage to work to make things other than they are."[12] When we understand God's wrath (which is declared over 500 times in more than 380 contexts in almost all the First Testament books), we are more able to respond to the world's injustices and oppressions with the right anger and proper courage.

Fretheim notes that there has been scholarly discomfort with the theme of God's wrath ever since Philo and Marcion. These days, a popular and mushy Christianity wants God to be only loving. However, as Fretheim urges, we need to retain the theme of God's wrath to be able to speak with weight and seriousness about the violent and deplorable state of the world. "The way things are" is not what God intended or created.

Most important, Fretheim's exploration of various facets of the wrath of God seeks to hold together dimensions of that theme that are often separated—"personal and natural; personal and political; wrath and grief; emotion and reason; covenant and creation; historical and eschatological." Among Fretheim's astute observations, the following are forceful for our purposes:

1. God's anger (in contrast to that of humans, which is infected with sin) is always exercised in the service of life, is always relational, and is a sign that God takes His relationship with Israel seriously.
2. Divine anger is connected, especially by the prophets, with divine grief. "God mediates judgment so that sin and evil do not go unchecked in the life of the world, but God does so at great cost to the divine life." *YHWH*'s anger and tears go together to show that harsh words of judgment are matched in God not by an inner harshness, but by profound grief. If we do not realize that God's anger is flooded with sorrow, then our own anger is less likely to be restrained from harshness.
3. God as judge is not neutral—the personal and political must remain linked, but not be collapsed—for the judge behind the bench is the spouse of the one tried (as in Hosea 2).
4. God's anger at Israel involves more than their covenant relationship with *YHWH*, for "Israel's sins have a devastating effect on the entire cosmos."

---

12. Quoted by R. M. Brown, *Religion and Violence*, 2d ed. (Philadelphia: Westminster Press, 1987), xxii, without citation (Fretheim's footnote).

5. God's anger is historical—provoked by specific acts or situations. Though God's faithful people are promised deliverance from *eschatological* wrath [that is, wrath at the time of final judgment], they might get caught in experiences of *historical* wrath. At such times, they can take comfort in God's promise, "I have loved you with an everlasting love; therefore I have continued my faithfulness to you" (Jer. 31:3).

6. Although the motivation for God's wrath is not explicit in all biblical texts, in about half of the settings the cause is wickedness of human beings toward others; 75% are marked by infidelity to God. *Never* is wrath vented to protect God or because the LORD's moral sense is offended. The Scriptural question-and-answer formulas show that wrath is rooted in human sin.

7. Over 70 times God's anger is part of Israel's prayers in the Psalms. The fact that Israel can raise objections, as well as their penitential acknowledgments, shows how relational God is; human beings can stand in the face of divine anger and have their say.

8. "Because God regularly gives motivations for the divine anger, wrath is not a divine attribute." If wrath were an attribute of God, that would entail an eternal dualism of wrath and love.

9. Anger is also *not* simply emotional since there are reasons for it, nor is it irrational since the First Testament shows that *YHWH*'s actions serve God's purposes.

10. The fact that God is angry because His will is not being done demonstrates that His will is resistible.

11. Because God is patient and slow to anger, there is a delay in time between the provocation of *YHWH*'s wrath, its execution, and its coming to an end. During that time, God is open to His wrath being turned away or limited when Israel is repentant or takes action or when someone such as Moses stands in the breach. Valuing these human contributions, God reassesses. God, too, can stand in the breach. Hosea 11 enables us to see that "the Godness of God is such that God chooses to take the wrath into the divine self and suffer it there rather than letting it go forth to destruction."

12. Wrath is personal and natural (see Psalm 78, which juxtaposes God's involvement and natural causes), and these should not be split apart. *YHWH*'s anger works through the natural order. The phrasing of God "giving [Israel] up" to the consequences of their sin is not arbitrary; sin itself leads to a significant level of negative fallout. God might see to the movement and at other times withdraws, but God is not removed from the process.

13. God uses human and nonhuman agents to express wrath. Sometimes *YHWH's* wrath is vented against agents that go overboard. God risks to be associated with violence; since there is an interdependent order of freedom in creation and room for genuine human decision, the latter sphere can be overstepped.

14. God's wrath is part of His saving purposes. It is vented as *YHWH's* circumstantial will in relation to sin, as opposed to God's ultimate will. One of the goals of divine wrath is to end indifference to oppression and thereby make a future possible to those who have no hope. God would prefer to avoid wrath altogether and has no pleasure in anyone's death—even the death of the wicked. Anger lasts a moment, but God's love is everlasting.

Fretheim's concluding remarks sent me back to Abraham Joshua Heschel's powerful work on the prophets, which eloquently summarizes and clarifies what we have learned:

> The anger of the Lord is instrumental, hypothetical, conditional, and subject to His will. . . . Far from being an expression of "petulant vindictiveness," the message of anger includes a call to return and to be saved. . . . It is not an expression of irrational, sudden, and instinctive excitement, but a free and deliberate reaction of God's justice to what is wrong and evil. For all its intensity, it may be averted by prayer. There is no divine anger for anger's sake. Its meaning is . . . instrumental: to bring about repentance; its purpose and consummation is its own disappearance.[13]

Heschel's and Fretheim's careful attention to the texts encourages us to be similarly careful when we read passages in our meta-narrative of faith. When we are careful, we will continually find a sweeping basis for hope as we discover more and more the undergirding of the LORD's saving purposes (even—and especially—when God is angry). Moreover, we will more frequently be aroused from our lethargy and indifference to oppression and challenged to live more profoundly our focal concerns for the sake of participating in God's gracious work to make a future possible to those without hope.

We can't choose ourselves to be the instruments of God's divine wrath, as Miroslav Volf noted in a conference response to Fretheim's presentation

---

13. Abraham J. Heschel, *The Prophets,* vol. 2 of paperback ed. (New York: Harper & Row, 1962), 66.

of his essay. But in response to God's immense grace, we can commit our-selves to obey *YHWH*'s commands (see chapter 6) and thereby be avail-able for God to use us in His purposes to feed the hungry and shelter the homeless.

Praise and Lament

The poetic literature in the First Testament underscores the themes we have already sketched, especially the foundation of our hope in God's character and actions of grace. The command in Psalm 46:10 to "be still" (literally, "cease striving") and know that *YHWH* is God—who "makes wars to cease" by breaking bows and shattering spears—reminds Israel that they are to depend upon the God of Jacob as their fortress rather than on themselves.

A prominent motif in all forms of biblical poetry is that God's people can hope in Him, rather than in themselves or wealth, because of the LORD's *chesedh*, or "steadfast love."[14] In Psalm 62, for example, together with verses of lament the poet also declares with confidence,

> For God alone my soul waits in silence,
>   for my hope is from Him.
> He alone is my rock and my salvation,
>   my fortress; I shall not be shaken. . . .
>
> Trust in Him at all times, O people;
>   pour out your heart before Him;
>   God is a refuge for us.   *Selah*
>   . . . if riches increase, do not set your heart on them.
>
> Once God has spoken;
>   twice have I heard this:
> that power belongs to God,
>   and steadfast love [*chesedh*] belongs to you, O Lord.
>   (62:5–6, 8, 10c–12a)

In the laments also, as noted in the section above, God's wrath appears—often with pleas for it to be abated or with repentance because it is deserved. Then the psalmists find hope in knowing that *YHWH* will be merciful.

---

14. For deeper exploration of this motif, see Marva J. Dawn, *I'm Lonely, LORD—How Long? Meditations on the Psalms*, 2d ed. (Grand Rapids: Wm. B. Eerdmans Publishing Co., 1998).

On the human side, the psalmists speak both of the fear with which they observe illness, death, or God's actions in nature and also of the love with which they adore their covenant God. This dialectic frees them to hope, for they know that God's interventions will be directed on their behalf—or, when they are guilty, that the LORD will hear their confession.

Perhaps the strongest suggestions of God's searching love are in the intimate imagery of the Song of Songs. We can't discuss here the proportions of human love poetry and analogous portrayal of God contained in the text, but the book's appearance in the canon hints that spiritual overtones of God's tenderness and passion with regard to us are present.

Even Job's sufferings do not call God's character into question. Neither his "friends" nor Job himself let his suffering negate their confidence that God is not unjustly violent.[15]

Very important for our purposes here is the preacher *Qohelet*'s rejection of the life of accumulation. He recognizes that amassing all sorts of possessions, pleasures, persons, and positions turns out to be the same sort of vanity as everything else (Ecclesiastes 2). Would that we could learn so well that lesson about our society's commodities.

The Preacher also observes "all the oppressions that are practiced under the sun. Look, the tears of the oppressed—with no one to comfort them! On the side of their oppressors there was power—with no one to comfort them" (4:1). In these words he summarizes the two kinds of despair we noted in chapter 1—the overt despair of those with nothing and the covert despair of those with too much. Only with the unfettered hope given us by the LORD can we escape both despairs and turn, instead, to be genuine comforters for both sides.

Proverbs and the Psalms are vigorous in calling us to that comforting. This morning a psalm in my prayers included these words:

> How blessed is the one who acts wisely toward the poor;
> The LORD will deliver that person in the day of trouble.
> (Ps. 41:1, my translation; see also, e.g., Psalms 72, 78, 82)

---

15. During the responses to a panel in the Mennonite Scholars' meeting at the American Academy of Religion/Society of Biblical Literature annual meeting in Denver on November 17, 2001, Denny Weaver stressed that social location is critical. He asserted that even the African American slaves did not see suffering as evidence of God's violence. Their suffering did not call into question the character of God but led instead to deeper trust. Theodicy, Weaven suggested, is the construction of the wealthy.

Psalm 41 was followed by this prayer: "Lord Jesus, healer of soul and body, you said, 'Blessed are the merciful, for they shall obtain mercy.' Teach us to come to the aid of the needy in a spirit of love, as we have been received and strengthened by you; and to you be the glory and praise now and forever. Amen."[16]

Our hope in the LORD, who heals and receives and strengthens, is unfettered. In response to His gifts, may we love God with lives of genuine praise integrally connected with love for the needy.

The Minor Prophets

If the focal concerns of God's people are primarily the love of God and the love of neighbors, then the minor prophets are necessary these days, for most of their prophetic denunciations arise because Israel has lost sight of those commitments. Since there is not enough space in this short chapter for a full exploration of the seers' oracles, I have chosen to focus on the warnings of one representative prophet, Amos—the dresser of sycamore trees who did not want to be a prophet, but was compelled to speak the LORD's words.

After doom oracles directed to Damascus, Gaza, Tyre, Edom, the Ammonites, Moab, and Judah for their idolatries and violences, *YHWH* vents justified wrath against Israel

> because they sell the righteous for silver,
>   and the needy for a pair of sandals—
> they who trample the head of the poor into the dust of the earth,
>   and push the afflicted out of the way . . .
>
> (Amos 2:6c–7b)

The LORD's strongest denunciations and some of the most stirring calls to compassionate action occur in Amos 5:

> Therefore because you trample on the poor
>   and take from them levies of grain,
> you have built houses of hewn stone,
>   but you shall not live in them;
> you have planted pleasant vineyards,
>   but you shall not drink their wine.

---

16. From *The Roman Missal* (International Committee on English in the Liturgy, Inc., 1973), as cited in *For All the Saints*, vol. 3: *Year 2: Advent to the Day of Pentecost*, 619.

For I know how many are your transgressions,
    and how great are your sins—
you who afflict the righteous, who take a bribe,
    and push aside the needy in the gate.
Therefore the prudent will keep silent in such a time;
    for it is an evil time.

Seek good and not evil,
    that you may live;
and so the LORD, the God of hosts, will be with you,
    just as you have said.
Hate evil and love good,
    and establish justice in the gate;
it may be that the LORD, the God of hosts,
    will be gracious to the remnant of Joseph. . . .

I hate, I despise your festivals,
    and I take no delight in your solemn assemblies.
Even though you offer me your burnt offerings and grain offerings,
    I will not accept them;
and the offerings of well-being of your fatted animals
    I will not look upon.
Take away from me the noise of your songs;
    I will not listen to the melody of your harps,
But let justice roll down like waters,
    and righteousness like an everflowing stream.
                                     (5:11–15, 21–24)

These verses are critically important for our purposes because they display clearly how our two focal concerns are intertwined. We do not really love God if we do not live justly. Our worship of God is hypocritical if we trample on the poor. In this present "evil time," why do our churches not hear this word from the LORD? How can we who claim to be God's people come to worship without an uneasy conscience when so many in the world are hungry?

The LORD says to us, too,

Alas for those who are at ease in Zion,
    and for those who feel secure on Mount Samaria,
the notables of the first of the nations. . . .

> I abhor the pride of Jacob
>   and hate his strongholds;
>   and I will deliver up the city and all that is in it. . . .
>
> Do horses run on rocks?
>   Does one plow the sea with oxen?
> But you have turned justice into poison
>   and the fruit of righteousness into wormwood.
>   (6:1, 8c–d, 12)

We who live in what is thought to be the present "first of the nations," we who are at ease, do we know how much the LORD abhors our pride? Do we realize how contrary to our creation it is that we have "turned justice into poison"? Therefore:

> Hear this, you that trample on the needy,
>   and bring to ruin the poor of the land, . . .
>
> The LORD has sworn by the pride of Jacob:
> Surely I will never forget any of their deeds.
> Shall not the land tremble on this account,
>   and everyone mourn who lives in it,
> and all of it rise like the Nile,
>   and be tossed about and sink again, like the Nile of Egypt?
>   (8:4, 7–8)

Verses 9 and 10 give a formidable description of the "day of the LORD," a day of judgment and wrath. But the worst element of God's wrath is this:

> The time is surely coming, says the Lord GOD,
>   when I will send a famine on the land;
> not a famine of bread, or a thirst for water,
>   but of hearing the words of the LORD.
> They shall wander from sea to sea,
>   and from north to east;
> they shall run to and fro, seeking the word of the LORD,
>   but they shall not find it.
>   (8:11–12)

Perhaps this is a famine we are presently experiencing in North America and Western Europe, where Christianity is declining and where we don't seem to be paying much attention to how the poor of the world are being trampled by our overabundance.

Amos does not end his oracles with despair, however. His prophecy takes a dramatic turn in 9:8, which promises,

> The eyes of the Lord GOD are upon the sinful kingdom,
>> and I will destroy it from the face of the earth
>> —except that I will not utterly destroy the house of Jacob,
>>>>> says the LORD.

There is hope only because *YHWH* will "restore the fortunes of my people Israel" (9:14a). That is our only hope, too. God will restore us, in spite of our sinfulness, but only because the meta-narrative of our faith builds on this foundation in the First Testament to tell us the story of God reconciling the cosmos in Jesus.

The Story of Jesus

As with the preceding sections, it is impossible adequately to survey the narratives about Jesus and their references to our themes. I will only sketch the main doctrines formulated from the Gospels to stress my basic biblical theses—that grace is God's primary character toward us and therefore we have hope; that a proper fear keeps us from trusting ourselves or other false hopes; that we love God more fully in response to knowing the Triune hope; that in loving our neighbors we pass on hope to them.

Incarnation

Who could even begin to comprehend the immensity of this mystery? British writer Dorothy Sayers emphasizes that Jesus was "in fact and in truth, and in the most exact and literal sense of the word, 'the God by whom all things were made.'" Thus, she declares:

> [F]or whatever reason God chose to make man as he is—limited and suffering and subject to sorrows and death—He had the honesty and the courage to take His own medicine. Whatever game He is playing with His creation, He has kept His own rules and played fair. He can exact nothing from man that He has not exacted from Himself. He has Himself gone through the whole of human experience, from the trivial irritations of family life and the cramping restrictions of

hard work and lack of money to the worst horrors of pain and humiliation, defeat, despair, and death. When He was a man, He played the man. He was born in poverty and died in disgrace, and thought it well worthwhile.[17]

If the eternally existent Word loved us so much as to reduce Himself to such disgrace and despair; if His Father loved us so much as to give us His Son to be the means by which our failures to share that path are forgiven; and if the Spirit loved us so much as to be the means by which that gift was communicated in conception (see Matt. 1:18–25), then these truths cannot help but draw us to the Triune love and flood us with hope. And the more we contemplate the poverty, humility, adversity, and receptivity of the wee Child in the manger, the more we learn to love God and our neighbors, especially those suffering deprivations.

As we ponder the scene, however, we find a healthy fear: If we had been in Bethlehem that night, would we have been stuck in a fancy hotel room and thereby missed the Child in the stable? That recognition of the problem of our wealth helps us respond with even greater love. As Dietrich Bonhoeffer wrote,

> We have become so accustomed to the idea of divine love and of God's coming at Christmas that we no longer feel the shiver of fear that God's coming should arouse in us. We are indifferent to the message, taking only the pleasant and agreeable out of it and forgetting the serious aspect, that the God of the world draws near to the people of our little earth and lays claim to us. The coming of God is truly not only glad tidings, but first of all frightening news for everyone who has a conscience.
>
> Only when we have felt the terror of the matter, can we recognize the incomparable kindness. God comes into the very midst of evil and of death, and judges the evil in us and in the world.[18]

Lost in wonder, love, and praise, how can we help but be like the shepherds as "they made known what had been told them about this child" and

---

17. Dorothy Sayers (1893–1957), *Creed or Chaos?* (London: A. Wattsins; New York: Harcourt, Brace & Co., 1st American ed., 1949), as cited in *For All the Saints*, 156.

18. Dietrich Bonhoeffer, "The Coming of Jesus in Our Midst," in *A Testament to Freedom: The Essential Writings of Dietrich Bonhoeffer*, ed. Geoffrey B. Kelly and F. Burton Nelson (San Francisco: HarperSanFrancisco, 1995), as quoted in *Watch for the Light: Readings for Advent and Christmas*, ed. the Bruderhof (Farmington, Pa.: The Plough Publishing House, 2001), December 21.

as they continued "glorifying and praising God for all they had heard and seen, as it had been told them" (Luke 2:17, 20)? Notice the emphasis in both verses on what "had been told them."

This biblical pattern of promise and fulfillment, repeatedly stressed in the Gospel accounts, caught me this year as I preached on Matthew's undergirding sentence "All this took place to fulfill what was spoken by the Lord through the prophet" (Matt. 1:22). What overwhelming hope lies in the faithfulness of the divine Word! The grand meta-narrative we're sketching here is not taken from dead words on a printed page, from past events that no longer pertain. This is a lively story, constantly present and fulfilled in new times, a story that enfolds us in its vitality and eternally present hope.

Do our ease and comfort block us from discovering afresh what Good News this is? Do our frantic preparations for the "holidays" prevent the kind of pondering necessary to receive this Child and the hope He brings? Does our trust in the various kinds of commodities of this season keep us from glad and generous proclamation of Good News to the innkeepers and kin, the shepherds and census takers and soldiers of our own Bethlehems?

Commission and Mission

I used these two words instead of "ministry" in order to stress the Triune involvement in Jesus' life on earth. His teaching and healing and ultimately His suffering and death were initiated with a Triune presence both in His baptism and at His temptations in the wilderness. Furthermore, Jesus referred to Himself most often with the title *Son of Man*, which announces God's eschatological promises (especially in Daniel 7) and transmits a deep significance rooted in Israel's struggle for freedom, for justice for the oppressed.[19] Receiving the One who bears that title pulls us into the center of the Trinity's kingdom purposes.

Momentously important for our purposes here is Jesus' initial proclamation as He began His ministry: "The time is fulfilled, and the kingdom of God has come near; repent, and believe in the good news" (Mark 1:15). How must He have announced these things that Mark puts the first two verbs in the Greek perfect tense and the last two in continuing imperatives? Literally, the text thus proclaims that the "opportune time" has been "made replete"—all its fullness of opportunity is, and remains, available

---

19. See William C. Placher, *Jesus the Savior: The Meaning of Jesus Christ for Christian Faith* (Louisville, Ky.: Westminster John Knox Press, 2001), 27–29.

to us. Furthermore, the "reign of God" is at hand, initiated in Christ's presence and unceasingly accessible to us. Therefore, Jesus calls us to "be repenting" and to "be believing" or "continue entrusting" ourselves to the Good News.

That is our unfettered hope in a nutshell. No matter what happens in our lives, still the reign of God has begun. God's future aeon has already broken into this present age, and we can participate by grace in its gifts. Let us so fear (repent) and love (believe) God that we receive and live this Gospel!

Christ's mission invites us to participate, to spread the hope of this Good News. Jesus sent His disciples out to proclaim the kingdom and to heal (Luke 9 and 10 especially). Ultimately, that is entirely what our lives are about if we are Christians. That is why our focal concerns are so important, equipping us to restrict dimensions of the technologized, commodified society in which we live so that they contribute to healing and to expanding God's reign, rather than be allowed to fetter life and promote other gods instead.

There is a necessary fear in Christ's mission. His cries of "Woe to you, scribes and Pharisees, hypocrites!" ring true for us; do we "tithe mint, dill, and cummin, and have neglected the weightier matters of the law: justice and mercy and faith" (Matt. 23:23)? Do we miss the hope in the narrative of Jesus because we are not participating in the glorious work of His kingdom's justice?

Affliction

That involvement will embroil us in afflictions, just as it did Jesus. We misunderstand His life on earth if we place His sufferings only at the end. We are taught to think that way, I greatly regret, by what seems to be a misplaced comma in the Apostle's Creed and a changed phrase in the Nicene. The version of the Apostle's Creed most commonly used says,

> He suffered under Pontius Pilate,
>   was crucified, died, and was buried.

We should say instead,

> He suffered,
>   under Pontius Pilate was crucified, died, and was buried.

Similarly, in newer versions of the Nicene Creed, we confess,

> For our sake he was crucified under Pontius Pilate;
> he suffered death and was buried,

when, lamentably, He suffered throughout His earthly life. Older versions of the creed said that "he suffered and was buried."

Jesus did not only suffer at death or under Pontius Pilate. He suffered at His birth in a poor stable, when He was a refugee from Herod, in the misunderstandings of His family, when the disciples were unable to comprehend Him and His mission, in His homelessness and fatigue, from the incessant pushiness of the crowds and the constant critique of the religious leaders, and so forth. And what a suffering it must have been to empty Himself, as Paul says in Philippians 2, of His equality with God. Similarly, we diminish His sufferings on the cross when we limit them to the physical or even the spiritual. Imagine the emotional weight of bearing all our accusations and rejections, the sin of the whole world—of being "[f]or our sake . . . made to be sin [He] who knew no sin" (2 Cor. 5:21). Envision the temptations hurled along with the scorn and abuse of the bystanders; why not take again Your divine power and hurl a few lightning bolts at them?

We don't want to ponder the extent of Christ's afflictions because we don't want to bear them ourselves. We are like Peter, rebuking Jesus for forecasting the fullness of His agony (Mark 8:32); Peter wanted a triumphant Messiah, not One calling him to follow Him into hardship.

Since I'm writing this section in Advent, the approach of Christmas pulls me into Peter's fright: Oh, Jesus, don't let this happen to You—because, if we follow You, we will be called to divest ourselves of comfort and warmth, to find ourselves in a cattle stall, a place of muck and cold, humility and poverty and persecution. That stirs new repentance (I really am not ready to follow Him there) and new hope: He welcomes me anyway and receives my worship, deficient as it is.

Passion

Reading the Gospel accounts of Jesus' betrayal, trials, scourgings, mockings, crucifixion, and death never lets us even remotely understand the profound significance of these events. We need the ponderings of the early saints in the Epistles, the ruminations of the early patristic writers, the reflections of reformers and mystics and contemporary theologians. Perhaps even more, we need the creations of the artists in poetry and drama, instruments and voice, fabric and paint and clay.

For example, listen to the opening movement of Johann Sebastian Bach's *St. Matthew Passion* as the orchestra plays a haunting lament above an insistent throbbing in the string basses. Then, behold! as the choirs join antiphonally to call us, question that call, and answer with stark simplicity:

> Come, you daughters, help me lament;
> See!   Whom?   The Bridegroom.
> See Him!   How?   As a Lamb.
> See it!   What?   See His patience.
> Look!   Look where?   On our guilt.
> Look on Him.   Out of love and grace
> He gathers the cross to Himself to bear it.[20]

Meanwhile, a children's chorus is singing the chorale,

> Lamb of God, pure and holy,
> Who on the cross didst suffer,
> Ever patient and lowly,
> Thyself to scorn didst offer.
> All sins Thou borest for us,
> Else had despair reigned o'er us;
> Have mercy on us, O Jesus! O Jesus![21]

What immensity of grace, intensity of compassion, and surprising hope it is that in this deplorably clashing scene of mockery, brutal torture, and holiness all three Persons are working out the Triune purposes of our redemption!

One of our first responses is fear, for we know that we join Judas and Peter as betrayers and deniers. Why don't the heavens and hell respond with cataclysmic upheavals? The libretto and Bach's fervid music ask when Jesus is handed over to the soldiers,

> Have lightnings, have thunders disappeared into the clouds?
> Then open the fiery abyss, O hell!

---

20. The translations in this section of the *St. Matthew Passion*'s libretto by C. F. Henrici (who went by the pseudonym Picander) are mine, with great help from my husband, Myron Sandberg. Since I am writing this section in Advent, I have discovered that listening to the entire *St. Matthew Passion* in Advent helps us more consciously prepare for the true meaning of the humble birth we will soon celebrate.

21. This is the most common early English translation of Nikolaus Decius's 1531 chorale text "O Lammes Gottes, unschuldig."

Demolish, ruin, devour, shatter
With sudden rage
The treacherous betrayer, the murderous throng!

We have to grieve our part in the proceedings against Jesus. With a graceful and stately, slow and undulating triple meter, a richly sonorous alto sings for Peter,

Have mercy on me, my God.
Regard the depth of my tears!
Behold here,
Heart and eyes weep before You
Bitterly.

Underneath, the string bass plucks a solemn pulse of repentance, and, above, a solo violin plays an intensely expressive weeping.

Our fear and remorse are wondrously relieved by the multiple meanings of the very afflictions we caused. To the melody you might know as the hymn "Ah, Holy Jesus," the chorus sings this staggering truth:

How extraordinary indeed is this penalty!
The good Shepherd suffers for the sheep;
The Lord, the Just One, settles the debt
For His servants.

And why was Jesus brought to trial and death in the first place? In response to Pilate's question "Why, what evil has He done?" the soprano soloist answers:

He has done all things well:
To the blind He gave sight,
The lame He caused to walk,
He told us His Father's Word,
He drove the devils away,
The grieving He has comforted,
He received and accepted sinners.
Besides this, Jesus has done nothing.

Can we respond with anything but adoration? Such an unfathomed overflowing of grace inundates us with hope. The more ardently we receive this hope, the more fervently we love God. We join the chorus in these hymn verses:

O sacred Head, now wounded,   What language shall I borrow
With grief and shame weighed down, To thank Thee, dearest Friend,
Now scornfully surrounded   For this Thy dying sorrow,
With thorns, Thine only crown.   Thy pity without end?
O sacred Head, what glory,   O, make me Thine forever!
What bliss, till now was Thine!   And should I fainting be,
Yet, though despised and gory,   Lord, let me never, never
I joy to call Thee mine.   Outlive my love for Thee.[22]

We dare not place our hope in our own ability to respond with love. Our only hope is that if the mercy of Jesus was so deep as to hang for us, it is strong enough to hang on to us.

We stand before the cross immeasurably indebted, extraordinarily calmed, and earnestly committed to speaking and living its meaning. We join the bass soloist in this meditative recitative of praise for God's salvation for Adam and Noah and all of us:

At evening, when it was cool,
Adam's fall was made manifest;
At evening then the Savior came down to him.
At evening, the dove came back
And carried an olive leaf in her beak.
O beauteous time, O evening hour!
The culmination of peace is now made with God,
For Jesus has finished the work of His cross.
His body sinks to rest.
Ah! beloved soul, please
Go, let the Savior's lifeless body be given to you.
O salutary, O precious keepsake!

It seems to me that these last phrases refer to how we—like Joseph of Arimathea asking Pilate for Jesus' corpse—in our remembrance shall carry His dead body as a precious Gift.

---

22. This is the English translation commonly found in mid-20th-century hymnal of verses 1 and 8 of Paul Gerhardt's (1656) German chorale "O Haupt voll Blut und Wunden," based on the 12th-century Latin hymn by Bernard of Clairvaux.

In order to safeguard this treasure, we join the bass soloist in this aria and urge,

> Make yourself pure, my heart;
> I will bury Jesus myself.
> For He shall now in me
> Forever and ever
> Have His sweet rest.
> World, get out! Let Jesus in.

It would be a mistake (and the German doesn't include it) to translate the first line as if we would purify ourselves *from sin*. That would be to fetter our hope once again. Instead, this song of commitment depicts the same theme as Søren Kierkegaard's *Purity of Heart Is to Will One Thing*. The image urges us to command the world to depart so that we can instead focus entirely on Jesus. The repeated pleas to our hearts to be single are reinforced in Bach's music by the oboes' penetrating and steadfast call, and the bass soloist's command for the world to get out is firm and strong. Only by sending away the world and its paradigm and idolatries can we let Jesus in as fully as He wants to come—with all the hope He has procured for us in His Passion.

Resurrection

If we are not remotely capable of comprehending the hope in the Passion, even more is it totally unbefitting to try to capture the hope of the Resurrection. Contemplate earnestly all these things that God's raising of Jesus from the dead accomplished:

the fulfillment of Jesus' oracles concerning His own fate and thus the confirmation of His Word;

the final defeat of *all* the principalities and powers, including the last enemy, Death;

the commencement of the mopping-up operations, in which the vanquished powers are exposed, disarmed, and triumphed over in daily life (a process carried on by us when we expose and disarm the device paradigm and commodifications of our culture);

the initial realization of the First Testament promises concerning the work of the Messiah to deliver us thoroughly from "sin, death, and the power of the devil" (as Martin Luther would say);

the turning point toward culmination in God's reconciliation of the
entire cosmos;

the opening of an eternal future to all God's people;

the building of our hope because we know that we, too, shall rise.

How we trivialize all this with our Easter egg hunts and bunnies, our commodifications of the splendor!

Perhaps we do so because we feel an element of fear in the Resurrection. Like the Virgin Birth, it is so extraordinarily unprecedented, it shat-
ters all our categories for understanding. It is the breaking of *GOD* into
the world, and we can hardly bear it.

Moreover, we can hardly even begin to live it. What the world needs, to
give it hope, is the vision of contemporary saints persisting as resurrected
people (in spite of hindrances and hardships), conveying in every dimension of their lives the magnificent hope of Christ's presence and reign.

Ascension

A grand and hope-creating event in Luke and Acts is the Ascension of
Christ. Most churches don't even celebrate it, and, as a result, we don't realize how crucially necessary it was and remains.[23] Once again, permit me
simply to outline for further reflection key reasons why it was necessary:

If Jesus had not ascended, He could not be present with us every-
where.[24] Thus, Christ continues to invade our technologized,
commodified world with a reality more real than that world is.[25]

By ascending to His Father, Jesus' total obedience and the completion of his earthly/human work on our behalf were affirmed. (Heb.
1:3; 10:12; 12:2)

---

23. For a more thorough exploration of all the gifts that Ascension conveys, see Douglas Farrow, *Ascension and Ecclesia: On the Significance of the Doctrine of the Ascension for Ecclesiology and Christian Cosmology* (Grand Rapids: Wm. B. Eerdmans Publishing Co., 2000);
and chapter 7, "The Call to Be Formed and Transformed by the Spirit of the Ascended
Christ," in Marva J. Dawn and Eugene H. Peterson, *The Unnecessary Pastor: Rediscovering
the Call* (Grand Rapids: Wm. B. Eerdmans Publishing Co., 1999).

24. On being more aware of Christ present in our midst, see Luke Timothy Johnson,
Living Jesus: Learning the Heart of the Gospel (San Francisco: HarperSanFrancisco, 1999).

25. Jones, "Liberated by Reality," 27.

In the Ascension, Jesus took up again the fullness of His deity; it was the end of the *kenosis*, the total emptying of His self-imposed self-limitation. (Phil. 2:5–10)

As ascended Lord, Jesus reigns over all the principalities and powers. (1 Pet. 3:22)

From that position of power Jesus will come again. (Matt. 26:64; Acts 1:11)

At that position with His Father, Christ intercedes for us. (Rom. 8:34; Heb. 8:1–2)

Unless Jesus had ascended, the Holy Spirit would not have been sent to us. (John 16:5–15; Acts 2:33)

The result of that pouring out of the Spirit, furthermore, has been all God's gifts to the Church. (Eph. 4:7–11)

Moreover, that gifting leads to the fulfillment of Jesus' astonishing promise that we, the Church, will do even greater works than He. (John 14:12)

That final gift, due to Jesus' return to His Father and their sending of the Spirit, is one reason that we fear the Ascension. We don't want to be left with the responsibility to continue Jesus' work. Like the disciples, we would rather see Jesus with us in the flesh; then, we think, we could trust Him more fully.

At His Ascension, Jesus commissioned His followers to be His witnesses throughout our home territory and to the ends of the earth (Acts 1:8). But He made this comment in a way that gives us invigorating hope, for it is accompanied by the promise of power when we receive the Holy Spirit, and, instead of a command demanding that we be witnesses, a future verb assures us that we indeed *shall* be. We fetter hope when we depend on our own power or ability to witness.

Christ's Spirit and the Church

As astounding as everything else in the Scriptures is the descending of the Holy Spirit on Pentecost and the infilling of the disciples—along with the promise that this same Spirit power is available to us. We certainly don't usually experience that strength and mastery in all its fullness because we so often rely on ourselves.

The early Christians recognized the Empowerer's forceful work through them because, under oppression and coming primarily from the lower classes, they didn't own much or have much influence by themselves. The Church in nations of poverty, conflict, and disease experiences it similarly today, as we noted in chapter 4, for in those places Christianity is flourishing.

Our society, in contrast, stifles the Spirit. It seduces us into thinking that the perfect life for which we yearn can be found in accumulating and achieving more. But the only perfect life is new birth and Holy Spirit empowerment for a resurrected and centered life.

In the gift of Pentecost we again behold the pattern of God's promises and fulfillment. Think of all the texts by which God pledges to rescue us from ourselves, such as Ezekiel 11:19–20 (which promises a new spirit so that God's people can obey the commandments); 36:22–28 (which pledges cleansing, a restoration, a new heart, and a new spirit); or 37:13–14 (which vows both resurrection and God's own spirit within us). Joel, whom Peter quotes in his sermon on Pentecost, is even more expansive, promising visions and prophecies and dreams to young and old, men and women, slave and free, all flesh.

Another element of hope in the Spirit's coming is that Jesus forms His body into a community by the Comforter's enabling. Thus, we are able to do greater works than Jesus because we don't do them alone. There are many of us who follow Jesus and carry on His mission.

Regrettably, we often miss this plurality because we have been trained by our culture to read the Bible singularly. With the books of Timothy, Titus, and Philemon comprising the only major exceptions, most of the rest of the Bible is written in the plural. We are not called to be witnesses and justice builders by ourselves. We go into the world separately, perhaps, but together—knit in mutual support and prayer by the Holy Spirit's enabling.

Pentecost outpouring is, however, frightening. The Spirit might call us and empower us to do something we don't want to do, we think. Nevertheless, that attitude too constricts the Spirit, for the promise that we are made new includes our desires if we let the Paraclete have full sway in our lives. And when we are not yet able to answer God's call gladly, the Spirit sustains us and endures with us for the meanwhile.

What tremendous hope the gift of the Holy Spirit is for us as we seek to resist and reform the fettering encroachments of our technologized, commodified society! The people of Thessalonica agitatedly shouted about Paul and Silas, "These people who have been turning the world upside down have come here also" (Acts 17:6). May that be said of us also, for the Paraclete's enabling can work through us to set the world actually right side up!

The Battle for Genuine Christian Life

This brief sketch of the biblical meta-narrative cannot even begin to introduce all the aspects of the Christian life set out by the New Testament letters, the Acts of the Apostles, and The Revelation. For our purposes here, it is important to note especially five elements found in these books.

1. The early Christian writers insisted that to live the way of Christ was difficult. First of all, it was necessary for new believers decisively to "put away" or "lay aside" the old life in ordinary society and its sins (e.g., Rom. 13:12; Eph. 4:22, 31; Heb. 12:1). They should make "no provision" for the temptations of the world and the flesh (Rom. 13:14).

2. Then, Christians should "put on" or "clothe" themselves in new practices and virtues and in the armor of God (Rom. 13:14; Eph. 4:24; 6:11, 14, 15; Col. 3:12, 14; 1 Pet. 5:5). Within a short time from its founding, the Church developed deliberate practices of catechesis for the sake of helping new believers to develop these attributes and disciplines. It was important that believers be willing to submit to God and to each other in order to nurture these mature habits of faith.

3. The biblical writers stressed how powerful is the battle we must wage against societal forces. Believers should constantly realize that "like a roaring lion your adversary the devil prowls around, looking for someone to devour" (1 Pet. 5:8), and thus they should "resist him" (1 Pet. 5:9; Jas. 4:7), "not make room for the devil" (Eph. 4:27), "stand against the wiles of the devil" (Eph. 6:11), and be careful to "escape from the snare of the devil" (2 Tim. 2:26).

4. In order to resist and escape evil forces in society and beyond, early Christians were repeatedly warned to watch and pray (1 Cor. 10:12; Eph. 6:4; 1 Thess. 5:17; 1 Tim. 2:8; Jas. 5:13–16; Jude 1:20). Moreover, biblical writers continually offered a model to their readers as they frequently mentioned their own prayers on behalf of their letters' recipients.[26]

---

26. For further elaboration of these disciplines of putting off, putting on, submitting, watching and prayer, and resisting the devil, see Philip Carrington, *The Primitive Christian Catechism* (Oxford: Oxford University Press, 1940).

5. A final theme that resounds through the rest of the New Testament after the Gospels is the sure hope that can be found in Jesus. Although Christians are warned to be wary of the devil, they can also always be confident with the writer of 1 John that "the Son of God was revealed for this purpose, to destroy the works of the devil" (3:8). Only in Christ is there unfettered hope that the obstructions to the life we truly want can be and are destroyed.

Telling This Story in Our Times and Place

The meta-narrative of the Christian faith is a great gift to our neighbors and the source of abounding hope. Its constant reiteration of the world's foundation in grace challenges our society's notions of what is valuable. Meanwhile, that grace frees us to entrust ourselves to no other, lesser hopes.

However, the meta-narrative also constantly challenges and indicts us. We can't, for example, read or preach Luke 1 without realizing that when Mary sings, "The rich He has sent empty away," her words also refer to our society and its vanities and perhaps to us, unless we have been mindful of our accumulations.

How do we speak this story in and to a society that trusts its wealth? Douglas John Hall (using Paul Tillich) contends that notions from previous eras—such as "fate and death," which was dominant in the classical period, or "guilt and condemnation," paramount for the medieval period—are not primary predicaments in our times. Tillich and Hall name "meaninglessness and despair" as the foremost anxiety and suggest that we ought to address this distress primarily in our mission to the world.[27] I disagree.

Conversations on airplanes and elsewhere convince me otherwise— that people still wrestle mightily, but often ineffectively, against guilt. Where will they hear a sure and lasting word of hope except in the Good News of forgiveness through Christ's reconciling work? Similarly, especially since September 11, 2001, but also whenever terminal illness or other tragedies strike, everyone struggles with questions of their fate and worries about their death.

Thomas Long also disagrees. He does not accept Hall's dismissal of the categories of fate and death, guilt and condemnation; he insists they are

---

27. Douglas John Hall, "Despair as Pervasive Ailment," in *Hope for the World*, ed. Walter Brueggemann (Louisville, Ky.: Westminster John Knox Press, 2001), 84.

still as relevant as hopelessness.[28] In fact, he asserts, "I believe that God loves us so much that God *will* judge us" (15, emphasis mine).

A great proportion of people in our society feel guilty about their bondage to commodities. We need to nudge them a bit further into despair over their guilt by helping us all to see that God not only doesn't like our overindulgences, but also judges them, especially because we accumulate stuff and experiences to the detriment of much of the rest of the world.

That may sound cruel, but the truth is that we don't see how good the Good News is unless we know we are desperate for it. That is why people often don't think they need to think about God until they come face to face with their own deaths. Since the death rate is the same for everyone—one per person—sooner or later everyone must question what it means for them. Then the hope of the Christian meta-narrative is not simply "pie in the sky in the bye and bye after we die." It is instead the recognition that eternal life has already begun when the Spirit leads us to Christ, who draws us into His own intimacy with His Father.

This is not to deny that despair and meaninglessness reign in our culture. Long offers cell-phone calls as an example—suggesting that most calls are made not from necessity or utility, but because of boredom and loneliness. The greeting I frequently hear from phone users in airports, "Whazzup?" surmises, as Long observes, that there must be action and meaning somewhere else and the caller has to find it somehow (15).

Long quotes Karl Barth, whose declaration summarizes how we find unfettered hope: "For those to whom God wills to be all in all, God strips everything else" (16). This is, indeed, a source of hope, for the fact that God IS all in all is enough to make the promise of our being dismantled Good News.

Trinitarian Hope

How can we summarize the fullness of the Christian meta-narrative and the sureness of the hope it conveys? The key is a full Trinitarianism.

The meta-narrative of the Triune God enables us to live differently as God's people. I can't in this short chapter expound on the connections of

---

28. Thomas G. Long, "A Response to Douglas John Hall" (following a reprint of Hall's chapter from *Hope for the World*), *Journal for Preachers* 25, 1 (Advent 2001): 14. Page references to this article in the following paragraphs will be given parenthetically in the text.

the persons of the Trinity or the practical consequences of the doctrine,[29] but I must emphasize that our hope does not reach its potential if it is not Trinitarian. Nor can we pass on hope to our neighbors unless we introduce them to the Three in One.

To name only the Father as Creator is to miss the Son as the creative Word and the Spirit as creative breath. To see only the Son in the Passion is to risk turning His Father into a patriarchal oppressor. To know only the Spirit's intercession in sighs and groans is to disregard our ascended Lord's role at the right hand of His Father. Only in completely entrusting ourselves to who God is as Three Persons in one God can we, each as individual Christians and as the corporate Church, recover our true identity.

In his remarkable memoir of his first three years in ministry in a small country congregation, Duke Divinity School homiletics professor Richard Lischer describes the Trinity window in the Cana church:

> At the center of the window was a triangular area in which was inscribed the word *DEUS* (God). In the area around the center were smaller triangular areas, one with the word *PATER* (Father), another with the word *FILIUS* (Son), and a third with *SPIRITUS SANCTUS* (Holy Spirit). These three were connected by three little highways running to *DEUS*, and on each highway was the word *EST* (is). Rimming the circle and connecting the three persons were more highways—between the Father and the Son, the Son and the Spirit, and so forth, and on each of these were the words *NON EST* (is not).
>
> God is persons and nothing else. There is no waxy residue of divinity that is not wrapped up in these three persons, Father, Son, and Holy Spirit. That's who God is. God is (*est*) each of these three persons, but the persons are distinct from one another (*non est*). God is both: alone in majesty and at the same time forever radiating love through each person of the Trinity. Our window's geometric design seemed to say, "Any questions?"
>
> We are only able to love each other because the Father loves the Son through the Holy Spirit. We want to be with one another as friends, lovers, and neighbors for the same reason. That's not an argument that would appeal to most theologians, but that's what the Trinity meant for us.

---

29. Besides, others have accomplished the task much more eloquently and wisely. See especially Catherine Mowry LaCugna, *God for Us: The Trinity and Christian Life* (San Francisco: HarperSanFrancisco, 1992).

. . . We believed there was a correspondence between the God who was diagrammed in that window and our stories of friendship and neighborliness. . . .

An aerial photographer once remarked that from the air you can see paths, like the canals on Mars, that crisscross pastures and fields among the farms where neighbors have trudged for generations, just to visit or help one another in times of need. These, too, are the highways among *Pater*, *Filius*, and *Spiritus Sanctus*, grooved into human relationships. The word religion comes from the same root as "ligaments." These are the ties that bind.[30]

Only in the fettering by those divine and human ties—drawn in by the Trinity's tether and inextricably connected with our neighbors—can we live with unfettered hope.

We have seen throughout this chapter the goodness and faithfulness of the Trinity's ties to us. The meta-narrative of our faith immerses us in hope as it shows us God's promises and constancy in fulfilling them. With the writer to the Hebrews we can challenge each other in the Christian community, "Let us hold fast to the confession of our hope without wavering, for He who has promised is faithful" (Heb. 10:23).

---

30. Richard Lischer, *Open Secrets: A Spiritual Journey Through a Country Church* (New York: Doubleday, 2001), 81.

Chapter 6

How Can We Learn to Live
the Language of Focal Concerns?

We began this book with a recognition that our society is ill—that the technologized, commodified society amasses all sorts of bondages in accumulations and all kinds of fetterings in false hopes from which we can't seem to escape. In chapter 2 we learned that this illness is not merely a problem with technology or commodities; rather, it is caused by the destructive paradigm that controls their connection and, in turn, controls our societal ethos as we withdraw away from engaging in practices that contribute to our focal concerns and depend instead on devices that produce deluges of commodities. In chapter 3 we contemplated the nature of focal concerns and steps by which they can reform our technologized, commodified society. Also, we named the focal concerns of Christianity as the love of God and the love of the neighbor. However, as we confessed in chapter 4, corporate churches and, correlatively and consequently, individual Christians often fail to live according to those focal concerns. In chapter 5 we saw that the meta-narrative of Christianity is large enough to enable us truly to find hope again, for the grace of the Triune God is sufficient to deliver us from our bondages and to free us to make more careful choices in all matters of life for the sake of living according to our focal concerns.

Now, in this chapter, we can turn to particular practices of Christianity by which we are lifted into hope and by which our character can be more deeply formed for the sake of developing culture positively and keeping the ravages and bondages of our technologized, commodified society in check. Especially we are concerned in this book for how those practices can work toward justice, toward correcting the imbalances that exist in the world between those who have too much and those who have too little.[1]

To organize this discussion of Christian practices, I have chosen to follow the pattern of the Ten Commandments. These mandates, underscored in both biblical Testaments, keep us centered in our focal concerns for loving God and the neighbor. Their meanings suggest various practices to be shared in Christian communities and families, in order to deepen those practices in all of our lives and every aspect of them—for the sake of genuine love and worship of God and for the sake of the world.

This categorization of practices is, of course, artificial, for a great proportion of the practices included in this chapter fulfill many of the ten in their dense overlap. Also, it is impossible to include every Christian practice, for we live inspired by the Holy Spirit, who is always doing a new thing. The practices sketched here are chosen merely to spark your own creativity and generosity, your own thoroughness in letting every aspect of life be formed in the mind of Christ, to the end that we all live intentionally and intensively by our focal concerns and thereby fulfill God's Law by the Spirit of grace.

Because my primary concern is to shake us and our communities from our bondage to the technological milieu's device paradigm and consequent commodifications, I will especially highlight the constant interplay of those considerations in these practices. May they give us all suggestions so that Christianity in the wealthier nations can find a way out of our societal morass, that we might more thoroughly know who we are as Christians and thereby return to the principles of justice and peace we saw in our meta-narrative.

We do engage in these practices as individual believers; however, they become more deeply rooted in our lives if we ourselves are anchored in a Christian community that supports them and us. Christian moral formation happens by the grace of God through the agency of many people. If we have insufficient mentors and models, aides and associates, we are much more likely to be formed by our society and its technological, commodifying paradigm. Furthermore, among myriads of other gifts, the

---

1. Great books on the practices of the Christian faith already exist. I only add one more because of the emphasis in this book on focal concerns as a means to reform and resist our larger society's paradigm. See, above all, Dorothy C. Bass, ed., *Practicing Our Faith: A Way of Life for a Searching People* (San Francisco: Jossey-Bass, 1997); and Dorothy C. Bass and Don C. Richter, eds., *Way to Live: Christian Practices for Teens* (Nashville: Upper Room, 2002).

community is a crucial component for proclaiming the meta-narrative so that we know our identity as kingdom people and for guiding us in making decisions.

I am totally convinced that the main reason that churches fail to live by their focal concerns is because their members are not deeply committed to each other in genuine communities formed by the biblical meta-narrative. I am equally convinced that the main reason individual believers fail to live by our focal concerns is because we are not well enough immersed in genuine communities that practice the faith.[2]

Trembling Freedom

We can only begin to be free by knowing that we are not free and will never be until we are ultimately delivered from our society's temptations and our propensity to sin. Jacques Ellul stressed this, too, in his book on technological bluffs. He emphasized that "the only way to find a narrow passage in this enormous world of deceptions (expressing real forces)"— that is, the principalities and powers—is "to have enough awareness and self-criticism to see that for a century we have been descending step by step the ladder of absolute necessity, of destiny, of fate." Ellul follows Hegel, Marx, and Kierkegaard in saying that "we show our freedom by recognizing our nonfreedom."[3] Martin Luther knew, too, that our best hope for deliverance from human fatality is by assuming and admitting that we are in bondage to sin (in all its manifestations) and cannot free ourselves.

Are we, then, hopelessly "shut up, blocked, and chained by the inevitability of the technical system which is making us march like obedient automatons thanks to its bluff?" Ellul answers Yes and No. First, he says, let's be realistic that we are caught in a system that is too intertwined, complex, universal, and autonomous for us to think we can master its machineries.

However, Ellul exhorts, we can also begin to discern that every example of growth at some extreme reaches the point of imbalance and rupture. Moreover, "the gigantic bluff is self-contradictory and it leaves a

---

2. There is not space in this book to discuss practices by which we can deepen our church's community life. See, instead, Marva J. Dawn, *Truly the Community: Romans 12 and How to Be the Church* (Grand Rapids: Wm. B. Eerdmans Publishing Co., 1992; reissued 1997).

3. All the quotations from Ellul in this section are from *Technological Bluff*, 411–412.

margin of chaos, it covers gaps without filling them, it gives evidence of mistakes, and it has to multiply deceptions to veil the absence of feedback in the system."

Consequently, we who serve the Gospel can reveal the fracture lines and revel in them. Also, with humility and weakness and "by the sole aptitude for astonishment, we profit from the existence of little cracks of freedom, and install in them a trembling freedom which is not attributed to or mediated by machines or politics, but which is truly effective," so that we bring to humankind the new thing for which everyone hopes (often without knowing that)—the kingdom of God.

I love that phrase, *trembling freedom!* The Church is the developer of "trembling freedom"! We who live in the new creation of the Trinity's interventions offer each other and the wider world the hope of release from our bondage to the technological paradigm and its commodifications and into the trembling freedom of God's kingdom (which then gives us the capacity to choose whatever technologies and commodities are useful and good for our purposes as God's servants and stewards).

A Language to Put Trembling Freedom into Society's Cracks

Throughout this chapter, I will be thinking of growth in the Christian life as comparable to learning a language.[4] An excerpt from *The Inextinguishable Symphony* discloses how powerfully an alternative language can offset the destructive effects of an inimical culture. When the Kulturbund had to close in Frankfurt, its final concert began with a stirring speech by conductor Julius Prüwer, which was greeted with a three-minute standing ovation. Then:

> [T]he concert took off and never really came back to Earth. Something extra-musical was at work on stage, some mysterious force that every performer has encountered at one time or another. The weight of the here and now dropped away, leaving each musician light and free to soar to the highest reaches of imagination. From this height, the mind relinquished its hold over the human apparatus and left the heart and soul in command. The printed notes on the scores were no

---

4. I learned the idea originally from George Lindbeck, *The Nature of Doctrine: Religion and Theology in a Postliberal Age* (Philadelphia: Westminster Press, 1984). See also William H. Willimon, "World Makers: A New Way of Seeing and Naming," *Christian Century* 118, 24, August 29–September 5, 2001, 6–7.

longer the merest black dots on white paper but cairns on the path of a wonderful journey of discovery shared by musicians and listeners alike. For Günther, the climax came in the finale of the Tchaikovsky Fifth, when the great striding melody seemed to lead the way to a victory that not even Caesar or Napoleon could have imagined, a triumphant expression of the human spirit that a million brown-shirted men bearing hooked-cross flags could never hope to extinguish.[5]

Even as the Nazis could only threaten the bodies of the instrumentalists and audience but never efface the power of the musical language they shared together, so the technologizing, commodifying threats of our culture cannot expunge the Holy Spirit power in the language of the Christian meta-narrative. And those who speak it find a trembling freedom by which to resist and reform societal systems.

How Well Do We Speak the Christian Language?

Because I am a realist, I am strongly convinced that the language of the technologized, commodified culture is extremely dangerous, for it is exceedingly inimical to the Gospel. We must know how strong the battle is, as did the early Christians whom we considered at the end of chapter 5. We cannot ignore how firmly our lives are entangled in the technological milieu's structure and the distractions and endowments of consumption, for we have supported this arrangement and are enduringly loyal to it. We also know that our friends and neighbors support it. Consequently, Borgmann argues, "It would take superhuman strength to stand up to this order ever and again. If we are to challenge *the rule of technology*, we can do so only through *the practice of engagement.*"[6]

Since I am a *hopeful* realist, I believe that our only hope lies in the work of God. However, we participate in God's reign with our engagement when we rename our world according to the vocabulary of our meta-narrative from God's Word.

How well do our churches and we speak and live this different language?

How well we speak it depends on how thoroughly our lives are shaped by the Christian community immersed in it. Just as with learning a language, practice makes us better at it. Then, what could be a momentary

---

5. Goldsmith, *Inextinguishable Symphony*, 112.
6. Borgmann, *Technology and the Character of Contemporary Life*, 207, emphasis his.

good choice can instead become a habit. Through such engagement, our lives and church life are ordered toward our focal concerns. The Church's practices (in Borgmann's terms) "guard" our double focal concern and "shelter it against the vicissitudes of fate and our frailty." Underscoring the necessity of these spiritual disciplines, "we must say that without a practice an engaging action or event can momentarily light up our life, but it cannot order and orient it focally."[7]

Schooling by Immersion: Multiform Illumination

As this chapter's overview of the Ten Commandments will reveal, the Christian faith language is different from the world's in most dimensions of life. The more we read the Bible and let it redescribe our life, the more we discover a unique language about such aspects as our money, time, sexuality, work habits, meaning in life, purpose, and hope. To live this language requires active engagement.

I am unceasingly grateful for my parents because of all the ways they formed my brothers and me in the language of faith. I will use their example here, not to say that their methods were necessarily the best, but simply to illustrate the importance of schooling in the faith by immersion. By their practice, various aspects of the life in Christ were for me illuminated in multiple ways.

First, they trained us in simple *habits*. We always prayed before and after meals (in restaurants, too) and before sleep. Participating in weekly, public worship was never questioned (partly because Dad was the organist/choir director). Tithing was established when we first began to receive an allowance and started delivering newspapers.

How can I ever stress enough the importance of developing such habits in children and new believers? Because we always prayed at mealtimes, we were made aware from earliest memories that God was the provider for our needs. That has caused us (coupled with the habits of the "clean plate club") not to waste food and to be mindful of the needs of others.

Tithing is an excellent habit to instill in children. By it we learned from the very beginning that all money is God's and lent to us for our stewardship. We discovered early in life that first taking out an offering of 10 percent for God never left us with insufficient funds for the rest of life. Consequently, since we never disputed tithing, as we grew older the question became how much beyond a tithe we could share with others.

---

7. Ibid.

As we grew older, childhood habits blossomed into more mature *practices*. At the Lutheran elementary school we attended (and of which Father was principal and both parents were teachers), the simple memorizing of Bible passages advanced into practices of meditation and spiritual reading. Attending worship expanded into the discipleship sustenance of receiving the Lord's Supper and being nurtured by sermons, hymns, prayers, and community life.

Meanwhile, we were enveloped in long-standing *traditions* of the Church. We participated in Advent vespers, midweek Lenten services, Maundy Thursday observances of Christ's initiation of His Supper (I learned footwashing later from the Mennonites), Good Friday Tenebrae services, and Easter sunrise celebrations (and later Easter vigils). These imprinted upon our minds and hearts the fundamental doctrines of the faith.

Those doctrines were illuminated even more both in the sanctuary where we worshiped and in our home by *works of art*. There were Christian symbols on the altar paraments, banners, furniture carvings, and our walls. We saw renditions of Bible stories in stained-glass windows, paintings, and sculptures. Also, we learned deep doctrines by singing them—in ancient hymns as well as new compositions by my father. And the books that carried our faith had an honored place in our home. From childhood we knew the elevated status of Bibles, hymnbooks, and the catechism.

At the same time, our family observed some of our own particular *customs*. The Church has for a long time utilized Advent wreaths with purple (symbolizing Repentance), pink (Joy), or blue (Hope) candles for the four Sundays of the season and white for Christmas. At our home, however, there was also a short red (for the saints) candle for every single day of Advent. We also followed particular family (mostly German) customs concerning the Christmas tree and honored the Christ Child (definitely *not* Santa!) coming to our house on Christmas Eve as the Light of the world. These customs especially helped develop in all of us a strong resistance to the commercialization of the holy day. Advent was for waiting, and Christmas was a night and morning of worship far more than a time for opening presents.

The customs and traditions, as well as the Bible teaching we received, immersed us in the *manners* of faith, the customary behaviors or bearing of Christians in their relation to the world. For example, we discerned from our parents' frugality and simple living the importance of caring for justice and greater sharing of the world's resources. Correlatively, one cannot read the Bible extensively without discovering that the manners of reconciling and peacemaking are at the core of faith. Through advanced training, my brother learned these skills best of all and is now the executive director of the Lutheran Peace Fellowship.

All these elements together formed a Christian *culture* in our family and church life. All the ideas, customs, skills, arts, and teachings of God's people contributed together to create a special form of civilization. This led to moral development, improvement in behaviors, refinements of mind, controlling of emotions, fostering of interests, cultivations in tastes. Just as training helps a sensitive person be repulsed by bad art, so my parents' guidance schooled their children to be naturally repulsed by such things as pornography and cheating. Just as certain things "weren't done in Israel," so in our home certain elements of the surrounding milieu were forbidden not so much by command as by strongly cultivated consciences.[8]

Mostly from my parents' *modeling and mentoring*, we learned that God's commands "are not burdensome." We saw constantly that they served God not from mere obedience, but from love and a positive sense of duty to carry out their calling as part of the priesthood of all believers. They had a vocation and the gifts to fulfill it. They didn't mind being different from the world around them. Consequently, they also began equipping their children for various forms of ministry and witness as members of an alternative community.

The boldly italicized words in the above paragraphs do not represent clearly distinct analytical categories. I use them merely to illustrate the many ways in which we become engaged in the life of faith. For the rest of this chapter I will use the summary word *practices* to denote any of a variety of means by which we attend to our focal concerns.

My parents were not perfect, of course (and their children didn't always learn the lessons that were available), but they manifest how Christian communities enfold their members in many kinds of engagement. It is most desirable that children first learn the practices of the Church in their homes. At the beginning of his explanations to the commandments, the creed, the Lord's Prayer, and other chief Christian doctrines in his *Small Catechism*, Martin Luther wrote, "as the head of the family should teach them in a simple way to his household."[9] Do our

---

8. On practices for raising children, see Marcia J. Bunge, ed., *The Child in Christian Thought* (Grand Rapids: Wm. B. Eerdmans Publishing Co., 2001); and Dawn, *Is It a Lost Cause?*

9. Martin Luther, *Small Catechism: A Handbook of Christian Doctrine* (St. Louis: Concordia Publishing House, 1943), 5, 9, 12.

churches actually equip parents for their role as nurturers of their children's spiritual life? Especially do we help parents teach their children the meaning of their baptism?

Practices Begin with Baptism

I apologize to those whose conception of baptism is different (a subject which cannot be addressed here), but it seems to me that baptism is the crucial starting place for developing a genuinely Christian way of life that inculcates moral virtues and skills for keeping technologies and commodities in the background.

I choose the Christian discipline of baptism to begin because it is one of two practices specifically commanded by Jesus. It also graphically demonstrates, and undergirds us to remember constantly, that the Christian life flows from grace.

When I was 29 days old, my parents brought me to baptism. I couldn't do anything to receive it, earn it, deserve it. Totally by grace, the Triune God washed me in mercy, forgave me utterly, adopted me as His child, took up residency in me, initiated me into His Body, and ordained me into the priesthood of all believers. I could never be able to pay God back for all those gifts, nor does God want me to try.

Baptism therefore frees me to respond to the immensity of Trinitarian grace by loving God and loving my neighbors. Because in my baptism I became inhabited by the Spirit and a "priest" in God's service, it orders my life and initiates my commitment to live according to the focal concerns God mandates. Because baptism is not merely a rite, but also includes the whole life inaugurated by that rite, it is a source by which to challenge constantly my involvement in the technologized, commodified society. Daily I renew my baptismal covenant because the Trinity is always faithful to God's side of the relationship. Daily that grace and hope empower me to ask about everything: Is this appropriate to my baptized life?

Baptism thus equips us to engage in other practices that enable us to live as Christians in a technologized, commodifying world. In the pages that follow I discuss various practices (though certainly not all) that clear the space for our focal concerns and help us limit the influence of, and the destructions caused by, the device paradigm that controls our world. May these examples equip us constantly to ask what might be the dangers of our present milieu and what the Church is in response. How could our local churches and our own ministries foster these practices for the sake of counteracting the harmful effects of our environment?

Fear and Love

In his catechism Martin Luther explicated the first commandment by asking, "What does this mean?" and wisely answering, "We should fear, love, and trust in God above all things."[10] His responses to that same question for each of the other nine commandments all begin with the phrase "We should fear and love God that we may . . ." or "may not. . . ."

I am convinced that "fear and love" is the necessary combination that will enable churches in wealthier nations to recover their focal concerns. Unless we keep fear in this crucial dialectic, we let love become romanticized and mushy, instead of tough and demanding. Without a sense of how much we deserve God's wrath, we don't take seriously enough the severe temptation that Mammon presents. Without a healthy fear of the bondages of the technologized, commodifying society, we do not know thoroughly enough the power of God's love and cannot appreciate to the full the genuinely unfettered hope of the Gospel.

Good biblical fear helps us to observe the prohibitions mandated by the Ten Commandments. Love enables us to respond to God and to neighbors with the positive outworking of these statutes. Indirectly we will see this dialectic constantly in operation as we consider practices that fulfill the Law in truth and hope.

You might find the following listing of the Ten Commandments a bit unfamiliar because various denominations number them differently by dividing either Exodus 20:3–6 or 20:17 into two. I am observing the latter division because this is the way it is split in the Hebrew text (with the Hebrew letter *samekh* between the commandments), and therefore that is Martin Luther's ordering, which I learned as a child. For our purposes here, this grouping is also significant because it puts greater emphasis on the sin of coveting, which seems to be one of the most common temptations in a commodity-laden and commodifying culture.

1: "You Shall Have No Other Gods Before Me"[11]

Actually, all the practices of the Church could fall under this commandment, for everything that we do that is particularly *Christian* is a way of loving God. Moreover, even the many specific practices designed explic-

---

10. Ibid., 5.

11. All biblical quotations in this chapter are from the New Revised Standard Version. The Ten Commandments are cited from the listing in Exodus 20.

itly for the sake of keeping God primary in our lives also have the effect of changing us so that our relations with our neighbors are different, too. Thus, corporate worship and private prayer, as examples, deepen our love for both God and the neighbor. In fact, I won't even discuss prayer further in this outline, not because it is not a crucially weighty practice, but because everything becomes prayer (or at least "putting legs on our prayers") when we live according to our focal concerns.

Concerning the practice of corporate worship, I simply must stress again[12] that, if we stayed mindful not to have other gods before our Triune God, many congregational worship "wars" could be avoided. Indeed, perhaps *most* of the conflicts churches have over worship involve arguments over *our* preferences for various styles or tastes (instead of *God's*) or idolatries of numbers, Mammon, people, community position, buildings, or other societal gods.

One such "other" god might be the use of the newest technology in worship. Our focal concern of desiring to love God by having no other gods before Him helps us discern what technological tools are useful for the worship service. Remembering our disdain for "mass communication," which merely relays information rather than offering genuine communication, we will use such things as media clips in worship carefully—making sure that their intended message is actually received. The question must remain whether worshipers actually encounter God and are brought by the worship service to know more deeply the fullness of Triune grace and love, so that they may respond with love for God and neighbor. What people experience (in awe or other emotions) from the use of multi-media must be connected in some way to the true God, to the divine Word.

Language specialists have observed that emotions are based on our ability to name them, that they can be understood by us only when we have a word for them. For that reason, worshipers must be immersed in a church community that teaches them the faith language and practices that enable them to encounter God, hear God, receive God, respond to God, have no other gods before God.

The various technological or other idolatries related to corporate worship can be thwarted and counteracted if churches train children and new believers in the purpose and meaning of the practice. Two superb

---

12. See, for more thorough explication, my *Reaching Out without Dumbing Down* and *A Royal "Waste" of Time* and chapter 5, "The Heart of God Revealed in Worship," in *Is It a Lost Cause?* An excellent new resource is Russell F. Mitman's *Worship in the Shape of Scripture* (Cleveland: Pilgrim Press, 2001).

resources to help form worshipers are Robbie Castleman's *Parenting in the Pew*, which gives excellent suggestions for enabling children to participate more fully in worship, and Linda Witte Henke's *Marking Time*, which offers forty Christian rituals that can be engaged in at home to celebrate or grieve together many of our experiences in life.[13]

Henke's book includes rituals of Celebration for not only birth and baptism, engagement and marriage, but also pregnancy, an infant's naming and homecoming, and family reunions. Her rituals for Consecration embrace a child beginning school or starting to date or drive and an adult retiring or preparing a will. Rites for Encouragement include sensitive prayers for unemployment and the adoption process, to confess wrongdoing, and to mark the transition to an assisted-care residence. Finally, rituals for Comfort offer a salutary embrace for those experiencing such difficult times and situations as miscarriage or an infant's death, an experience of violence, or when a loved one's life support is removed.

I have listed many examples from Henke's book to illustrate how she teaches us that the practice of worship in the home encompasses every dimension of life. I have already adapted her rituals for a graduation party, a family reunion, and to celebrate someone's new job. Her rites are strongly based in the Scriptures and firmly rooted in the language of faith. They also demonstrate that loving God by worshiping meanwhile offers to our family and neighbors genuine solace, uplifting affirmation, and wise counsel. At the same time, they call all of us who participate into deeper prayer, new commitments to God and neighbor, and faithful living in the midst of a contrary society.

Children who grow up in households using such rituals will know that all of their times are in God's hands. Strengthened by that grace in the practice of worship, they will be formed to respond with lives of love and service to others.

---

13. Robbie Castleman, *Parenting in the Pew: Guiding Your Children into the Joy of Worship*, rev. ed. (Downers Grove, Ill.: InterVarsity Press, 2001); and Linda Witte Henke, *Marking Time: Christian Rituals for All Our Days* (Harrisburg, Pa.: Morehouse Publishing, 2001). Other excellent resources include the "Logos" midweek school program involving worship skills along with Bible teaching, games and sports, and common meals (Logos System Associates, 1405 Frey Road, Pittsburgh, Pennsylvania 15235) and the "Children in Worship" program for three- to eight-year-old children that engages them in worship practices and in learning about the Church year and the life of Jesus. See Sonja M. Stewart and Jerome W. Berryman, *Young Children and Worship* (Louisville, Ky.: Westminster/John Knox Press, 1989); and Sonja M. Stewart, *Following Jesus: More about Young Children and Worship* (Louisville, Ky.: Westminster John Knox Press, 2000).

The Key Is What God Has Done and Is

The command to have no other gods before the Trinity reminds us not to trust ourselves even for the formation of character in opposition to our society and for the sake of living according to our focal concerns. It is easy to think that we can accomplish growth by our own strenuous efforts.

Studying our meta-narrative, we realize that God is the one who acts, the Spirit is the one who inspires, the Christ in us changes us. Perhaps the best summary of letting God be the only God even in our desire to be faithful is Paul's "I have been crucified with Christ; and it is no longer I who live, but it is Christ who lives in me. And the life I now live in the flesh I live by faith in the Son of God, who loved me and gave Himself for me" (Gal. 2:19b–20). We nullify the grace of God (and thus put ourselves before God) when we think either our forgiveness (justification) or our improvement (sanctification) can be accomplished by us.

Not only in worship or in how our churches and families "work on" character formation but also in every aspect of daily life, we are tempted to put other gods before the true God. One practice, therefore, that is crucial for me (and perhaps for you) is that of consciously entrusting our work to God. In a commodifying society that stresses accomplishments, we can easily spiritualize that and develop grandiose Messianic complexes (of which I know I'm guilty at times). We can be set free only by remembering that God is the One who does the work through us. For example, instead of hoping that this book will change the world (a hope that would surely disappoint me), I can hope that God will work in me and through me as I write (which God has promised to do if I get out of the way). Then, if the book also challenges a few people to rethink their lives in terms of focal concerns, I can simply say, God be praised!

But that requires constant death—to self, to ambition, to image, to every other sort of idolatry (such as Mammon) fostered by our technologized, commodifying, device-paradigmed society. As we can see, to love God without any other gods is a demanding focal concern. If we could keep the first commandment, nothing in our culture could fetter us.

Gracious God, we constantly fetter our love for You by dabbling with other gods. Our only hope is Your forgiveness. May Your gracious love stiffen our resistance against idolatries, deepen our love for You, and increase our hope in an unfettered future. Amen.

2: "You Shall Not Make Wrongful Use
of the Name of the LORD Your God"

A Jewish rabbi taught me that the Hebrew people did not say God's name (*YHWH*) because they did not want to think they could control God or to lose the Otherness of God. Their concern (genuine biblical fear) makes me realize how much I blaspheme God's name and thereby profane the Triune character. A society that controls everything by inventing more technological quick-fixes increasingly invites this desecration.

In this technologized, commodified society, many Christians want a similar quick-fix to their own spiritual hungers. This often leads to symptoms of anxiety, overwork, isolation, loneliness, meaninglessness, manipulation. In contrast, the Church's worship and other practices sketched below invite trust through the turmoil, listening for God's directions against problems, community engagement in mission.

They also invite us to follow Jesus in an arduous way. Ben Johnson and Glenn McDonald note that Jesus first wept over Jerusalem and then entered it to die. Consequently:

> To call a local church into the mission of Jesus is to call its members into the same two behaviors. First we cry. Then we die. We let our hearts be broken with the things that break the heart of God. Then we die to the comfortable patterns of life that insulate us emotionally and geographically from those for whom Christ died.[14]

The hope of the Gospel frees us to die to ourselves, our ambitions and comforts. Then we can become truly engaged in the broken-hearted and hopeful mission against the world's injustices that the name of God reveals.

We need the Church's practice of Bible reading and meditation to learn more clearly (though, we acknowledge, always inadequately) who the Trinity is and how God is free and wild (uncontrollable by us) and tenderhearted toward the oppressed. Through these two practices we are urged to give up our commodifying tendencies toward God and toward the neighbor.

Meanwhile, these practices, along with those of prayer and worship, cause us to be formed (by God's grace) to have a character more in keep-

---

14. Ben Campbell Johnson and Glenn McDonald, *Imagining a Church in the Spirit: A Task for Mainline Congregations* (Grand Rapids: Wm. B. Eerdmans Publishing Co., 1999), 85.

ing with God's. The more we learn God's names of Love and Provider and Creator, the less we are able to treat people as commodities, to ignore the world's cries for justice, to hoard the gifts of the creation for ourselves.

How we read the Bible makes a big difference. Frederick Niedner, theology professor at Valparaiso University, cites Paul Griffiths's distinction between "consumerist readers" [fettered by our society] and "religious readers" of the Bible. The former, more prevalent in this time controlled by the device paradigm, move quickly through texts "in search of things that will excite, titillate, entertain, empower, and give them some advantage over others." In contrast,

> [Religious readers] assume they have come into the presence of a text with inexhaustible depth. They read with reverence, humility, obedience and the presumption that difficulty in understanding reveals more about their limitations than the excellence or effectiveness of the text. Religious readers incorporate, internalize and memorize texts. They read slowly, hoping not to miss anything.[15]

As a result, religious readers are formed by the grace and genuine hope of the meta-narrative more into the character of the Triune name.

This practice of religious reading also equips us with much practical wisdom for engaging in other practices that challenge the commodifications of our society. If we "incorporate, internalize and memorize texts," as Niedner urges, we are formed, for example, to "share [our] bread with the hungry, and bring the homeless poor into [our] house; when [we] see the naked, to cover them" and thereby never to turn away from any human being's needs (Isa. 58:7).

Honoring God's name also invites us into practices of wonder and faithful speech, in contrast to, and to counteract, the advertising and commodifying talk of our jaundiced, commercialized culture. I connect wonder to faithful speech because our society perpetrates the reduction of words' meanings and thus constantly reduces things, people, and God. Overinflated words do not carry wonder; they attempt to advertise. True words simply convey genuine reality; thus, when we want to speak of God, our speech always becomes tinged with amazement, a sense of both intimate immanence and mysterious transcendence.

---

15. Frederick Niedner, "Ground Zero: Forming Students through the Bible," *Christian Century* 118, 13, April 18–25, 2001, 19. See also William H. Lazareth, ed., *Reading the Bible in Faith* (Grand Rapids: Wm. B. Eerdmans Publishing Co., 2001).

We honor God's name with such astonished and astonishing words, rooted in the meta-narrative of redemption history. We introduce our neighbors to the Trinity best if our speech is thus truthful. Our practice of witness[16] thereby contributes to our focal concerns of loving both our neighbor and God (by honoring the Triune name) and constantly challenges our commodifying culture.

Moreover, our dual focal concern challenges the whole congregation to recover its mission to engage in the practice of witness by word and deed. If we bear the name *Christian*, we dishonor the name of Christ if our way of life does not invite the world to take Him seriously. Particularly in connection with the major concern of this book, we take His name in vain if we are not characterized by a poverty, mercy, and compassion that will contribute to righting the economic imbalances of our technologized world.

The practice of witness might lead to the practice of martyrdom. I was staggered by the statistic that 45 million of the 70 million martyrs who have died for their faith in Christian history were persecuted in the 20th century.[17] Are we willing to be heckled, threatened, brutalized, or even sacrificed for the Name?

Can we be so committed to our focal concerns that we ignore such mocking comments as "Are you that technologically incapable?" or "What are you, a Luddite?" and so forth? When we refuse to participate in society's commodifications, to buy into the wired world, or to value the "stuff" our neighbors find precious because these don't contribute to our focal concern for God's name/character, are we submissive to the flak for the sake of loving our neighbor?

Underscoring my prior decision to include martyrdom here, my morning devotions today offered an example of how it brings together our dual concern for the love for God and neighbor in combat with prevailing paradigms of power, whatever they might be in each era. Early Christian bishop Fulgentius of Ruspe (468–533), preaching about Stephen, the first martyr, asserted, "His love of God kept him from yielding to the ferocious mob; his love for his neighbor made him pray for those who were stoning him."[18]

---

16. A superb book on evangelism is John Bowen's *Evangelism for Normal People* (Minneapolis: Augsburg Fortress Publishers, 2002).

17. David B. Barrett, George T. Kurian, and Todd M. Johnson, eds., *World Christian Encyclopedia*, 2d ed. (Oxford: Oxford University Press, 2001), cited by James Billington, "Divided We Grow," *Books and Culture* 7, 6 (November–December 2001): 20.

18. Fulgentius's sermon is quoted in *For All the Saints*, 140–141.

Holy God, how often we dishonor Your name by yielding to the ferocious mob! Our only hope is Your forgiveness. May that grace free us to resist the temptations of common blasphemies—until the day when we truly hallow Your name in an unfettered future. Amen.

3: "Remember the Sabbath Day, and Keep It Holy"

I have discovered in my own observance of the practice of Sabbath keeping, directly mandated by the third commandment (in the Hebrew numbering), how it contributes to Christianity's focal concerns by giving me space, time, and freedom to love God and my neighbor. In light of the unfettered hope that Sabbath celebrates—in its reminder that it is the LORD who sanctifies us (Exod. 31:13) and in its foretaste of the perfect Sabbath rest that still remains for us (Heb. 4:9)—I spend a full Sabbath day away from work, its worries and messiah complexes, our society's incessant pressure to accomplish, the efficiency of our accelerated culture, the bombardment of the media, its commodification of my attention.

One of the promises of the technological age is that its inventions will annihilate space and time—erasing distances with faster jets and erasing waiting with e-mail and faxes and faster computers. What our society has discovered instead, with no time and space, is a vast emptiness and a loss of genuine community. In the practice of Sabbath keeping, time and space are restored as hallowed time and the holy place of community. In these we can be attentive to our focal concerns and rethink our involvement in the wired, consumerist society.

Since I have previously written an elaboration of the actual practice of Sabbath keeping that emphasizes how it counteracts our technologized, commodified culture,[19] I want to focus here instead on another practice related to the day and our focal concerns. Worship is, of course, a key dimension of the Sabbath, and one crucial (but not sufficient!) aspect of worship is the practice of preaching.

Ben Campbell Johnson and Glenn McDonald suggest in this description how, in practicing their craft before and on the Sabbath day, preachers love God and their neighbors:

> In a world of techno-sophistication that daily erodes the last vestiges
> of wonder in ordinary life, hungry souls yearn for a message from

---

19. See Marva J. Dawn, *Keeping the Sabbath Wholly: Ceasing, Resting, Embracing, Feasting* (Grand Rapids: Wm. B. Eerdmans Publishing Co., 1989).

God. The mandate of the preacher is to live with such integrity in the presence of God and to study the Word with such energy and giftedness that when he or she finally stands to speak, those who listen will experience an in-breaking of the invisible world that literally brings their frantic lives to a stop, and sends them away transformed by their response to the gospel.[20]

Such preaching requires a martyrdom of sorts, death to ourselves. One of the two authors says, "I know that on Sunday mornings either I get out alive or the truth gets out alive. There can be only one survivor."[21]

Remember my comments above about faithful speech. Do we preachers love our neighbors and an eternal God revealed in the One whose name is Word if our words are ephemeral or if we refuse to die to ourselves so that the truth survives? How instead could we more faithfully proclaim a God who rejects trivializing conceptions (in the sense of our society's Baalish idolatries) but who is revealed in poetic symbols, literary metaphors, the natural world, human history, and human images in community?

Preaching is just one of the many practices and gifts of the Sabbath day that enfold us in the drama of redemptive history.[22] The day's "Ceasing" from our labors imitates God's pattern set in the very fiber of our creation. Its "Resting" in grace reminds us that our deepest reprieve is made possible by the freedom purchased for us by Christ's supreme sacrifice of life and death. Its "Embracing" of a Sabbath way of life thrills us with the possibilities made available to us in God's pouring out of the Spirit into our lives. Its "Feasting" prepares us for that great day when this unfettered hope is fulfilled and we banquet face to face with the Trinity in God's eternal and cosmic reign.

Meanwhile, we do not practice the Sabbath well when we let our society's technicization and consumerism clutter its rest or prevent us from ceasing. We miss the Sabbath's hope when we embrace instead our society's paradigm and turn the day itself into a device to produce certain commodities of feelings and pleasures or when we embrace a way of life that keeps others from rest and well-being. We feast only partially when we do

---

20. Johnson and McDonald, *Imagining a Church in the Spirit*, 101.
21. Ibid., 102.
22. For an excellent discussion of preaching as drama and as offered by pastors who are "theologians of the cross," see Michael Horton's *A Better Way: Rediscovering the Drama of God-Centered Worship* (Grand Rapids: Baker Book House, 2002).

not share it or if we celebrate by means of technologized hype, instead of wonder and praise.

LORD of the Sabbath, our only hope is the forgiveness our Sabbath worship acclaims. May Your grace free us to keep Your Sabbaths, until the day when our hopes are fulfilled in Your perfect future rest. Amen.

4: "Honor Your Father and Your Mother"

In chapter 2, I noted how the development of the technological milieu has caused parents to lose the natural authority they held when their children needed them to learn skills to survive. The device paradigm of our culture has also eroded parent-child relationships, for young people can easily envision their parents only as the device from which they can derive commodities of toys, money, clothes, or technological gadgets.

The tools of contraception developed in a technologized society have also contributed to the decline of family relations, for they have changed the way some parents view their children—not as gifts to be stewarded but as a choice to be made according to their own pleasure and convenience.[23] Easy acceptance of the alternative of abortions has reduced our society's valuing of life even more. And now, with the commodification of medicine (e.g., if patients are treated as numbers) and of the elderly (e.g., if their families heedlessly relegate their care to nursing homes) and with the escalation of interest in euthanasia, our culture's respect for life has been drastically diminished.

Alternatively, the Christian practice of honoring one's parents contributes in many ways to our focal concerns of loving God and the neighbor and, in many more ways, challenges our society's disrespect for some persons. To esteem our parents, simply because God mandated it and whether or not they "deserve" it, equips us with skills for loving both God and neighbors even when we don't like them. Honoring parents teaches us, too, how hard it is for God to love us and why we are so dependent upon grace.

---

23. In a review of three historical studies of contraception, Sam Torode states, "If sex and fertility are inseparable by nature, then all attempts to control fertility by 'liberating' it from sex will prove ultimately unsatisfying and destructive." He concludes by asking if the history of contraception is "better described as a story of increasing bondage to doctors, scientists, and corporations, and increasing disregard for the sanctity of life and the human person." See Sam Torode, "Sex and Science: Does Making Love Still Lead to Making Babies?" *Books and Culture*, 7, 6 (November–December 2001): 8.

Fulfilling this commandment challenges our society because honoring parents requires time and engagement, the practices of patience and discernment, and not merely consumerist gifts. To obey them teaches us respect for proper authority (a necessary practice to counteract many of the tendencies the wired world fosters to disregard boundaries).

Of course, these comments do not mean that we should obey parents who misdirect us. In those cases, our dual focal concern to love God and the neighbor overrules such mistaken obedience. But even bad parents should be honored for bringing their child to life, though their offspring must look beyond them to find a perfect parent only in the heavenly Father.

Besides, as Christians we are able to honor our parents with many kinds of biblical love:

> *racham*—Hebrew for "womb" compassion, deep tender mercy toward another;
> *storgē*—the Greek noun for the blood love of parents and children;
> *agapē*—intelligent love selflessly directed toward the needs of the other;
> *philia*—friendship love, deepened by shared focal concerns;
> *philadelphia*—brotherly/sisterly friendship love;
> *philostorgē*—blood-tied friendship love, tenderhearted affection.

With all these kinds of love in the midst of a culture starved for intimacy, Christians can offer our parents and our neighbors the genuine kinship devotion we all crave.

One of the most essential gifts in the practice of honoring parents for this technologized, commodified culture is that it reminds us to seek the wisdom of those who have gone before us. So many of the practices by which we engage in various kinds of focal concerns are dying out in our society, but respect for our elders cautions us to look more closely at the value of these habits and to cherish them lest they be totally lost.

In our churches, to honor our parents reminds us that they knew many things about worshiping God by which our love for Him might be increased. In our communities, our elders knew many things about the practices of civility, courtesy, friendship, and hospitality that would challenge the sterility of our fast-paced milieu and deepen our love for the neighbor.

The busy-ness of our technologized lives and the fetterings of our society's commodifications keep us, however, from honoring our parents as well as we would like. Our only hope is God's forgiveness and theirs, which free us now to grow in grace and in our ability to honor well—and an unfettered future when love will be perfected as hope is fulfilled.

5: "You Shall Not Murder"

The utter simplicity of this commandment hides its immense mandate to care for human life and well-being. Martin Luther's splendid explanation to the commandment hints at the many practices for which it appeals: "We should fear and love God that we may not hurt nor harm our neighbor in his body, but help and befriend him in every bodily need."[24]

The prohibition against hurting or harming our neighbor suggests the practices of non-violence, truthful speech, upbuilding attitudes, non-oppressive business methods (such as honest scales, just rents, fair laws, upright contracts, products with no hidden flaws). To be directed to befriend our neighbors for the sake of serving their every bodily need propels us to help our neighbors near and far to have decent jobs, warm housing, adequate food, clean water, proper medicine, worthwhile opportunities for meaningful engagements, spiritual teaching. To fulfill these goals requires Christian practices of simplicity on our part, compassion, solidarity, partnership, generosity (which we will consider more thoroughly below in connection with the seventh commandment).

It is essential here that we recall the various kinds of violences caused by our technologized, commodified milieu—how, for example, the amassing of commodities in the First World is generally at the expense of the well-being of residents of the Two-Thirds World or even the working poor of our own nation.[25] I think it is important, therefore, for churches to stir up the practice of righteous anger at these injustices which harm our neighbors. Then this anger needs to be channeled into various kinds of engagements that work to right the imbalances and restore true justice.

Closely connected with the economic harms to our neighbors are the more direct violences of war, ecological destructions, and ruination of local jobs caused by globalization. History shows us the inherent propensity of

---

24. Luther, *Small Catechism*, 6.
25. For a heart-rending and change-motivating insider's view of the situation of the working poor in the United States, see Barbara Ehrenreich's *Nickle and Dimed: On (Not) Getting By in America* (New York: Metropolitan Books, 2001).

violence to beget more violence if it is used to end violence.[26] Christians have a specific call from Jesus to avoid human violence and to engage instead in love for the enemy (see, e.g., especially Matt. 5:38–48).[27]

The topic is much too gigantic for us to address here, but we can at least recognize that in a world that multiplies violence with technological advancements in the precision and power of deadly instruments, in a world that amplifies harm to the neighbor with increasingly monstrous gaps between the rich and the poor, in a world that impairs neighbors with globalized destruction of their indigenous cultures, in a world in which injury to our own personhood is caused by technological developments that crush our own life-giving engagements, Christians need to wake up to how much our enculturation abets these various forms of murder!

What can we do? Our only hope arises because God is angry and is working to bring good to our neighbors. In the grace of Triune forgiveness, we can learn skills of discernment about which particular dimensions of the global problems we can address—knowing that we are only a small part of the Lord's Body, but can offer an essential contribution nonetheless.

But are we angry enough about the world's overt and covert violence? And does our unfettered hope in the Triune God's cosmic re-creation undergird our every little effort to befriend our neighbors?

6: "You Shall Not Commit Adultery"

One might wonder what the sixth commandment has to do with this book's main opposition to the invidious economic injustices of our world, but, in fact, it is directly related. North American sexual behaviors are prime examples of the commodifications of our society, for genital sexual "relationships" have become for many simply another commodity to consume on a Friday night, and sexual techniques often replace commitment.

---

26. This comment was made by Duane Friesen during his presentation as part of a panel at a Mennonnite Scholars gathering discussing the question "Is God Violent?" at the American Academy of Religion/Society of Biblical Literature annual meeting in Denver on November 17, 2001.

27. For suggestions of means by which we might do that, see Glen Stassen, ed., *Just Peacemaking: Ten Practices for Abolishing War* (Cleveland: Pilgrim Press, 1998); and Ken Butigan, with Patricia Bruno, O.P., *From Violence to Wholeness* (Las Vegas: Pace e Bene Franciscan Nonviolence Center, 1999).

Moreover, sexual addictions frequently reflect the vacuum that develops in people's lives with the absence of genuine friendships.[28]

As Jacques Ellul brilliantly prophesied fifty years ago, the increase in technicization has created an environment that fosters a corresponding decrease in intimacy—in our skills, time, and social fabric for intimacy—with the result that we reverse the poles of intimacy and technology. Because deep inside we know that we offer and are enfolded by less intimacy (as Ellen Ullman showed us in chapter 1), we try to create that intimacy with the only tools we know—which are influenced by the device paradigm. For example, sexual union, which is most satisfying as the culminating expression of growing intimacy in many other human dimensions, has been ripped out of that context and placed as the initiating act for "relationships." Since it then has no supporting and sustaining intimacies, it must be improved by dealing with the very act itself—that is, by improving techniques to make "sex" more exciting.

Even as we technologize our intimacy, so also we intimize our technology. We advertise our technological toys and tools with sexy models or cozy images designed to make them appear less sterile. Remember that Ellen Ullman named her computers.

In great contrast, the Christian practice of sexual chastity requires disciplines of patience, honesty, and fidelity. It fosters the kind of quality engagement over time that allows genuine intimacy in friendships and family relationships, especially genital union, to thrive.

Consequently, the Christian practice of faithfulness in marriage is a gift to the larger society—not only because of the stability it provides the spouses and any children the marriage might create, but also because it is another protest against the "instant gratification" ethos of our commodified culture. People who choose deliberately not to participate in our society's consumption of genital excesses (in the flesh as well as in the media) have habits of restraint and moral carefulness that affect many other dimensions of life.

On a larger scale, parents and churches that train their youth to make godly moral choices for sexuality equip them also not to commodify their other choices—about careers, education, and other aspects of life frequently thought of with the "bottom line" mentality of our culture. Instruction for the practice of sexual faithfulness also provides a platform for consideration of the principalities and powers of the culture, for we

---

28. That the absence of genuine social sexuality causes a desperation for genital sexuality is the main thesis of my book *Sexual Character*.

must equip our youth with resistance to the entire "instant gratification" ethos of our society's ads and pressures to purchase commodities.

We can also enable them to see the intertwining of the powers—of technology and Mammon, war and rape, sexual and high-tech-gadgetry consumptions, advertising and addictions, political and economic oppressions. Thus, we recognize the intertwining of all God's commandments as well, for the LORD's prohibitions of adultery and killing are closely connected. Even as we equip young people to see that their sexual choices might be more harmful to others than they might think, so we can help them ask how many of their popular choices (such as certain fashionable clothes made in sweat shops) might be harmful to their global neighbors. Does their employment of various techno-tools and toys enable them to honor their parents? to keep the Sabbath? to love God above anything and everything? to keep from stealing other people's music? to keep their sexual fantasies in check?

Additionally, we discover more and more deeply that God's commands are not burdensome, for they are indeed given us for our own good. We don't teach the commandments to spoil people's fun but to propose the most abundant life possible, a life lived according to God's good designs. How rested and calm we would be if we kept Sabbath; how much more secure we could be if there was no murder in our world; how profoundly genuine loves would flourish if we were all faithful and chaste! How everything would be better if we would allow no other gods to displace the true God! As the 14th-century Christian mystic Richard Rolle wrote in *The Fire of Love*, "Since the human soul is capable of receiving God alone, nothing less than God can fill it, which explains why lovers of earthly things are never satisfied."

One indirect connection of the sixth commandment with economic injustice concerns the issues of homosexuality. Though these issues require careful discussion, let's recognize that the present-day prolonged fights over homosexuality in many mainline church bodies distract us from larger questions. As theologian Shirley Guthrie said, "You've got self-righteous people on all sides arguing with other self-righteous people. God is saying No to . . . these little trivial debates we're having in the church while hundreds of thousands of people are starving to death."[29] Not only do the debates, important though they might be, take up an enormous amount of time, but also denominations have spent inordinate

---

29. Shirley Guthrie, quoted in "Voices of 2001," *Christian Century*, 118, 35, December 19–26, 2001, 6.

amounts of money on task forces, study materials (often biased on one side or the other, depending on the denomination), and additional meetings for the endless discussions. Meanwhile, more children and adults weaken and perish.

Lord God, forgive us. Stir us to practice faithfulness—in sexual matters, as well as economic—until you lead us to that bright future where marriage is no more, but we will perfectly love you, and where there will be no more hunger and sorrow and loneliness. Amen.

7: "You Shall Not Steal"

Once again, the consummate simplicity of this commandment conceals its enormous charge to protect the neighbor's livelihood. Martin Luther's superb explanation suggests many of the practices by which we can live in accordance with this statute: "We are to fear and love God so that we do not take our neighbor's money or property, or get them in any dishonest way, but help him to improve and protect his property and means of making a living."[30]

As before, we are driven to fear when we realize how much the entire technological, increasingly commodifying nature of our society both directly and indirectly deprives our global neighbors of adequate property. We can't read the meta-narrative of our faith without recognizing how much this global injustice arouses God's wrath against our wealth.

How shall we respond? Of course, the solution to the immense bodily needs of a great proportion of the world is not merely to give away more of our money, but rather totally to de-sacralize Mammon in our own lives so that it doesn't have such a hold on us. Then, freed from the fetters of our society's gods, we could follow the practice of the Macedonian Christians. Paul's description of them begins with grace and overflows with their liberality as he writes to the Corinthians,

> We want you to know, brothers and sisters, about the grace of God that has been granted to the churches of Macedonia; for during a severe ordeal of affliction, their abundant joy and their extreme poverty have overflowed in a wealth of generosity on their part. For, as I can testify, they voluntarily gave according to their means, and

---

30. *The Small Catechism by Martin Luther in Contemporary English: A Handbook of Basic Christian Instruction for the Family and the Congregation*, rev. ed. (St. Louis: Concordia Publishing House, 1968), 4.

even beyond their means, begging us earnestly for the privilege of sharing in this ministry to the saints—and this, not merely as we expected; they gave themselves first to the Lord and, by the will of God, to us. (2 Cor. 8:1–5)

Notice that any response in order to fight against the world's stealing and to restore the livelihood of our global neighbors is best offered if we begin with grace and continue with giving of ourselves in partnership and solidarity. These two words, *partnership* and *solidarity*, are used so often in our society that they have almost become trite, but I mean by them that we must engage *with* our neighbors in restoring justice, for only then is it truly built.[31]

Albert Borgmann emphasizes that in a culture in which much "activity is in the service of consumption, of increasing it and of deepening its hold on us," the most important virtue we need to combat global stealing is moral courage, which must become, he says, a habit or a moral competence that we repeatedly test and exercise. He cites William Ian Miller's definition of courage as "the willingness to suffer discomfort or disgrace in the defense of what is right and good." When such moral courage is regularly employed by means of many decisions against the inroads of consumerism, it develops into the practice of fortitude for the long haul.[32]

It is that willingness to suffer that we seem to lack these days, and therefore the abhorrent economic injustices of our world remain. However, we will not be able to change and get serious about altering our way of life if we beat ourselves mentally or load ourselves with guilt about living where the standard of living is high. That is also not the way of our meta-narrative, which starts with grace and frees us with hope to be generous in pursuing actively and lovingly the well-being of our neighbors near and far.

The Scriptures invite us to know all that God in Christ has done for us so that we are set free to follow Jesus and become more generous by the Spirit's enabling. As we saw in chapter 5, Jesus came, lived, suffered his

---

31. For an important review of two books with very different approaches to how churches should do justice in communities of poverty, see Carl S. Dudley, "Choices for Churches," *Christian Century*, 118, 31, November 14, 2001, 32–34; and the books, Dennis A. Jacobsen's *Doing Justice: Congregations and Community Organizing* (Minneapolis: Fortress Press, 2001), and Ryan Streeter's *Transforming Charity: Toward a Results-Oriented Social Sector* (Indianapolis: Hudson Institute, 2001).

32. Albert Borgmann, "Everyday Fortitude: Beyond Heroism," a review of William Ian Miller's *The Mystery of Courage* (Cambridge, Mass.: Harvard University Press, 2000), *Christian Century*, 118, 31, November 14, 2001, 20 and 22.

whole life, obeyed the Triune purposes, and thus died a completely aton-ing death on the cross. He rose triumphant, ascended again to His right-ful place in the fullness of His deity, and will come again to take us home into an unfettered future.

Amazing gifts! As a result, I owe Jesus my life, now and forever. What can I do but give Him all that I make, think, and have, all that I do and say, all that I am and am becoming?

If I really understand these truths, I am set free to give Jesus 100 per-cent of me and mine. Then, having offered all to Him (which was His in the first place!), I'm also freed to use it however and wherever seems best. I discover I need less for myself and perceive how much richer it is to give resources away.

When Jesus said, "Where your treasure is, there your heart will be also" (Luke 12:34), He offered a great promise. Give away more, His words suggest, and your heart expands.

Thus, our dual focal concerns for God and neighbor dialectically stretch our generosity. Resting in Triune grace, we can become more formed in the Christian community to center our lives in God and thereby let our focal concerns guide all our thinking about what really matters in the world and what just clutters up our lives. The critical importance of being thus oriented around worthy focal concerns is exceptionally appar-ent when we compare the simple and authentic way that Mother Teresa lived in the world with the vain and destructive ambitions of high-powered executives such as those of the recently collapsed Enron corporation.

My prayer for this book is that its attention to our Christian focal prac-tices will help to deepen our generosity and compassion. Since focal prac-tices connect us more closely with the real world, they enable us to become more intensely engaged with those who suffer hunger, disease, and oppression. The technological environment can easily insulate us from the true plight of those who are poor and forgotten—and often that leads to astonishing hardness of heart. Instead, constant questioning by means of our focal concerns enables us to find just ways to respond to grace by using our specific resources for the sake of the neighbor.[33] May our commitment to our focal concerns free us from the bondage of

---

33. Several studies that help us think more deeply about these issues are these: Craig L. Blomberg, *Neither Poverty nor Riches: A Biblical Theology of Material Possessions*, New Studies in Biblical Theology, series ed. D. A. Carson (Grand Rapids: Wm. B. Eerdmans Publishing Co., 1999); Rodney Clapp, ed., *The Consuming Passion: Christianity and the Consumer Culture* (Downers Grove, Ill.: InterVarsity Press, 1998); David P. Gushee, ed.,

accommodation to our culture's paradigm, as well as free us from thinking that we have to achieve restoration all by ourselves.

Dorothy Day, founder of the Catholic Worker movement to feed and house the destitute, once translated Jesus' words this way: "If you continue in my word, you are truly my disciples; and you will know the truth, and the truth will make you *odd*" (John 8:31–32). If we live the Christian practices of discernment and fortitude, generosity and collaboration for the sake of the poor, we will be viewed as odd in a society dedicated to consumerism.

Once the Internal Revenue Service audited my husband's and my tax return because, our kind questioner explained, suspicions were aroused by the large amount of charitable donations in comparison with the income level on our report. Why should that be a surprise? My husband and I know that we would have to give away *lots more* to follow Jesus, who had "nowhere to lay his head." Because of the immense hope His grace creates, divesting ourselves of the burden of too much money and property is a great delight—but it probably does seem strange to those who buy into our culture's notion that happiness grows in proportion to the level of possessions.

Wouldn't it be terrific if the IRS was dazed by every Christian's tax return? Just think of all the ministry our churches and organizations that care for the world's needy could do!

Can our church communities engage in careful discussions to consider more thoroughly how we, personally and corporately, might be formed by God's grace to share our wealth for the world's sake? How might we also encourage our government to build peace by working for justice instead of relying on power and war? Can our church budgets and tax returns exhibit the oddness of disciples following the One who at His birth was laid in a manger, in His adult life had nowhere to lay His head, and at His death was laid in a borrowed tomb?

Martin Luther once chided his congregation in a Christmas sermon,

> There are many of you who think to yourselves: "If only I had been there! How quick I would have been to help the baby!" . . . You say that because you know how great Christ is, but if you had been there at that

(continued) *Toward a Just and Caring Society: Christian Responses to Poverty in America* (Grand Rapids: Baker Book House, 1999); George S. Johnson, *Beyond Guilt: Christian Response to Suffering*, rev. ed. (Minneapolis: Augsburg Publishing House, 1989; self-published in 2000); and Ron Sider, *Just Generosity: A New Vision for Overcoming Poverty in America* (Grand Rapids: Baker Book House, 1999). For an excellent and extremely helpful review of books that offer suggestions for working alongside the urban poor, see Mark R. Gornik's "Practicing Faith in the Inner City," *Books and Culture*, 7, 4 (May–June 2001): 10–12.

time you would have done no better than the people of Bethlehem. . . . Why don't you do it now? You have Christ in your neighbor.[34]

Oh, Christ, may we see You in the poverty of Your manger and of our global neighbors. For all our failures to work for justice, we hope daily for Your fresh forgiveness. Empower us by Your grace and Your example to live the Jubilee, bringing economic restoration to the poor and liberation for the oppressed. Change us radically, fill us with fortitude, and open our minds, hearts, and wallets for the sake of Your will that the hungry be fed—until the day when all suffering shall cease in the culmination of Your gracious reign. Amen.

8: "You Shall Not Bear False Witness Against Your Neighbor"

A very touching story about the eighth commandment occurs in Kate Seredy's second novel about farm life on the Hungarian plains. During World War I, in the face of a blockade of Germany by France and England, the Hungarian government asked the country's farmers to take in as many children, "the most helpless of sufferers in the war," as they could feed. The Nagy family, who had already taken in six Russian prisoners to help as farm workers (who fast became friends), welcomed six German children to their household, besides other sick women and children for a total of twenty people by the end of the war.[35]

One of the German boys, Hans, wrote to his mother in the fall of 1917,

> These people do not hate anyone. In our school in Berlin we were told that Russians and English and French are monsters. That is not true, Mother. The six Russians, especially my best friend Stana, are like German men, like Papa. They like to laugh and play with us and they like to work. Maybe the French and English men are the same. Our teacher told us a lie about the Jews too. Herr Mandelbaum, the storekeeper in the village, is not selfish and rich and bad. He is very old and small and he has lost two sons in the war. Herr Nagy, Jancsi's father, is giving him money now to pay for goods in the store because Herr Mandelbaum has no more left. He bought war bonds to help the

---

34. Roland H. Bainton, *The Martin Luther Christmas Book* (Philadelphia: Westminster Press, 1948), 38.

35. Seredy, *Singing Tree*, 207. Page references to this book in the following paragraphs will be given parenthetically in the text.

country. If he is helping Hungary, isn't he helping Germany too? We are allies. And nobody in the village pays him for anything and he does not keep books. He just remembers what people owe him, Jancsi says, but now he often forgets because people have no money. . . .

I do not hate Russians now, Mother, and I think that Jews are very kind and good. When I grow up I want to be a teacher and teach what Grigori is always saying. He says that people are all the same in Russia and Germany and Hungary and that we are all brothers. It's true, Mother. Why did our teacher in Berlin lie to us? (221–222)

His mother responded that she was praying for Herr Nagy and Hans's Russian friends every night. "Tell them that I want to thank them for teaching my boy to love instead of to hate. Forget all your teacher in Berlin has told you. Be very good, little Hans, to deserve the kindness and love of these good people" (223).

False witness has been borne throughout history, of course, and it has led to both minor injuries and major crimes of persecutions, oppressions, wars, and resultant poverty. It is, however, amplified exceedingly these days by the power of the Internet.

A pacifist friend told me that while looking for my address on the Net he found instead, to his astonishment, a set of virulent attacks on me. (I don't read them; it's too depressing.) Had I done anything so wicked as to deserve such hate-mongering? I've read some of the reviews that speed through the wires and have often wondered if the persons writing them actually read the book I wrote. But the "democracy" of various sites and chat rooms removes the overseeing of an editorial board or a library committee or any other sort of public accountability, so all kinds of false witness can be printed onto millions of screens without any possibility for defense.

In my case, the damage done actually relates to this book's concern for the poverty of the world. Erroneous reviews might cause fewer people to buy my books, so that fewer royalties go to the charities to which those royalties are designated to help in their work against poverty.

Is it false witness to the neighbor when we enter Internet chat rooms with an imaginary identity? At a conference I asked high school students how many of them had "best friends" in chat rooms, and a large proportion of them raised their hands. I asked them what difference it made in friendship if the other person didn't really know who they were—and vice versa. They didn't answer at first, but the surprised and then troubled expressions on their faces suggested, as did their later comments, that they recognized a deep problem.

Ponder all the false witnessing in our nation's political sphere—and how many people have had their careers destroyed by polls or by lies and their amplification through the ever-present media. Polls are especially destructive because false witnesses can remain anonymous.

How can we respond to false witness in any postmodern form? Martin Luther gives us help again with this explanation to the commandment: "We are to fear and love God so that we do not betray, slander, or lie about our neighbor, but defend him, speak well of him, and explain his actions in the kindest way."[36]

Do we have the courage to defend on screen a person attacked on the Internet? Do we have the moral fortitude to offset false witness with words of praise and commendation? When we engage in the practice of truth telling as one way that our lives are centered in the focal concern of loving our neighbor, then we must counteract all forms of betrayal, slander, or falsehood when and where we encounter them.

Another practice that is essential in these days of global information is that of speaking a word of knowledge for the sake of loving our neighbors. Reading James Scott's *The Weapons of the Weak*, mentioned in chapter 1, made me realize how easily we can have false assumptions about people in poverty.

Listening to political speeches or even news reports that describe the followers of Osama bin Laden or Palestinian resisters or any other notorious person or group, I realize that false witness is easily given about a country's enemies. We are tempted to satanize the foe and fail to account for the desperation of those in poverty or struggling under oppression. Into an atmosphere of hate, can we speak what we know—as did a local specialist on Afghanistan who helped a radio audience to recognize more deeply the plight of sufferers in that land?

An older version of Luther's catechism ended his explanation to the eighth commandment with the phrase "put the best construction on everything." That is a superb description of the kind of words Christians will want to employ in opposition to a culture that gives false testimony constantly—not only about people but also about its commodities, its technologies, its practices, its hyped hopes.

Putting the best construction on everything doesn't mean naively ignoring what is destructive. Instead, it is a practice by which lies are exposed, but the person perpetrating them is treated with love and compassion.

---

36. *The Small Catechism by Martin Luther in Contemporary English*, 4.

We have all borne false witness or failed to defend those who are maligned. Our only hope is God's gracious forgiveness, which motivates us to develop more careful habits of honest speech, defense of the innocent, and gentle dissent to hate—and the unfettered hope that someday the truth will be known.

9: "You Shall Not Covet Your Neighbor's House"

As a child whose friends memorized another ordering, I wondered why Martin Luther divided the commandments differently from founders of other Christian denominations. It is striking, however, that the arrangement used in this book is so apparent in the Hebrew text of Exodus 20. Commandments 5 through 10 all begin with the Hebrew word for "not." This is followed by the verbs for murdering, committing adultery, stealing, testifying (with the words for "witness" and "false" being the last two words in the sentence, respectively), and two occurrences of the verb for coveting. Before each word *not* is a separated Hebrew letter *samekh*.

This discovery makes me think (as I frequently do) that the Bible is written especially for the 21st century, for certainly coveting is one of the most frequent sins in a society that bombards us constantly with commercials for all the commodities we could accumulate. This also continues to be an age of ostentatious luxury, opulent houses, four-car garages, private luxury yachts, and advertisements that promise we can have it all.

We certainly need two commandments against coveting!

It seems to me that the first of the two emphasizes that we should not covet things or inanimate objects, while the second focuses on people and creatures or living beings. That distinction names my guilt more fully, as it perhaps does yours.

Years ago I coveted a neighbor's actual house—when I needed a bigger study. Now that I have a larger work place, however, I've wished for newer bathroom fixtures or a greenhouse for my husband. I have also coveted the sunshine flooding through someone's south-facing picture window, the view of the mountains from another's porch, the physical warmth of someone's home, or my good friend's warmer car. Equally sinful are covetings of less tangible things—someone's healthy body that can produce adequate heat, the huge number of copies another person's books sell, recognitions or accomplishments or any other possessions. It is amazing how much we covet when we stop to ponder it.

How can we resist this cultural plague, abetted as it is by all the media bombardments and technological developments of new commodities? To

do so is especially crucial, for our coveting often leads to new possessions—and, consequently, less care for those in the world with so little.

Four Christian practices especially enable us to combat coveting and to
focus instead on loving our neighbors and God. The first is gratitude. If
we are ardently thankful for all the blessings the Trinity has given us, we
find ourselves loving God too much to complain and crave more.

The second practice is contentment. Just as gratitude needs to be developed as a habit in a culture that beckons us always into whining, so contentment is a trained art. It seems to me to be based in discernment
(another Christian practice) between our genuine needs and our wants
and in trust (still another Christian practice) in the form of belief that God
cares about our every need and will provide whatever is necessary for us
to live out our focal concerns of loving Him and our neighbor.

The third and fourth practices are to "rejoice with those who rejoice"
and "weep with those who weep" (Rom. 12:15). If we learn truly to rejoice
in another's good blessings, we are able to resist jealousy, envy, coveting,
discontentment. For example, when I celebrate how beautifully the person
next to me is swimming, I find myself less covetous of non-crippled legs'
swifter kick. On the other hand, when I let my own bodily coldness keep
me weeping with refugees who are far colder at their inadequate camps in
more brutal temperatures, then I become not only less covetous, but also
more generous for the sake of meeting their needs through relief agencies.

One of the worst effects of coveting is that it spoils relationships. Not
only do we make enemies of those who possess what we want, but also our
attempts to satisfy our desires lead us away from other practices that
engage us in our focal concern to love our global neighbors. Rejoicing and
weeping turn enemies back into friends and those we might ignore back
into subjects of our attention. These habits also invite us more deeply into
God's heart, for the Creator delights in giving gifts to His children and
the Comforter grieves over the pain of the world. Are our hearts broken
by the things that break the heart of God? We need to resist temptations
to covetousness in order to be shaken out of our complacency and to grow
in our care for the poor.

What are the belongings that you covet? How might the habits of gratitude, contentment, rejoicing, and weeping refocus your attention (and
your resources) on loving God and your neighbors? Our only hope in the
face of our covetings and complacencies is God's complete forgiveness,
which frees us to practice compassion and generosity instead—until the
day when all our needs and desires become one in the future fulfillment
of our hope to belong completely to God.

10: "You Shall Not Covet Your Neighbor's Wife, or Male or Female Slave, or Ox, or Donkey, or Anything That Belongs to Your Neighbor"

It is obvious to me as I write that I can't really keep these last two commandments distinct, for the examples of health I used in the previous section could as well have been placed here. I only know that in this present society I need two commandments against coveting.

How might we, however, covet people and creatures? The coveting of spouses is quite obvious in a culture with high rates of marital infidelity, divorce and remarriage, and other tangible results of the initial desire.[37] Coveting of a neighbor's "slaves" happens all the time, as evidenced by corporations luring away another company's workers. Oxen and donkeys we don't need much anymore, but do we perhaps covet another person's brain power or training by which she accomplishes her work? I know that sometimes I also find myself coveting another person's friends, since many of mine live far away.

The practices by which we might become more thoroughly engaged in our focal concerns of loving God and the neighbors instead of coveting persons and what or who attends them again include gratitude, contentment, rejoicing, and weeping. With people, we might extend those with the additional practices of friendship, hospitality, and solidarity.

To avoid coveting someone else's spouse, the solution is not to love that person less, but to love him more—to love him genuinely as a friend, instead of falsely as a potential lover. Of course, that is easy to say and immensely hard to do, but I believe it is possible (and have seen it happen) by the grace of God. Such friendship is a severe discipline—and thus friendship of the truest sort. That is also the kind of friendship profoundly needed in our society, which tends to turn people into devices, useful only for the commodities of work or pleasure they produce.

Similarly, our means for combating coveting of someone else's friends (perhaps you are guilty of this, too) is to be a better friend ourselves and,

---

37. The multitude of destructions to our society and children are documented by such books as Barbara Defoe Whitehead's *The Divorce Culture* (New York: Alfred A. Knopf, 1996) and Judith Wallerstein, Julia Lewis, and Sandra Blakeslee's *The Unexpected Legacy of Divorce: A 25-Year Landmark Study* (New York: Hyperion, 2000). For both critique and positive strategies by which churches can help to build a "critical marriage culture," see Don S. Browning, Bonnie J. Miller-McLemore, Pamela D. Couture, K. Brynolf Lyon, and Robert M. Franklin, *From Culture Wars to Common Ground: Religion and the American Family Debate*, 2d ed. (Louisville, Ky.: Westminster John Knox Press, 2000).

especially, a friend to those desperate for relationships or needy for care. Jesus particularly tells us that we serve Him when we are friends with prisoners and the sick, with the homeless and hungry.

Our society is starved for friendship, in the ancient sense of that word. Perhaps that is why the two most mentioned movies opening at the end of 2001 were based on the books *Harry Potter and the Sorcerer's Stone* and *The Fellowship of the Ring*, in which both Harry and the hobbits of Tolkien's trilogy rely on their friends to meet the challenges that face them. Deeper friendships with others would decrease our need to compete with them or to covet their gifts.

Hospitality is a frequently misused word in our society, and it is misused to our detriment. It is often taken to mean inviting to our home those who have invited us. Such tit-for-tat entertaining is hardly the sort that leads to "entertaining angels without knowing it" (Heb. 13:2). Biblical hospitality is often extended to strangers and usually leads to them becoming friends. How different our attitudes toward injustice in the world would be if we welcomed the poor into our homes for a meal or to stay, and how quickly such a practice would stifle our coveting![38]

Hospitality moves into solidarity in Hebrews 13:1–3. These verses impress us with their continual widening of the community of relationships:

> [1]Let mutual love continue. [2]Do not neglect to show hospitality to strangers, for by doing that some have entertained angels without knowing it. [3]Remember those who are in prison, as though you were in prison with them; those who are being tortured, as though you yourselves were being tortured.

Only by genuine companionship in suffering can we recover from the coveting and consequent over-indulgence and gluttony of our society.

Dietrich Bonhoeffer (1906–1945), leader of the Confessing Church in Germany and martyr for his participation in the plot to assassinate Hitler, wrote from prison about what he called an "experience of incomparable value":

> We have for once learnt to see the great events of world history from below, from the perspective of the outcast, the suspects, the maltreated,

---

38. The best book I've ever found on the subject of hospitality is Christine D. Pohl's *Making Room: Recovering Hospitality as a Christian Tradition* (Grand Rapids: Wm. B. Eerdmans Publishing Co., 1999).

the powerless, the oppressed, the reviled—in short, from the perspective of those who suffer. The important thing is that neither bitterness nor envy should have gnawed at the heart during this time, that we should have come to look with new eyes at matters great and small, sorrow and joy, strength and weakness, that our perception of generosity, humanity, justice and mercy should have become clearer, freer, less corruptible. We have to learn that personal suffering is a more effective key, a more rewarding principle for exploring the world in thought and action than personal good fortune. This perspective from below must not become the partisan possession of those who are eternally dissatisfied; rather, we must do justice to life in all its dimensions from a higher satisfaction, whose foundation is beyond any talk of "from below" or "from above."[39]

I pray that in this book I have revealed the crucial importance of finding our higher satisfaction in the unfettered hope of God's eternal grace. May that free us to enter into the experience of those "below"—the outcasts, the maltreated, the powerless, the hungry, all who suffer. In a world of such glaring injustices, why do we waste our time coveting?

Gracious God, our only hope is in Your forgiveness. May Your mercy free us from our bondage to envy, wrongful desires, insatiable greed, and the idolatry of commodities. Empower us by Your love to love our neighbors with a willingness to join with them in their sufferings—until the day when our dreams are unfettered in Your completed plan to make the cosmos whole again. Amen.

The Lord's Supper

How do we find strength to engage in all the practices by which, fulfilling the Ten Commandments, we may attend centrally to our focal concerns to love God and the neighbor and thereby restrict, resist, and reform the technological, commodified society in which we live?

First, let us remember that the practices I sketch above are not meant to be a list of all we should do. These are simply some of the means by which we attend to our ends. Nonetheless, they are important habits, and I frequently broke into prayer while writing because only God by the Spirit can form them in me. Our churches, however, can also pay more

---

39. Dietrich Bonhoeffer, *Letters and Papers from Prison*, rev. enlarged ed. (London: SCM Press, 1971), as cited in *For All the Saints*, 41–42.

attention to the disciplines by which the community can be the sort of milieu in which these practices are modeled and experienced.

Moreover, I discussed a large assortment of practices so that we can be elated by all the wonderful ways through which God works. Grace frees us to practice prayer, worship, tithing, memorization, Scripture reading, meditation, spiritual reading, hearing (sermons and the Word and instruction), participating in the Church's traditions and our customs, footwashing, creating art and music, Advent waiting, frugality, simple living, building justice, reconciliation, peacemaking, modeling, mentoring, training of children, baptism and the living of the baptismal life, entrusting our work to God, learning God's names, sharing bread with the hungry, bringing the homeless poor into our own homes, clothing the naked, always attending to the needy we encounter, wonder, truthful speech, witness, martyrdom, Sabbath keeping, preaching, patience, discernment, obedience, respect for authority, seeking the wisdom of our elders, civility, courtesy, non-violence, upbuilding attitudes, fair business practices, simplicity, compassion, solidarity, partnership, generosity, righteous anger, sexual chastity, purity, honesty, fidelity, faithfulness in marriage, restraint, moral carefulness, giving ourselves to each other, fortitude, collaboration, defense of the neighbor, speaking words of knowledge, gentle dissent to hate, gratitude, contentment, trust, rejoicing, weeping, compassion, friendship, hospitality. And these are only a selection of the habits, virtues, customs, practices, and manners through which God works for the healing of the world.

How does God sustain us?

Christ has given us one exceedingly special gift by which our hope is continually nurtured, and that is His Supper. I am using that name for the meal here because it puts the focus on the Lord's gift rather than on our thanks (the meaning of the Greek *eucharisteo*).

Albert Borgmann recognizes that this supporting feast, this sacred practice, "consisted in the regular reenactment of the founding act, and so it renewed and sustained the order of the world." Christianity began as Jesus went beyond the Passover meal and declared a new covenant in the bread and wine.[40] Thus, Borgmann insists, "the eucharistic meal, the Supper of the Lamb, is [Christianity's] central event, established with the instruction that it be reenacted."[41]

---

40. See John D. Zizioulas, *Being as Communion: Studies in Personhood and the Church* (Crestwood: St. Vladimir's, 1985), 20–21.

41. Borgmann, *Technology and the Character of Contemporary Life*, 207.

As our central event, the Lord's Supper sustains us as it constantly conveys forgiveness, reminds us of Christ's past and present work on our behalf, incorporates us into the present community of His Body, and offers us a foretaste of the feast to come when we will participate with Him in the culmination of His glorious reign.

At the table, we find our Bethlehem—which means "House of Bread"— and God Himself incarnated for us in bread and wine and community. The meal's gifts fill us with unfettered hope, which empowers us to return to the world around us eager both to challenge and to serve it.

Living Our Meta-Narrative for the Sake of the Technologized, Consumerist Society

When we understand the paradigm undergirding our technological milieu and its consumerism, then we can in contrast clear a space for our focal commitments and thereby use the commodities of the technological milieu wisely. We can discern which gifts of that world contribute to our engagement in practices of Christian faith and life and those which might hinder our ministry and proclamation. This is essential because we can so easily become overwhelmed by all the possibilities available to us in the commodious world and fail to choose carefully what is appropriate to our calling and character, our faith formation and our desire to pass that faith on to all those for, to, and with whom we minister. We serve the world best by clearing space for our focal concerns of loving God and the neighbor, engaging in spiritual practices directed toward those commitments, and thus limiting our involvement with elements of our society in order not to succumb to its idolatries.

All the practices suggested by the Ten Commandments—most especially by the prohibitions against killing, stealing, and coveting—contribute profoundly to our focal concerns of loving God and the neighbor and challenge the reign of the technological, commodifying milieu and the hideous economic imbalances it causes and fosters.

As we learned from Augustine in chapter 5, may our hope, gathered from the meta-narrative about, and our relationship with, the covenant God, have the beautiful daughters of anger and courage—anger at the way things are and courage to change them. Only as a community can we have enough courage to engage in the practices of faith. Only by grace are they possible to us. But when hope and grace bear fruits of righteous anger and courage, the injustice of the world could be changed.

Chapter 7

The Only Unfettered Hope
Is Eschatological

G. K. Chesterton once quipped, "It is always easy to let the age have its head; the difficult thing is to keep one's own."[1] How in a technologized, commodified society, which constantly binds us in false hopes, can Christians maintain and live a truly unfettered hope, especially for the sake of combating the world's injustice?

We have noticed all kinds of fetterings in chapter 1, and we learned that the only way through them is to escape the paradigm, sketched in chapter 2, by living according to our focal concerns. We have emphasized the focal concerns of the Church in chapter 3, but recognized in chapter 4 how much churches fail to live by them. In chapter 5, we rejoiced in the basis for true hope in the meta-narrative of our Christian faith, and in chapter 6 we noted seventy practices by which, empowered by the hope of the Gospel, we can attend to our focal concerns and challenge the culture by which the whole world is mired in despair.

Now, let us celebrate our unfettered hope—define it more closely, understand its pattern, test it against suffering, consider how it can reform our churches and challenge the surrounding society, and pray that it might inflame our lives.

"Sketch of a Phenomenology and a Metaphysic of Hope"

This section heading is the title of a chapter in *Homo Viator* by philosopher Gabriel Marcel (1889–1973), whose work helps to explain why the hopes of our society are always disappointing. Marcel distinguishes

---

1. Chesterton, *Orthodoxy*, 107.

between having genuine hope and using the phrase *I hope* merely to express my wishes; those desires come from roots in the depths of what I am, but the reasons for true hope are exterior to myself.[2] Hope that is based on my own desires becomes often a calculation (of the sort our society fosters!) about the chances or probabilities that what I want will happen.

Hopes in our society are usually stated in the form "I hope that . . . ," which is very different from "I hope" as an absolute statement. This parallels the difference between "I believe that . . ." and "I believe" (32). Do we believe or hope *that* things might become better, or do we believe, and hope in, God? Hope transcends any laying down of conditions.

Hope is a mystery. In our hoping, we dare not be presumptuous. By hoping, we aren't let in on special secrets, nor do we know God's purposes by special enlightenment. To presume such special knowledge "does not take into account all that there is of humility, of timidity, of *chastity* in the true character of hope" (35, emphasis Marcel's). This is why so many hopes in our society prove empty: people try to define them by rationalistic investigation.

Hope is often deprecated as mere illusion or as simply related to one's physical vitality, as if the healthy can be more truly hopeful. However, as Marcel asserts, "The truth is that there can strictly speaking be no hope except when the temptation to despair exists. Hope is the act by which this temptation is actively or victoriously overcome" (36). Consequently, to hope doesn't necessarily mean that we *feel* hopeful. It is, instead, not to capitulate "before a certain *future*" according to our own judgment or society's (37).

Our society confuses hope with stoicism, as if we ourselves could fulfill our hopes by sheer grit. The power and greatness of stoicism is that it enables one to rise above the future, but Marcel points out its limitation: "the stoic is always imprisoned within himself. He strengthens himself, no doubt, but he does not radiate." That phrase intrigues me, for the Gospel's unfettered hope does indeed fill us with dazzling Joy.

Stoicism is basically inward-turned. The stoic "bears himself— . . . above all he controls his interior life—as though he had no neighbours, as though he were concerned only with himself and had no responsibility towards anyone else" (38). This is why the stoic response of the wealthy to our own fetterings—for example, that we will simply "bite the bullet" and use our technological expertise to develop a way to get ourselves out

---

2. Gabriel Marcel, *Homo Viator*, reprint (Gloucester, Mass.: Peter Smith Publisher, 1996), 29. Page references to this book in the following paragraphs will be given parenthetically in the text.

of whatever binds us—hinders us from sharing true hope with the poor. True hope is more than merely a stiffening.

Genuine hope includes both non-acceptance of the present situation and patience. "He who stiffens and rebels does not know how to take his time," but the person who hopes can actually relax and not let a trial constrict her (39).

Marcel's reference to hope's patience reminds me of an insight stirred in conversation with a Canadian. He asked why the French uses *espérer* (to hope) in a text where English Bibles say "wait." Because the Hebrew word is translated both ways, it struck me that the two, hoping and waiting, must remain dialectically together. To wait without hope is to be without God. To hope, but not be willing to wait, dismantles true hoping because we try ourselves to bring about what we hope for. But hopeful waiting or a waiting hope is genuine eschatological hope—enabling us to wait because what we hope for is already initiated in Christ and will be fulfilled by Him.

As Marcel notes, since hope does not depend on what is in me "but much more on what arises independently of my possible action," hope "has the power of making things fluid" (41). This is partly the reason hope can't be held by those enslaved by the device paradigm. Another reason is that hope correlates with the security of *Being*, contrary to the radical insecurity of *Having*.

Thus, Marcel names the *only* source from which "absolute hope springs": the God Who is "infinite Being." Because we are creatures, true hope arises as our response to God, to Whom, we recognize, we owe everything we have and upon Whom we "cannot impose any condition whatsoever without scandal."

> From the moment that I abase myself in some sense before the absolute Thou who in his infinite condescension has brought me forth out of nothingness, it seems as though I forbid myself ever again to despair, or, more exactly, that I implicitly accept the possibility of despair as an indication of treason, so that I could not give way to it without pronouncing my own condemnation. Indeed, seen in this perspective, what is the meaning of despair if not a declaration that God has withdrawn himself from me?

Such an accusation is incompatible with the character of the absolute God, and "in advancing it I am unwarrantably attributing to myself a distinct reality which I do not possess" (47).

Notice how thoroughly Marcel's comments demolish all our human pretensions. Invincible hope, he emphasizes, can arise only "from the ruins of all human and limited hopes" (48). Would we Christians be more able to give up our fettered, finite, human hopes if we realized that to hang on to them is to reject the absoluteness of our Thou, to commit one more form of treason against the Triune God?

When Marcel underscores that hope "is not interested in the *how*," he shows us another reason why true hope is contrary to our society, enslaved as it is to the quick-fix mentality of the device paradigm. Marcel acknowledges that hope is "fundamentally untechnical," for "technical thought, by definition, never separates the consideration of ends and means. An end does not exist for the technician, if he does not see approximately how to achieve it" (51).

An inventor or discoverer says about a problem, "There must be a way, and I'll find it," but someone who hopes says, "It will be found." Hope doesn't mean that we create solutions, but that we appeal to the One who is the Creator and to all the resources in God's power (52).

Our society tempts us to think that there is no hope because we have no established experience by which to measure a way out. But "established experience" perceives time as only passing without carrying anything new; that is to be hopeless. Hope is part of a process (52).

Marcel's insights are attested by biblical assurances that God's promises enable us to wait for what has already begun. We saw in chapter 5's overview of the Christian meta-narrative that the fulfillment of all God's promises has begun in Christ, and therefore we wait/hope (with roots, as noted above, in one Hebrew word). We already have a beginning (all that Christ accomplished during His life on earth), and consequently we have unfettered hope as we look to, and participate in, the total fulfillment of all God's promises.

Despair, especially as it is experienced by our society, produces the sense that time is a prison, that it's closed in, "whilst hope appears as piercing through time." Consequently, hope has a prophetic character. It "draws its authority from a hidden vision of which it is allowed to take account without enjoying it." Thus the future and the present are reunited (53). Theology expresses this in the notion that God's future reign has already broken into this age in Christ.

Marcel also accentuates that hope, even if interior, is always associated with a community (59). This helps explain why hope is often so vibrantly displayed in poor communities, but absent in wealthier nations where people do not depend on each other and on God.

Though Marcel died before the last quarter of the 20th century, these words presciently recognize the destruction caused by the device paradigm and its focus on commodities:

> [T]o hope . . . is to live in hope instead of anxiously concentrating our attention on the poor little counters spread out in front of us which we feverishly reckon up over and over again without respite, tormented by the fear of being foiled or ruined. The more we allow ourselves to be the servants of Having, the more we shall let ourselves fall prey to the gnawing anxiety which Having involves, the more we shall tend to lose not only the aptitude for hope, but even I should say the very belief, indistinct as it may be, of its possible reality. In this sense it is no doubt true that, strictly speaking, only those beings who are entirely free from the shackles of ownership in all its forms are able to know the divine light-heartedness of life in hope.

Marcel doesn't think such liberation is available to many. The vast majority of people, he claims, are "destined to remain entangled in the inextricable meshes of Having" (61). He suggests that "if, however feebly, we remain penetrated by hope, it can only be through the cracks and openings which are to be found in the armour of Having which covers us: the armour of our possessions, our attainments, our experience and our virtues, perhaps even more than our vices" (62). This reminds us of Jacques Ellul's insight in *The Technological Bluff* that the system develops cracks, into which we can install a trembling freedom. Whenever all that we Have loses its hold on us (by the grace of God), we glimpse again genuinely unfettered Hope.

Finally, Marcel asks if hope is permissible where reasons for it are insufficient or lacking (64) and answers that to raise that question is to enter into the very processes of deliberating by calculations, the figuring of probabilities. But that is to distort the meaning of the word *hope*, for it can't be argued for as if one could inquire into the validity of the arguments (65). The very character of hope is that it challenges the evidence by which it is thought to be disproved (67).

In reading Marcel, I recalled the fall of the Berlin Wall. It was not possible to argue that it would fall, yet the prayerful hope that finally brought it down challenged the impossibility by which many discounted the hope of those who prayed.[3]

---

3. See Jörg Swoboda, *The Revolution of the Candles: Christians in the Revolution of the German Democratic Republic*, ed. Richard V. Pierard, trans. Edwin P. Arnold (Macon, Ga.: Mercer University Press, 1996).

Christians all are participants in the historical drama of our salvation, told in the meta-narrative of the Christian faith. God incorporates us into that drama so that we become participants in the eschatological reality of God's reign. It doesn't look like the Kingdom has come, but our hope challenges that lack of evidence, for we know that God has already begun the work of reconciling the cosmos, and we believe, hope, know that the Trinity will bring it to completion.

The reason this is our only *unfettered* hope is that daily life often keeps us from living according to our ultimate concerns. Borgmann claims that having centered his life in his focal concern, he has "clear and principled answers to life's endless and distracting demands."[4] But sometimes, as we all experience, those principled answers conflict—for instance, when I'm passionately engaged in writing this book (which contributes to my focal concern) and someone calls, wanting to visit. How do I know how important that conversation would be and whether it is the way I should love my neighbor at that time—especially when the writing, also being done for the love of the neighbor, is going strongly?

My only hope is the eschatological hope that now God's kingdom is characterized by forgiveness, and someday it will be characterized by the absence of such conflicts.

Hope Redescribes the World

The lectionary-assigned Gospel text for the Third Sunday of Advent in 2001 was Matthew 11:2–11, which tells of John the Baptizer, in prison, sending disciples to ask Jesus if He is the One who is to come. John is confused because Jesus doesn't match his expectations of what the Messiah should be.

But Jesus responds, "Go and tell John what you hear and see: the blind receive their sight, the lame walk, the lepers are cleansed, the deaf hear, the dead are raised, and the poor have good news brought to them" (11:4–6). This rings with joyful echoes of the First Testament Lesson for the same day, Isaiah 35:1–10. Therein the lame shall "leap like a deer"; the tongue of the speechless shall "sing for joy."

One of my favorite verses in all the Scriptures concludes the reading: "And the ransomed of the LORD shall return, and come to Zion with singing; everlasting joy shall be upon their heads; they shall obtain joy and gladness, and sorrow and sighing shall flee away." The same themes are

---

4. Borgmann, *Technology and the Character of Contemporary Life*, 214–215.

sprinkled throughout Isaiah (1:27, 25:8, 30:19, 51:11, 65:19) and appear twice in The Revelation (7:17 and 21:4). In the latter texts, the reason for such exultant gladness is made clear: because "the Lamb in the center of the throne shall be their shepherd," and "He [Himself] shall wipe away every tear from their eyes" (NASV).

On that day in Advent, Father Bob Rhodes preached that Jesus' answer to John encouraged the latter to see that the Messiahship was not about power, but about promises and their fulfillment in the great day of deliverance when people in the wilderness would be brought home. The *pattern* of Jesus' life and work, His presence, connected to the promises God had made to His people.

We, too, are in wildernesses, the priest said, and more so since September 11, 2001. We feel great sorrows, but those tears, too, will be no more when the promises of God are fulfilled [and thus, I add, we hope]. Moreover, when we become steeped in the stories of Jesus' mercy and compassion, then we follow in the same pattern and contribute to the healing of those who have sorrow and sighing.

The priest urged worshipers to read their Bibles every day and to pray, "Lord, reveal to me the pattern of your presence," so they could learn to see it in their daily lives. In the same way, can we learn to let the Bible's patterns redescribe what we see in the world? Can we see the pattern of the ways God works to fulfill promises? Can we, then, believe God for the future without seeing much evidence now? Can we hope simply because we believe God?

When the language of hope fills our lives, we manifest the "radiance" of which Gabriel Marcel wrote. We live true to who we are as the redeemed people of God. The result is that our hope changes our world because we really *live* the Gospel.

Near the end of his gripping story of Jewish musicians in Hitler's Germany, Martin Goldsmith reports on prevailing arguments over whether the Kulturbund caused people to misjudge the terror of the Nazis. One of the Goldsmiths' musician friends, Henry Meyer, insisted that the Jews didn't underestimate the Nazis, but the other way around. He said the Nazis made a big mistake in not realizing that "[i]f you let a full-blooded musician or any artist practice his profession, even under the force of the Gestapo, he comes alive, and that's what we did. . . . We were born to perform and when we did that we really lived."[5]

In baptism Christians are born to hope, and when we practice that, we really come alive!

---

5. Goldsmith, *Inextinguishable Symphony*, 299.

Do We Practice Our True Hope?

Let us each wrestle with whether and how we live our hope. Since God is the One who brings hope, creates hope, and promises the fulfillment of our hope, we can give up our false pride, false humility, false effort, false urgency, false responsibility, false guilt. This requires a certain kind of weakness,[6] a willingness to suffer, a certain kind of childlikeness.

One vignette in *The Heroic Face of Innocence*, collected works by Georges Bernanos, is a "Sermon of an Agnostic on the Feast of St. Thérèse." The book's main theme is that the world will be saved not by human intellectual accomplishments, technological advancements, political endeavors, genetic engineering, or theological astuteness, but by the radical innocence of spiritual childhood. Christ, for Bernanos, is the epitome and the source of such true childlikeness—Christ, whose power resides in total obedience to His eternal Father's will, and who asserted unequivocally, "Unless you change and become like children, you will never enter the kingdom of heaven" (Matt. 18:3).[7]

The Sermon is a brilliant indictment of Christians' failure to practice our hope, to be radiant with our baptismal confidence. The agnostic criticizes the congregation for not being interested in unbelievers, since those unbelievers are extremely interested in Christians. There is always the smallest chance that Christianity is right, he says, and, if so, "death would come as a devastating surprise to us."[8] After observing believers, however, the agnostic preacher mocks, many unbelievers have decided that they aren't very interesting after all. Christians disappoint unbelievers because, one can't help but notice, "the faith they profess makes little difference in their lives" (25).

The agnostic complains, "We're wondering what you do with the Grace of God. Should it not be shining out of you? Where the devil do you hide your joy?"

Then he pokes fun. "You generally talk in that acid, revengeful way, as though you hated us for the pleasures of which you have deprived yourselves. Can they be so precious in your eyes? Alas, we don't think so much of them" (26).

---

6. See Dawn, *Powers, Weakness, and the Tabernacling of God*.

7. Erasmo Leiva-Merikakis, "Foreword," *The Heroic Face of Innocence* (Grand Rapids: Wm. B. Eerdmans Publishing Co., 1999), ix.

8. Georges Bernanos, "Sermon of an Agnostic on the Feast of St. Thérèse," trans. Pamela Morris and David Louis Schindler Jr., in *The Heroic Face of Innocence*, 24. Page references to this story in the following paragraphs will be given parenthetically in the text.

The agnostic's ridicule must force us to ask, too, as we contemplate our role in this technologized, commodified world: Why do we Christians hide God's grace and the Joy it gives to us? Do we value the world's pleasures so much that we let them choke our hope?

The unbeliever proceeds by confessing, "[W]e worship the same calf"—which is not, he assures us, "the sign of an optimistic people." Instead, the whole world is "corroded by the same leprosy," the total inability "to conceive of the Resurrection" (26). In chapter 4 we saw signs of that leprosy in churches, but all the practices of faith in chapter 6 flourish richly when they are undergirded by the quickening of the Resurrection in our lives.

Next, he wonders why Christians don't notice—as unbelievers all do—that God "reserved His most stringent maledictions for some of the very 'best' people, regular church-goers" who never fail to fast and are very well instructed in their faith. Why doesn't that enormous paradox grab our attention (27)? Will Bernanos's book and mine help us to wake up to it?

What is most beyond understanding to agnostics, he claims, "is that you habitually reason about the affairs of this world in exactly the same way we do. I mean, who's forcing you?" Why do Christians act according to the world's principles, as if they had "no hope in another world." To live according to the laws of survival and the economics of society simply strikes unbelievers as "odd, incomprehensible" (29).

The only way out of the world's laws and economics, the agnostic reminds Christians, is "to become children yourselves, to rediscover the heart of childhood" (31). He looks to the saints for the reality of the Christian life, but needs the present language of our faith to express it. Finally, he chides, "I'm sorry to have to tell you that we [agnostics] pay dearly for your neglect" of your faith's hope and life (34), and again, "Because you do not live your faith, your faith has ceased to be a living thing. It has become abstract—bodiless" (36).

Embodied Faith, Living Our Hope

Bernanos's agnostic haunts me, just as does Nietzsche's comment "I'd believe in a resurrected Christ if I saw more resurrected Christians walking around." Has the faith of the wealthy nations of the world become so abstract? Must we persist in so failing to live our hope? Why does the Grace of God not shine out of us?

How might we so live according to our focal concerns that we help others caught in the bonds of the device paradigm to discover God's gift to us of unfettered hope? What are some ways that we can envision the mission of the Church to our society?

I'm writing this section on the morning of New Year's Eve and am, consequently, very conscious that the way forward is not by making New Year's resolutions about how we and our churches will reform. That is the fettered hope of our technologized, commodifying society. We want to be better by our own efforts, and we want to be able to measure the results by how well we keep our resolutions.

No. The way forward is to die more.

Martin Luther's "We should so *fear* and love . . ." shows us the way. Did you notice each section on the commandments in the previous chapter ended with confession and gratitude or a plea for forgiveness?

The way forward is to give up on ourselves, to recognize how badly we fail, to acknowledge our guilt, and then, freed by the unfettered hope of forgiveness and the promise of God's new future (already begun), we rise from that death to ourselves into newness of life, filled with Joy and Hope and thereby equipped for devotion to loving God and the neighbor.

We must begin with dying. And daily we see afresh how much more we need to die. In *Mere Christianity*, C. S. Lewis compares the process to having a toothache (much like aches we all experience from fetterings of society and ourselves). Lewis knew that if he went to his mother, she would give him aspirin to deaden the pain. However, he did not go to her—at least not until the pain became insufferable—and the reason was that she would no doubt take him to the dentist the next morning. He writes, "I could not get what I wanted out of her without getting something more, which I did not want. I wanted immediate relief from pain: but I could not get it without having my teeth set permanently right." Dentists wouldn't settle for dealing with the aching tooth; they would probe around and "not let sleeping dogs lie."

Lewis claims, "Our Lord is like the dentists." Give Him an inch and He'll take the whole yard. "Dozens of people go to Him to be cured of some one particular sin which they are ashamed of . . . or which is obviously spoiling daily life." He will remedy that, of course, "but He will not stop there. That may be all you asked; but if once you call Him in, He will give you the full treatment."[9] This is the pattern by which God changes the world: *repentance, forgiveness, new life, the full treatment!* Our daily recognition that we are inadequate, our constant death to our own efforts

---

9. C. S. Lewis, *Mere Christianity* (New York: Harper & Brothers, 1952), as cited in *For All the Saints*, 163–164.

to improve ourselves, and our consistent reception of God's immeasurable forgiveness emancipate us to be changed radically. We cannot and do not do enough about the injustice in the world, but repentance alerts us to the Kingdom of God at work in the world and to the mighty army of saints involved in what the Trinity is doing.

Unshackled from false hopes, we are empowered by truly unfettered hope in God's reign to continue in the pattern of fear and love. We are winged into ever higher reaches of loving our neighbors and God. We are deepened into our ability to participate with the whole Church throughout the world in the cosmic battle against injustice—knowing that the victory, which is God's, is already assured in Christ, who has defeated all the principalities and powers.

This is a theology of the cross, that only constant death to ourselves leads to a renewal of our love for God and the world. But we are freed to die by the hope of the Resurrection, the sureness of God's promise and reign.

Consequently, the Church's mission, in which we participate as individual Christians enfolded in the corporate community of churches, includes such elements as these:

1. Against the super-objectivity of technological logic and scientific hyper-rationalism, the Church bows before the mystery of the Triune God and His love.
2. In the face of all the idolatrous images of our monoculture, the Church receives, knows, and thereby is freed to live the meta-narrative of a historical Word, a Word which is authentic, particular, incarnated in one specific time and place, acting on our behalf and present with us now through the Spirit, present in bread and wine and community.
3. In a technological milieu that has led to a decrease in skills, time, and social fabric for intimacy, the Church knows that it is loved without limit by the Triune God who frees us to love our neighbor thoroughly with *racham*, *storgē*, *agapē*, *philia*, *philadelphia*, and *philostorgē*.
4. Against the destructions of family and home augmented by the wicked pace of the technological world, the Church is created as the genuine household of God, by the Spirit's uniting, which frees us to welcome the homeless and poor into our family.
5. Against the nihilism and arrogance of our technologized, commodifying world and its consequent moral paralysis, the Church receives authentic meaning and purpose from God's majestic reign, by which we are freed to respond in the true humility of obedience.

6. Against the technological milieu's primary criterion of efficiency, the Church is ushered by our unfettered hope into the language of patience, waiting, eternity.
7. Against the device of advertising, which produces the commodity of more consumption and demands that things be always new, the Church is not only ever new and millennia old, but timeless. Freed by eternal love and unfettered hope, God's people can limit themselves to those commodities that contribute to their focal concerns of loving God and their global neighbors.
8. Against the technological milieu's attitude that if we just find the right method we can fix things, the Church is freed by its unfettered hope to continue living with steadfastness and faithfulness and to "hang in there" when things can't be fixed. Moreover, we follow a Savior who invited us to take up our cross and follow Him, so we engage in mission for the long haul.
9. Against the passivity of an entertained, consuming world, the Church is stirred into action by the fullness of God's grace. We are freed by our unfettered hope to live as saints engaged in mission. We are always *being Church* for the sake of the world.
10. Against the economic disparity of our unjust, technologically oppressive world, the Church is freed by the overwhelming generosity of God's forgiving grace to practice generosity, critique the principality of Mammon, and build genuine *shalom*. Since *shalom* begins in Christ's work to reconcile us to God, that Hebrew word frees us to pass on the reconciliation. The word implies that if those to whom we speak it lack anything for their well-being, then we will do whatever we can to provide for them. *Shalom* connotes the fullness of God's peace spread into the world in sharing, contentment, fulfillment, wholeness. Thus, generous giving on the part of Christians not only builds justice in the world, but also frees us from the burden of idolatries.

These ten visions of the Church's mission are only a few examples meant to encourage your own formulations. Above all, the fullness of our unfettered hope frees the Church, in the midst of the technologized, commodifying society, to live as a "parallel culture." That phrase comes from Miroslav Václav Havel, president of the Czech Republic and, before that, dissident playwright under communist rule. He and his associate dissidents were asking, "How can we live the truth in a culture based on a fundamental lie, especially since the lie is in our heads? How can we begin to live into the truth?" They, as we in our gluttonous society, desired "so much more than just things. We want something to hope in, a reason to believe."[10] Mary Jo Leddy, Director of Romero House Community for Refugees in Toronto and a frequent commentator on human rights concerns, sketches as follows what happened when Havel and his friends set up parallel cultures (as did the Jews and others oppressed by Nazi and communist or similarly alien dominant cultures):

> They had underground study groups. They studied Plato. They had drama. They had music groups. They wrote novels and poetry, and published them underground. . . . It was not a counter-culture because, [Havel] said, it was impossible for us to live totally outside the system. You cannot live outside a culture. But you can create within it zones and spaces [in the cracks a "trembling freedom"] where you can become who you really are. It is in such places that one can speak the truth, where one can gather with others who share that truth. This went on for years, not without difficulties, but for years. Over time, the truth became stronger and stronger, and at a certain point people began to walk in the streets and to say to the system, "We don't believe you anymore." And the system fell. It fell, not because of the power of Western nuclear equipment, but because the people said within the system, "We don't believe you anymore." It was a vision that had been nourished within those parallel cultures.[11]

In the same way, against the materialism, the consumerism, the passivity, the injustice, the violence, and all the other dimensions of our technologized world alien to the Gospel, Christians understand themselves as citizens of two kingdoms, for we can't escape our society, nor do we wish to withdraw from it since we want to minister to it. Instead, we live in our wealthy society and also in the Kingdom of God, our parallel culture. And in that parallel culture, we tell the stories of our meta-narrative, we sing our songs, we pray our prayers, we proclaim in worship the truth—until we know that truth so well that we can say to the surrounding culture,

---

10. Havel is quoted in Mary Jo Leddy, "The People of God as a Hermeneutic of the Gospel," in *Confident Witness—Changing World: Rediscovering the Gospel in North America*, ed. Craig Van Gelder (Grand Rapids: Wm. B. Eerdmans Publishing Co., 1999), 311.

11. Ibid. See also Miroslav Václav Havel, *Living in Truth*, ed. Jon Vladislav (London and Boston: Faber and Faber, 1989).

"We don't believe your lies anymore," and that opens up a trembling freedom to change it!

How Do We Find the Endurance to Continue Living Our Eschatological Hope When Society's Cracks Are Small?

In chapter 6 we learned from Jacques Ellul the fitting image that our work as Christians is to insert "trembling freedom" into the small cracks in our society's overwhelming and controlling paradigm and structures. I return to that image now because we need to be realistic about how hard it is to live truly as a Christian grounded in hope in our technologized, commodified world. We need enormous patience, which, Albert Borgmann emphasizes, in turn requires a source of strength. Since patience is, like athletic endurance, "a habitual skill, acquired gradually and maintained through exercise," it is sustained by the hope of its reward in "vigor when, having endured the duress of reality, our strength is graced and confirmed by real splendor."[12] But what about the situation of living Gospel hope in a very resistant culture?

My own struggles with handicaps give insight, for certain focal practices are essential for survival, but offer no intrinsic reward—and nothing remotely like splendor. I thought of this after a painful time of swimming. I walked home utterly miserable in a winter rain storm as the tenacious wind kept ripping away my umbrella or turning it inside out. Why bother? Why not just stay home instead and work on this book? But every day that I stay home, it would become easier to skip the workout the next day—and the next, until the discipline that keeps my defunct systems in some operating condition is lost.

Three things keep me going: community, the vision of my body as a temple, and my unfettered hope that someday God will keep His covenant promise to make all things new.[13]

God's promise is most important for endurance with health handicaps. I keep knowing (when I consciously attend to it!) that this life is not all there is. That knowledge is not a "pie in the sky after you die" fantasy to help me ignore the present. It is a *sure hope* that what God has begun in Christ will be brought to completion when all sorrow and suffering and

---

12. Borgmann, *Crossing the Postmodern Divide*, 124–125.
13. For an elaboration of how we can have Joy in the midst of trials, see Dawn, *Joy in Our Weakness*.

pain are destroyed forever. Meanwhile, living in that unfettered hope frees us to endure suffering now.

Community is found in the group of us who usually swim at the same time; we continually affirm each other when we show up and wonder about each other when one is missing. These are my companions: Mary, fighting osteoporosis by walking and swimming; her husband, Ed, strengthening and stretching his limbs after delicate foot surgery; Bob, a philosophy professor, trying to balance medicines and blood pressure; Sue, recovering from a head injury; Sal, from Iraq, undergoing chemotherapy for lung cancer. No wonder these people quickly became good friends. We're in this together—this workout for survival. In the same way, members of our Christian communities support each other in the never-ending struggle to resist, restrict, and reform our societal milieu.

Envisioning my body as a temple also requires continuous reflection. Based on God's promises and supported by a community, this discipline is a combination of two biblical themes: caring for our bodies as well as we can so that they are fit vehicles for God's glory and "strengthening what remains" (see Revelation 3). My temple isn't getting any more beautiful or powerful by my workouts, but at least it's as good as it could be for the sake of larger concerns in ministry. The parallel to our Christian fight against injustice is similarly depicted by an early 20th-century protester against society's violence who once was told, "You might as well give up; you'll never change the world." He responded, "But at least I'll keep it from changing me." We might not make major changes in the injustices of the world, but we begin with clearing them out of our own spending habits and urging the same from others (including the larger forces of church bodies and governments) wherever we can, and then we look with hope to the surprises of God.

These three—unfettered hope in God's gracious and sure promises, a community to support us, and, because of these two, our present disciplined involvement—enable us from the wealthy side of the world to persist in fighting injustice. Those whose despair arises not because of the glut of Western society, but from the inadequacies of life in war-torn, disease-ridden, politically and/or economically oppressed lands rise above their trials because of the same—unfettered hope in God's grace, the enfolding of a community, their disciplined responses.

This is our eschatological hope: God's new reign has already broken in in Jesus, and we can be confident that God will fulfill His own purposes for the cosmos. That this reign has already broken in is to be demonstrated by the Body that Jesus left to "do greater things" than He in His name. In solidarity with our brothers and sisters throughout the world, we do those practical things that build justice—looking to the day of God's future reign when the outcasts and the poor will feast with the rich and powerful. As we work together, we envision all persons as temples—recognizing their gifts, discovering all that they can teach us, honoring their insights into faith, sharing their sufferings. We don't know the Joy of our Hope's fulfillment unless we know the Death of carrying a cross.

Sharing the Sufferings of the World Required and Requires a Cross

Perhaps the most beautiful portrayal of this dialectical nature of hope is given in Johann Sebastian Bach's "Christmas Oratorio," written in 1734. The sixth section of this set of cantatas for the three days of Christmas, New Year's Day, the Sunday after New Year's Day, and the Epiphany ends with a glorious cry of hope sung by the soloists and chorus. All of the soloists participate, singly at first and then together, to ask,

> What can hell's own terrors do now,
> What could the world and sin do to us,
> For we in Jesus' hands rest in stillness?[14]

Then the three trumpets sound a gloriously exhilarating call, stirring forcibly in our souls because of the addition of timpani. Into this rousing music, Bach inserts an amazing surprise.

The final chorus utilizes the melody of the hymn "O Sacred Head Now Wounded" (quoted in chapter 5)—an exquisite chorale tune used and harmonized differently five times in the *St. Matthew Passion*. Since the hymn would have been familiar, and since the *Passion* had probably been written seven years earlier and performed perhaps several times since then, the people participating in the "Christmas Oratorio" would certainly know how this particular melody conveyed profound images of the intense suffering of Jesus upon the cross. But to that well-known melody of anguish, Bach sets these words with a triumphant sound:

---

14. This and the following quotation from the "Christmas Oratorio" are my literal translations of Christian Friedrich Henrici's German libretto.

Now you are well avenged upon your enemy host,
For Christ has fully broken everything that opposed you.
Death, devil, sin, and hell are thoroughly reduced to nothing.
The whole mortal race now has its place with God.

Hope is possible because of the victorious work of God in Christ, especially on the cross. Death, devil, hell, the overwhelmings of the media and
other technologies, the shackles of money, the control of the device paradigm, the burden of accumulated possessions are all reduced to nothing.

In the Gospel's shining splendor and sheltering forgiveness, we are set
free. Therefore, in radiant Joy we willingly suffer for the sake of participating in the Triune God's work of bringing justice to the earth. In that
overwhelming and unfettered hope we pick up our own cross and live to
the hilt our focal concerns. All of life becomes more directed to loving
God and loving our neighbors. All of life is radiantly flooded with an
unfettered hope that keeps breaking out in justice and Joy!

Let us pray: Triune God, we are grateful for the grace-full privilege of
being citizens of Your eternal Kingdom and servants of Your enduring
purposes. Open up our minds to understand our culture more clearly.
Open up our hearts to love You more dearly. Open up our lives to invest
ourselves more thoroughly for the sake of serving Your world. May we
each, in our own particular place and ministry, expose the bluffs of the
technological, commodity-laden milieu and reject the idolatries, lies,
delusions, and diversions of our society. Thank You that Your forgiveness
is always with us and Your grace is always rich.

We pray that now You will enfold us in Your grace so that we can hear
what Your Spirit is saying to the Church. We pray for our churches—that
they might equip us all with hope to stand against the control of the device
paradigm, with courage to resist the onslaughts of media and technological bombardment, with tenacity to limit consumerism and the other
encroachments of our inescapable culture, and with skills continually to
clear space for our focal concern of loving You and our neighbors. May
Your people together be a parallel society for the sake of knowing, proclaiming, and living true hope—to Your honor and glory and for the sake
of the world, especially the poor. And we ask all of this confidently, eagerly,
expectantly, because of the victory of our resurrected Lord Jesus Christ,
who lives and reigns with You, Eternal Father, and Empowering Spirit,
one God, now and forever. Amen.

Works Cited for Further Study

Alley, Richard B. *The Two-Mile Time Machine: Ice Cores, Abrupt Climate Change, and Our Future*. Princeton, N.J.: Princeton University Press, 2000.

Barber, Benjamin R. *Jihad vs. McWorld: How Globalism and Tribalism Are Reshaping the World*. New York: Ballantine Books, 1996.

Barrett, David B., George T. Kurian, and Todd M. Johnson, eds. *World Christian Encyclopedia*. 2d ed. Oxford: Oxford University Press, 2001.

Bass, Dorothy C., ed. *Practicing Our Faith. A Way of Life for a Searching People*. San Francisco: Jossey-Bass, 1997.

Bass, Dorothy C., and Don C. Richter, eds. *Way to Live: Christian Practices for Teens*. Nashville: Upper Room, 2002.

Beaudoin, Thomas M. "Celebrity Deathmatch: The Church Versus Capitalism?" and "After Purity: Contesting Theocapitalism." In *Proclaiming the Gospel in a Wired World: The 2001 Princeton Lectures on Youth, Church, and Culture*, edited by Amy Scott Vaughn, pp. 1–29. Princeton, N.J.: The Institute for Youth Ministry of Princeton Theological Seminary, 2001.

Bellah, Robert, Richard Madsen, William M. Sullivan, Ann Swidler, and Steven M. Tipton. *Habits of the Heart: Individualism and Commitment in American Life*. Berkeley: University of California Press, 1985.

Bernanos, Georges. "Sermon of an Agnostic on the Feast of St. Thérèse." In *The Heroic Face of Innocence*, translated by Pamela Morris and David Louis Schindler Jr., pp. 23–41. Grand Rapids: Wm. B. Eerdmans Publishing Co., 1999.

Billington, James. "Divided We Grow." *Books and Culture* 7, 6 (November–December 2001): 20.

Blomberg, Craig L. *Neither Poverty nor Riches: A Biblical Theology of Material Possessions*. New Studies in Biblical Theology. D. A. Carson, series editor. Grand Rapids: Wm. B. Eerdmans Publishing Co., 1999.

Bonhoeffer, Dietrich. *A Testament to Freedom: The Essential Writings of Dietrich Bonhoeffer*. Edited by Geoffrey B. Kelly and F. Burton Nelson. San Francisco: HarperSanFrancisco, 1995.

Borgmann, Albert. *Crossing the Postmodern Divide*. Chicago: University of Chicago Press, 1992.

———. "Everyday Fortitude: Beyond Heroism." *Christian Century* 118, 31, November 14, 2001, 16–21.

———. *Technology and the Character of Contemporary Life: A Philosophical Inquiry*. Chicago: University of Chicago Press, 1984.

Bouma-Prediger, Steven. *For the Beauty of the Earth: A Christian Vision for Creation Care*. Engaging Culture Series. William A. Dyrness and Robert K. Johnston, series editors. Grand Rapids: Baker Academic, 2001.

Bowen, John. *Evangelism for Normal People*. Minneapolis: Augsburg Fortress Publishers, 2002.

Browning, Don S., Bonnie J. Miller-McLemore, Pamela D. Couture, K. Brynolf Lyon, and Robert M. Franklin. *From Culture Wars to Common Ground: Religion and the American Family Debate*. 2d ed. Louisville, Ky.: Westminster John Knox Press, 2000.

The Bruderhof, eds. *Watch for the Light: Readings for Advent and Christmas*. Farmington, Pa.: The Plough Publishing House, 2001.

Brueggemann, Walter, ed. *Hope for the World*. Louisville, Ky.: Westminster John Knox Press, 2001.

Bunge, Marcia J., ed. *The Child in Christian Thought*. Grand Rapids: Wm. B. Eerdmans Publishing Co., 2001.

Butigan, Ken, with Patricia Bruno, O.P. *From Violence to Wholeness*. Las Vegas: Pace e Bene Franciscan Nonviolence Center, 1999.

Capon, Robert Farrar. *The Supper of the Lamb: A Culinary Reflection*. New York: Harcourt Brace Jovanovich, 1967.

Carrington, Philip. *The Primitive Christian Catechism*. Oxford: Oxford University Press, 1940.

Carter, Stephen L. *Civility: Manners, Morals, and the Etiquette of Democracy*. New York: HarperPerennial, 1998.

Castleman, Robbie. *Parenting in the Pew: Guiding Your Children into the Joy of Worship*. Rev. ed. Downers Grove, Ill.: InterVarsity Press, 2001.

Chesterton, G. K. *Orthodoxy: The Classic Account of a Remarkable Christian Experience*. Wheaton, Ill.: Harold Shaw Publishers, 1994. First published in 1908.

Clapp, Rodney, ed. *The Consuming Passion: Christianity and the Consumer Culture*. Downers Grove, Ill.: InterVarsity Press, 1998.

Clausen, Christopher. *Faded Mosaic: The Emergence of Postcultural America*. Chicago: Ivan R. Dee, 2000.

Cormode, Scott. "Engaging Students." *Christian Century*, 118, 5, February 7–14, 2001, 19.

Dawn, Marva J. "The Concept of 'the Principalities and Powers' in the Works of Jacques Ellul." Ph.D. diss., University of Notre Dame, 1992. Ann Arbor, Mich.: University Microfilms, #9220614.

———. *Corrupted Words Reclaimed*. Grand Rapids: Brazos Press, forthcoming.

———. *I'm Lonely, LORD—How Long? Meditations on the Psalms*. 2d ed. Grand Rapids: Wm. B. Eerdmans Publishing Co., 1998.

———. *Is It a Lost Cause? Having the Heart of God for the Church's Children*. Grand Rapids: Wm. B. Eerdmans Publishing Co., 1997.

———. *Joy in Our Weakness: A Gift of Hope from The Book of Revelation*. Rev. ed. Grand Rapids: Wm. B. Eerdmans Publishing Co., 2002.

———. *Keeping the Sabbath Wholly: Ceasing, Resting, Embracing, Feasting*. Grand Rapids: Wm. B. Eerdmans Publishing Co., 1989.

———. *Powers, Weakness, and the Tabernacling of God*. Grand Rapids: Wm. B. Eerdmans Publishing Co., 2001.

———. *Reaching Out without Dumbing Down: A Theology of Worship for This Urgent Time*. Grand Rapids: Wm. B. Eerdmans Publishing Co., 1995.

———. *A Royal "Waste" of Time: The Splendor of Worshiping God and Being Church for the World*. Grand Rapids: Wm. B. Eerdmans Publishing Co., 1999.

―――. *Sexual Character: Beyond Technique to Intimacy*. Grand Rapids: Wm. B. Eerdmans Publishing Co., 1993.

―――. "Technological Devices or Engagement in Practices?" and "The 'Humiliation' of the Word or Its Restoration?" In *Proclaiming the Gospel in a Wired World: The 2001 Princeton Lectures on Youth, Church, and Culture*, edited by Amy Scott Vaughn, pp. 37–80. Princeton, N.J.: The Institute for Youth Ministry of Princeton Theological Seminary, 2001.

―――. *To Walk and Not Faint: A Month of Meditations on Isaiah 40*. 2d ed. Grand Rapids: Wm. B. Eerdmans Publishing Co., 1997.

―――. "What the Bible *Really* Says About War." *The Other Side* 29, 2 (March–April 1993): 56–59.

Dawn, Marva J., trans. and ed. *Sources and Trajectories: Eight Early Articles by Jacques Ellul That Set the Stage*. Grand Rapids: Wm. B. Eerdmans Publishing Co., 1997.

Dawn, Marva J., and Eugene H. Peterson. *The Unnecessary Pastor: Rediscovering the Call*. Grand Rapids: Wm. B. Eerdmans Publishing Co., 1999.

Dean, Kenda Creasy, and Ron Foster. *The God-Bearing Life: The Art of Soul Tending for Youth Ministry*. Nashville: Upper Room, 1998.

Dudley, Carl S. "Choices for Churches." *Christian Century* 118, 31, November 14, 2001, 32–34.

Ehrenreich, Barbara. *Nickle and Dimed: On (Not) Getting By in America*. New York: Metropolitan Books, 2001.

Ellul, Jacques. *The Ethics of Freedom*. Translated by Geoffrey W. Bromiley. Grand Rapids: Wm. B. Eerdmans Publishing Co., 1976.

―――. *The Humiliation of the Word*. Translated by Joyce Main Hanks. Grand Rapids: Wm. B. Eerdmans Publishing Co., 1985.

―――. *Money and Power*. Translated by LaVonne Neff. Downers Grove, Ill.: InterVarsity Press, 1984.

―――. *The Technological Bluff*. Translated by Geoffrey W. Bromiley. Grand Rapids: Wm. B. Eerdmans Publishing Co., 1990.

―――. "The Technological Order." Translated by John Wilkinson. *Technology and Culture* 3, 4 (Fall 1962): 394–421.

―――. *The Technological Society*. Translated by John Wilkinson. New York: Random House, 1964. French version published in 1954.

―――. *The Technological System*. Translated by Joachim Neugroschel. New York: Continuum, 1980.

Farrow, Douglas. *Ascension and Ecclesia: On the Significance of the Doctrine of the Ascension for Ecclesiology and Christian Cosmology*. Grand Rapids: Wm. B. Eerdmans Publishing Co., 2000.

Ford, David F. *The Shape of Living: Spiritual Directions for Everyday Life*. Grand Rapids: Baker Books, 1997.

Fretheim, Terence E. "Theological Reflections on the Wrath of God in the Old Testament." *Horizons in Biblical Theology* 24 (forthcoming).

Gilpin, Robert, with Jean M. Gilpin. *Global Political Economy: Understanding the International Economic Order*. Princeton, N.J.: Princeton University Press, 2001.

Gleick, James. *Faster: The Acceleration of Just About Everything*. New York: Pantheon, 1999.

Goldsmith, Martin. *The Inextinguishable Symphony: A True Story of Music and Love in Nazi Germany*. New York: John Wiley & Sons, 2000.

Gornik, Mark R. "Practicing Faith in the Inner City." *Books and Culture* 7, 4 (May–June 2001): 10–12.

Gushee, David P., ed. *Toward a Just and Caring Society: Christian Responses to Poverty in America*. Grand Rapids: Baker Book House, 1999.

Hacker, Andrew. *Two Nations: Black and White, Separate, Hostile, Unequal*. New York: Ballantine Books, 1992.

Hall, Douglas John. "Despair as Pervasive Ailment." In *Hope for the World*, edited by Walter Brueggemann. Louisville, Ky.: Westminster John Knox Press, 2001, 83–93.

Harris, Maria. *Proclaim Jubilee! A Spirituality for the Twenty-first Century*. Louisville, Ky.: Westminster John Knox Press, 1995.

Hartung, William. *And Weapons for All*. New York: HarperCollins, 1994.

Henke, Linda Witte. *Marking Time: Christian Rituals for All Our Days*. Harrisburg, Pa.: Morehouse, 2001.

Heschel, Abraham J. *The Prophets*. New York: Harper & Row, 1962.

Horton, Michael. *A Better Way: Rediscovering the Drama of God-Centered Worship*. Grand Rapids: Baker Book House, 2002.

Jacobsen, Dennis A. *Doing Justice: Congregations and Community Organizing*. Minneapolis: Fortress Press, 2001.

Johnson, Ben Campbell, and Glenn McDonald. *Imagining a Church in the Spirit: A Task for Mainline Congregations*. Grand Rapids: Wm. B. Eerdmans Publishing Co., 1999.

Johnson, Luke Timothy. *Living Jesus: Learning the Heart of the Gospel*. San Francisco: HarperSanFrancisco, 1998.

Jones, Tony. "Liberated by Reality." *Books and Culture*, 5, 5 (September–October 1999): 27.

Kalpakgian, Mitchell. "Why the Entertainment Industry Is Bad for Children." *New Oxford Review* 63, 2 (March 1996): 12–17.

Kenneson, Philip D., and James L. Street. *Selling Out the Church: The Dangers of Church Marketing*. Nashville: Abingdon Press, 1997.

Kuhns, William. *The Post-Industrial Prophets: Interpretations of Technology*. New York: Weybright and Talley, 1971.

LaCugna, Catherine Mowry. *God for Us: The Trinity and Christian Life*. San Francisco: HarperSanFrancisco, 1992.

Lazareth, William H., ed. *Reading the Bible in Faith*. Grand Rapids: Wm. B. Eerdmans Publishing Co., 2001.

L'Engle, Madeleine. *Walking on Water: Reflections on Faith and Art*. Commemorative ed. Wheaton, Ill.: Harold Shaw, 1998.

Lindbeck, George A. *The Nature of Doctrine: Religion and Theology in a Postliberal Age*. Philadelphia: Westminster Press, 1984.

Lischer, Richard. *Open Secrets: A Spiritual Journey through a Country Church*. New York: Doubleday, 2001.

Long, Thomas G. "A Response to Douglas John Hall." *Journal for Preachers* 25, 1 (Advent 2001): 11–16.

Mackay, Hugh. *Turning Point: Australians Choosing Their Future*. Sydney: Pan Macmillan Australia, 1999.

Marcel, Gabriel. *Homo Viator*. Reprint. Gloucester, Mass.: Peter Smith, 1996.

Miller, Donald E. "The Reinvented Church: Styles and Strategies." *Christian Century* 116, 36, December 22–29, 1999, 1250–1253.

Miller, William Ian. *The Mystery of Courage*. Cambridge, Mass.: Harvard University Press, 2000.

Mitman, Russell E. *Worship in the Shape of Scripture*. Cleveland: Pilgrim Press, 2001.

Mouw, Richard J. *Uncommon Decency: Christian Civility in an Uncivil World*. Downers Grove, Ill.: InterVarsity Press, 1992.

Neusner, Jacob. *Invitation to the Talmud: A Teaching Book*. Rev. ed. San Francisco: Harper & Row, 1984.

Niedner, Frederick. "Ground Zero: Forming Students through the Bible." *Christian Century* 118, 13, April 18–25, 2001, 16–20.

Noam, Eli. "Electronics and the Dim Future of the University." *Science: The Global Weekly of Research* 270, October 13, 1995, 247–49. Reprinted in *The Council of Societies for the Study of Religion Bulletin* 30, 4 (November 2001): 78–80.

Noble, David F. "Digital Diploma Mills: The Automation of Higher Education." *First Monday* 3, January 5, 1998 (http://www.firstmonday.dk). Reprinted in *The Council of Societies for the Study of Religion Bulletin* 30, 4 (November 2001): 81–85.

Noll, Mark A. "Who Would Have Thought?" *Books and Culture* 7, 6 (November–December 2001): 21–22.

Nouwen, Henri J. M. *In the Name of Jesus: Reflections on Christian Leadership*. New York: Crossroad, 1989.

Nyitray, Vivian-Lee. "Distance Learning: Proceed with Caution." *The Council of Societies for the Study of Religion Bulletin* 30, 4 (November 2001), 85–87.

Olsen, Charles M. *Transforming Church Boards into Communities of Spiritual Leaders*. Bethesda, Md.: Alban Institute, 1995.

Osborn, Robert T. "Theological Table Talk: The Possibility of Theology Today." *Theology Today* 55, 4 (January 1999): 562–570.

Pascal, Blaise. *Pensées*. Translated by A. J. Krailsheimer. New York: Penguin Books, 1966.

Placher, William C. *Jesus the Savior: The Meaning of Jesus Christ for Christian Faith*. Louisville, Ky.: Westminster John Knox Press, 2001.

Pohl, Christine D. *Making Room: Recovering Hospitality as a Christian Tradition*. Grand Rapids: Wm. B. Eerdmans Publishing Co., 1999.

Postman, Neil. *Amusing Ourselves to Death: Public Discourse in the Age of Show Business*. New York: Viking Penguin, 1985.

———. *Technopoly: The Surrender of Culture to Technology*. New York: Alfred A. Knopf, 1992.

Putnam, Robert D. *Bowling Alone: The Collapse and Revival of American Community*. New York: Simon & Schuster, 2000.

Schultze, Quentin. *Habits of the High-Tech Heart: Living Virtuously in the Information Age*. Grand Rapids: Baker Book House, 2002.

Schumacher, Frederick J., with Dorothy A. Zelenko, comp. and ed. *For All the Saints: A Prayer Book For and By the Church*. Vol. 3: *Year 2: Advent to the Day of Pentecost*. Delhi, N.Y.: American Lutheran Publicity Bureau, 1995.

Scott, James C. *Weapons of the Weak: Everyday Forms of Peasant Resistance*. New Haven, Conn.: Yale University Press, 1985.

Selles, Otto. "What's Cooking When Martha Stewart Meets the VeggieTales?" *Books and Culture* 7, 4 (July–August 2001): 8–11.

Sider, Ron. *Just Generosity: A New Vision for Overcoming Poverty in America*. Grand Rapids: Baker Book House, 1999.

Sivard, Ruth Leger. *World Military and Social Expenditures*. Solna, Sweden: Stockholm International Peace Research Institute, 1996.

Stassen, Glen, ed. *Just Peacemaking: Ten Practices for Abolishing War*. Cleveland: Pilgrim Press, 1998.

Stassen, Glen M., and David P. Gushee. *Christian Ethics as Following Jesus*. Downers Grove, Ill.: InterVarsity Press, forthcoming.

Stewart, David. "Nurturing Curiosity: A Librarian's View." *Christian Century* 118, 5, February 7–14, 2001, 18.

Stewart, Sonja M. *Following Jesus: More about Young Children and Worship*. Louisville, Ky.: Westminster John Knox Press, 2000.

Stewart, Sonja M., and Jerome W. Berryman. *Young Children and Worship*. Louisville, Ky.: Westminster/John Knox Press, 1989.

Stockholm International Peace Research Institute. Annual Yearbooks.

Streeter, Ryan. *Transforming Charity: Toward a Results-Oriented Social Sector*. Indianapolis: Hudson Institute, 2001.

Suzuki, David, and Holly Dressel. *From Naked Ape to Superspecies*. Toronto: Stoddart, 1999.

Swoboda, Jörg. *The Revolution of the Candles: Christians in the Revolution of the German Democratic Republic*. Edited by Richard V. Pierard. Translated by Edwin P. Arnold. Macon, Ga.: Mercer University Press, 1996.

Tierman, John. *Spoils of War: The Human Costs of the Arms Trade*. New York: Free Press, 1997.

Torode, Sam. "Sex and Science: Does Making Love Still Lead to Making Babies?" *Books and Culture* 7, 6 (November–December 2001): 6–8.

Ullman, Ellen. *Close to the Machine: Technophilia and Its Discontents*. San Francisco: City Lights Books, 1997.

von Rad, Gerhard. *Holy War in Ancient Israel*. Edited and translated by Marva J. Dawn. Grand Rapids: Wm. B. Eerdmans Publishing Co., 1991.

Wallerstein, Judith, Julia Lewis, and Sandra Blakeslee. *The Unexpected Legacy of Divorce: A 25-Year Landmark Study*. New York: Hyperion, 2000.

Whitehead, Barbara Defoe. *The Divorce Culture*. New York: Alfred A. Knopf, 1996.

Williams, Raymond B. "Getting Technical: Information Technology in Seminaries." *Christian Century* 118, 5, February 7–14, 2001, 14–17.

Williams, Rowan. *Writing in the Dust: After September 11*. Grand Rapids: Wm. B. Eerdmans Publishing Co., 2002.

Willimon, William H. "World Makers: A New Way of Seeing and Naming." *Christian Century* 118, 24, August 29–September 5, 2001, 6–7.

Wuthnow, Robert. *After Heaven: Spirituality in America since the 1950s*. Berkeley: University of California Press, 1998.

Yoder, John Howard. *The Politics of Jesus: Behold the Man! Our Victorious Lamb*. 2d ed. Grand Rapids: Wm. B. Eerdmans Publishing Co., 1994.

Yoder Neufeld, Thomas R. *Ephesians*. Believers Church Bible Commentary. Scottdale, Pa.: Herald Press, 2001.

———. *'Put on the Armour of God': The Divine Warrior from Isaiah to Ephesians*. Journal for the Study of the New Testament Supplement Series 140. Sheffield, England: Sheffield Academic Press, 1997.

Zizioulas, John D. *Being as Communion: Studies in Personhood and the Church*. Crestwood: St. Vladimir's, 1985.

Children's Literature

Juster, Norton. *The Phantom Tollbooth*. New York: Random House, 1964.

Lovelace, Maud Hart. *Heaven to Betsy*. New York: HarperTrophy, 1980. Originally published in 1945.

Schami, Rafik. *A Hand Full of Stars*. Translated by Rika Lesser. New York: Dutton Children's Books, 1990.

Seredy, Kate. *The Good Master*. New York: Viking Press, 1935.

———. *The Singing Tree*. New York: Puffin Books, 1939.

Spinelli, Jerry. *The Library Card*. New York: Scholastic Inc., 1997.

Scripture Index

Subject Index

abortion, 163
The Acceleration of Just About Everything
    (Gleick), 17
accumulation, 9–10, 123
Ackermann, Denise M., 111 n.3
addiction, 19, 26, 56
    to information, 8
    sexual, 167
advertising
    focused on saving time, 17
    interwoven with fabric of society, 51
affluent society, despair of, xv–xvi
Afghanistan, conditions before war on
    terrorism, 37
AIDS, consequences for poorer nations, 35
Apostle's Creed, 130
art, needed to understand Jesus' passion,
    131–32
arts, lose of transcendence in, 82
art works, 151
Augustine, on hope, 119
authority, loss of, 84
availability, 42

Bach, Johann Sebastian, 132–35, 198
baptism, 153
Barber, Benjamin R., 73 n.8, 99 n.28
Barth, Karl, 141
Being vs. Having, 186
Bellah, Robert, 83
Bernanos, Georges, 190
Bible
    consumerist readers vs. religious readers, 159
    meta-narrative offered in, 111, 140, 145–46
    unique language of, 150
    written mostly in plural, 138

Bible reading, results of, 158–59
biblical love, types of, 164
biblical poetry, 122–24
bin Laden, Osama, x, 61, 87
bluffs
    advertising media as leader, 19
    busy-ness, 15–16
    misuse of words, 13–15
    newness, 17–18
    technological milieu, 12–13
Bonhoeffer, Dietrich, 128, 179–80
Borgmann, Albert, xiv, 22, 23–24, 41–50, 99
    culture of the table, 58–59
    different approaches to common events, 103
    distraction vs. engagement, 48–51
    engagement in challenging rule of technol-
        ogy, 149
    extending sphere of engagement as third
        reform, 71, 72–73
    first reforming step of clearing space, 81
    impossibility of enclosing technology in
        boundaries, 57
    limits on technology freeing people from
        boredom, 55
    Lord's Supper as Christianity's central
        event, 181–82
    machinery, 93–94
    moral courage as most important virtue, 170
    parasitic and voracious delights, 102
    patience required, 196
    questioning link between technological
        work and education, 53
    reforming technological paradigm, 57–60, 69
    reform in simplifying context, 77
    relationships replaced by concealed
        machinery, 98